Concepts, Conversations, Critique

Seventh Edition

English 100 Program

University of Wisconsin—Madison

Department of English

D1371958

Bedford/St. Martin's   BOSTON ◆ NEW YORK

Contents

Award-Winning Student Essays

Narrative Essays

Informative/Synthesis Essays

Critical/Analytical Essays

Multimodal/Digital Essay

Working with Sources

English 100 Program Award Guidelines

Introduction to the English 100 Program

You may already appreciate the central role writing plays in your everyday life and academic career, as well as in other contexts. If you're already a strong writer, you might wonder why you are required to take a class like English 100. As this course will emphasize, writing is a socially situated practice that takes into account purpose, context, audience, and other factors that may inform why you write, what you write, and how you write. To put it more simply, new writing situations require new writing strategies.

Certainly, we all appreciate some general qualities of "good" writing—such as clarity of thought and language—but there are many more qualities of effective writing that connect to specific situations. So while the types of writing that you've done during high school or for other occasions have developed and focused your writing for that context and those experiences, you'll find that the writing you do at the university and beyond requires a variety of new and/or different strategies and practices. You will need to resituate both yourself and your writing.

As an introduction to college composition, English 100 prepares you to identify your purposes for writing and to make informed decisions about the choices you face when you write. What are the kinds of questions you need to ask in order to approach and execute your writing effectively? Even in the defined context of the university, purposes and decisions vary widely. Some writing strategies can be applied across courses, regardless of discipline, or within cocurricular and extracurricular activities, or even as you begin to create materials for your career beyond the university. But you also need to recognize when to use other strategies that may require specialized knowledge about how information is communicated or how arguments are made in specific disciplines.

AN INTRODUCTION TO *CONCEPTS, CONVERSATIONS, CRITIQUE*

This course reader—*Concepts, Conversations, Critique*—has two primary purposes: (1) to provide readings that help you consider issues and practices related to writing in college, and (2) to serve as a handbook for English 100.

First, the readings offer opportunities for you to engage with a variety of ideas, especially about writing. At the same time, they illustrate the kinds of intellectual work expected of you in this course. Some of the essays published here were written during 2013 by English 100 students. Each student essay includes commentaries by the author and the student's instructor. These materials provide a context to help you understand the writing assignment and the writing and revision process.

Second, some materials in this text serve as a type of handbook for the course, providing you with information about foundational practices, program policies, student support services, and other resources you may find useful as you join the UW-Madison community. At the back of the book, you will find information about the writing awards sponsored by the English 100 Program.

The essays in *Concepts, Conversations, Critique* range widely and include pieces that offer advice on drafting and editing, narratives about writing as both personal and social experiences, and explorations about the building of knowledge through writing, among other topics. Your experience with this reader is meant to be active. We want you to read with a critical eye, to question the ideas presented here, and to take these ideas and transform them into practices that will shape your writing. With this in mind, the first thing you might notice is that the essays are arranged alphabetically by author rather than, for instance, by theme or type. This organization encourages instructors to customize the choice of readings for your section of English 100 in ways that best meet the needs of your class. Some of the readings are interchangeable and overlapping in purpose to enable you to experience writing and reading as interrelated activities.

WRITING AS A PROCESS

English 100 is designed to emphasize writing as a process, and several of the essays here are meant to illustrate "writing practices." They provide ideas for approaching any writing project, but especially writing in this course. For example, readings suggest strategies you can use for invention (Greene; Kennedy, Kennedy, and Muth), drafting (Lamott), revision (Murray), and editing

2

(Zinsser). Invention, drafting, revision, and editing, of course, are stages of the writing process, and you will move through this recursive process several times during the semester as you explore and develop ideas; sharpen and clarify descriptions, narratives, and arguments; and, finally, present your work in clear, organized, and effective ways.

WRITING TO BUILD RHETORICAL AWARENESS

English 100 also emphasizes the development of rhetorical awareness, the understanding of how writing and language can be engaging and persuasive in particular situations. An important element of rhetorical awareness is understanding audience. In your classroom, you'll find opportunities to engage with a variety of audiences, from members of the peer review group who will respond to your drafts, to your instructor who will work closely with you on revisions, to your entire class and possibly others with whom you might share your research presentations.

English 100 is organized in three sequences, with each building on the rhetorical work of the one(s) before it.

Sequence 1. Concepts: Invention and Inquiry

In Sequence 1, you will use narrative strategies to explore concepts, ideas, and experiences. Narrative encourages you to draw evidence from a wide variety of phenomena in the world and also in your life. Assignments in Sequence 1 allow you to trace how an inkling of an idea that arises from curiosity or the material world can move to a fully realized line of inquiry. Effective communication with those around us depends upon the ability to take our own experiences and connect them to that of others in meaningful ways. One way to do this is by using specific and perhaps unique experiences as *evidence* for more general or common qualities or conditions. This is a process of abstraction that can begin the process of building knowledge.

Sequence 2. Conversations: Writing to Inform

Much of the writing you'll do in college is connected to texts produced by people who have ideas about the same topic on which you're working. Academic writing is often thought of as part of a conversation, because of the way writers and researchers build on, disagree with, and respond to one another's work. As understood in Sequence 2, writing that informs offers one way of organizing and making sense of a variety of information and thoughtful points of

3

view that a writer gathers about an event, topic, or issue. An important first step in this intellectual process is doing research to locate relevant material related to your interest. For instance, if you are interested in freedom of speech, you will need to learn where to look for sources that will help you understand the issues and arguments related to freedom of speech. Then you will need to choose sources that provide a range of perspectives you can investigate or study. The writing you will do in Sequence 2 will build this kind of information literacy and guide you through a process of learning to locate and use texts and/or other sources, as you identify and enter into written conversations that provide context for your own ideas and writing. Sequence 2 writing assignments will engage you in the process of summarizing, analyzing, and gradually synthesizing information so that others understand the knowledge you are discovering. This kind of writing – or this kind of purpose for writing – is valuable in many contexts within the university and workplace. It can also provide a foundation for further investigation and for developing your own contribution to an academic or other public conversation.

Sequence 3. Critique: Developing a Critical Approach through Research and Argumentation

The final sequence of assignments asks you to engage in research in order to develop a critical approach to a topic or issue, that is, to develop a way to investigate and analyze it. Part of your job will include designing and executing a research plan to guide your investigation. The writing you produce should make some form of an argument about your researched topic, supporting your views with specific reasons and evidence. It's important to note that making an argument does not assume you have reached a definitive answer. Arguments are also not only "pro and con." Arguments can be made as a way of exploring an issue and raising intelligent questions.

Sequence 3 builds on your earlier practice in using texts, considering audience and purpose, and incorporating others' ideas into your own writing. Rather than asking you to produce a report or "research paper," as you might have done in high school, it provides an opportunity for you to develop a critical perspective on a body of knowledge or craft a set of questions around a well researched issue. For example, one approach to the sequence might have you looking at ideas that you first formulated at the start of the semester about a topic, let's say freedom of speech, placing your ideas within scholarly conversations on the history of censorship and then critically testing your conclusions by interviewing a high school English teacher and a librarian for their views on banned books.

WRITING AT WISCONSIN

Writing at the University of Wisconsin-Madison happens in all kinds of locations and through a wide variety of practices, from sitting on the Terrace with your laptop, to using a pen and notebook in a lab, to being surrounded by papers and books in your dorm room or the library. As you begin your career at Wisconsin, you will see that writing is everywhere. Your experience writing in English 100 is an invitation to participate in the university community, contribute to scholarly conversations, and become an engaged learner. Welcome!

English 100 Program
Policies and Resources

ATTENDANCE

Attendance is required. English 100 is a small seminar-like course, and your presence matters, not only for your own learning but for your contributions to others' learning. You need to be in class, on time, and prepared for every meeting. For those unavoidable times when you are sick or otherwise unable to come to class, the attendance policy allows 3 absences without penalty in a MWF class and 2 in a TR class. It is always considerate to notify your instructor by email before an absence, and it is *your* responsibility to find out what you missed and to make up any required work. Excessive or habitual tardiness may be counted as an absence.

The final course grade may be lowered for each additional absence beyond the allowed absences (an A will become an AB; an AB will become a B; a B will become a BC, and so on). More than 6 absences in a MWF class or more than 4 absences in a TR class (the equivalent of 2 full weeks of class) may result in a student failing the course.

An instructor has the discretion to take into account *extraordinary* reasons for an absence, such as a severe accident or illness, a family emergency or death, a recognized religious holiday, or jury duty. (Be sure to talk with your instructor about such circumstances.) Documentation may be required. Too many absences for whatever reason will prevent you from completing the required coursework; in the case of excessive absences, your instructor may recommend that you drop the class.

DROPPING OR WITHDRAWING FROM THE COURSE

Dropping and withdrawing from a course are separate, formal administrative procedures, and it is the student's responsibility to initiate these procedures. If you simply stop attending class, *this is not the same* as either formally dropping or withdrawing from the course. Before choosing either option, a student should meet with his/her instructor and advisor.

ACADEMIC HONESTY AND PLAGIARISM

The University of Wisconsin-Madison and the English 100 Program expect students to present their work honestly and to credit others responsibly and with care. University policy states: "Academic honesty and integrity are fundamental to the mission of higher education and of the University of Wisconsin system" (Wisconsin Administrative Code 14.01). Plagiarism is a serious offense, and it can occur in drafts as well as in final papers. Because English 100 relies heavily on sharing knowledge and information in the learning and writing processes, it is important that students learn how to work with sources without plagiarizing. Plagiarism includes all of the following:

- cutting and pasting from another source without using quotation marks and citing the source;
- using someone else's words or ideas without proper documentation when quoting or paraphrasing;
- copying any portion of your text from another source without proper acknowledgement;
- borrowing another person's specific ideas without documenting the source;
- having someone rewrite or complete your work for you (which does not include getting and using feedback from a writing group or individual classmate);
- turning in a paper written by another person or obtained from an essay "service" or a World Wide Web site (including reproductions of such essays or papers); and
- turning in a paper that you previously wrote for another course, or turning in the same paper for more than one course, without getting permission from your instructors first.

In all of the above cases, plagiarism occurs when someone else's words and/or ideas are used without proper citation and documentation *no matter* what kind of text is the source of the words and/or ideas. That is, material must still be documented even if it comes from a source such as an e-mail, personal writing, oral or written interview, classroom conversation, or formal presentation or lecture—not just from a published source such as a book, journal, popular magazine, or Web site.

The University of Wisconsin-Madison has established a range of penalties for students guilty of plagiarism or academic dishonesty. These penalties include, as appropriate, a reduced grade, a failing grade for an assignment, a failing grade for the course, or even suspension or expulsion from the university. All instances of plagiarism are reported to the English 100 administration. For more information, see the Dean of Students Office, Academic Integrity Web page: **students.wisc.edu/doso/acadintegrity.html**.

UNIVERSITY GENERAL EDUCATION REQUIREMENTS: COMMUNICATION

English 100 fulfills Part A of the university's general education requirement in communication (commonly known as "Comm A"). The Comm A general education requirement seeks to prepare students in the communication skills (both written and oral) they will need at the university. Below you will find a description of the Comm A requirement itself and more detailed descriptions of the objectives and learning outcomes expected of a Comm A course such as English 100.

Part A. Literacy Proficiency: 2-3 credits at first-year level dedicated to reading, listening, and discussion, with emphasis on writing. While most incoming freshmen are required to complete course work to fulfill this requirement, students may be exempted from Part A by approved college course work while in high school, AP test scores, or placement testing. Students are expected to satisfy this requirement by the end of their first year.

Purpose: The first course is to be a basic course in communication skills at the college level, developing student abilities in writing and public speaking, for both exposition and argumentation. As such, the course is to serve as a general foundation in the central skills and conventions required for student success in a variety of subsequent course work, as well as in careers after college.

Objectives: The course will advance basic skills in:

- The four modes of literacy: writing, speaking, reading, and listening, with special emphasis on writing
- Critical thinking
- Information-seeking skills and strategies

These skills should be taught through continuous practice in the process of writing and speaking. Although the items listed below suggest a sequence, many or all of them are simultaneously learned in this process. Courses that satisfy the new University requirement must advance student skills in the following areas:

Planning

- Selecting, narrowing, and focusing topics
- Identifying and analyzing audience information needs
- Generating and organizing ideas
- Comprehending and analyzing texts

Drafting

- Learning structures of exposition and argument and the use of evidence
- Organizing and developing paragraphs, papers, and speeches
- Adapting writing and speaking for intended audiences
- Learning conventions of academic writing
- Mastering elements of grammar, usage, and style
- Preparing speeches for oral delivery
- Citing sources, avoiding plagiarism, and compiling accurate bibliographies

Revising

- Developing critical skills for reading and listening — in review of peer writing/speaking
- Revising and editing essays and speeches — for spelling, punctuation, grammar, style, organization, and logic
- Critiquing assigned readings and speeches delivered outside class

Information-Seeking Skills and Strategies

- Develop and adapt information seeking strategies in order to access information effectively.
- Evaluate information retrieved and select information sources appropriate to the particular research need.

(From *2011-2013 University Undergraduate Catalog* and the College of Letters and Science General Education Web site: **www.ls.wisc.edu/gened**. *Note*: "Information-Seeking Skills and Strategies" updated 2012.)

CAMPUS RESOURCES

There are a number of English Department and campus resources available to you that may facilitate your transition to college life and your success in English 100. Described below are some services that may be especially useful as you negotiate this large campus and the many demands that you face as a student.

The English 100 Tutorial

The English 100 Tutorial Program offers individualized writing instruction specifically geared for English 100 students. You can find more information about the tutorial program or schedule an appointment at the tutorial Web site: **www.english.wisc.edu /english100/tutorials.html**

English 100 students of all kinds, including experienced writers, frequently seek extra help with writing assignments beyond what is available in the classroom and during their instructor's office hours. Since the Writing Center is not funded to provide tutoring for Comm A courses like English 100, the Tutorial provides an opportunity for you to receive one-on-one help from experienced English 100 instructors. These instructors are willing to work with you on any issue related to English 100, from brainstorming ideas for a paper to revising strategies for a final draft. Please visit the Web site to learn how you can make tutorial sessions an effective part of your writing process!

Design Lab

Located in College Library, Design Lab (**designlab.wisc.edu**) is a media lab and design consultancy dedicated to improving students' digital communication skills. Through one-on-one and small group consultations, design consultants help students hone the conceptual, aesthetic, and technical skills they need to work effectively in digital media. If your English 100 class includes multi-modal assignments, you will want to consider making an appointment with Design Lab.

The Writing Center

While the Writing Center will not schedule appointments for English 100 assignments, it offers a wide array of free, one-time short classes on specific issues throughout the semester on topics such as improving style, email etiquette, writing literary analysis essays, writing resumes, etc. You can access this semester's Writing Center class schedule at **www.writing.wisc.edu**. You can also make an appointment with the Writing Center for assistance with assignments in other courses.

The McBurney Center

If you have a disability or particular circumstance that could impact your academic work, you may want to meet with a counselor at the McBurney Disability Resource Center. The McBurney Center is located at 702 West Johnson Street, Suite 2104 (263-2741). Students need to provide documentation of a disability to the center in order to receive official university services and accommodations. For more information, visit the center Web site: www.mcburney.wisc.edu/

Other Resources

Other helpful learning resources are listed at **www.learning.wisc .edu** and through the Division of Student Life: **www.students .wisc.edu**

The University Health Service offers a variety of counseling services. Their Web page is **www.uhs.wisc.edu**. To make an appointment or for emergency crisis intervention services, call 265-5600.

ENGLISH 100 COURSE DIRECTORS

Morris Young
Director of English 100 and Professor of English
6187C Helen C. White Hall
(608) 263-3367
msyoung4@wisc.edu.

Mary Fiorenza
Associate Director of English 100
Associate Faculty Associate
6183 Helen C. White Hall
(608) 263-4512
fiorenza@wisc.edu

Annika Konrad
Assistant Director of English 100
6189 Helen C. White Hall
konrad@wisc.edu

Anna Flock
Assistant Director of English 100
6189 Helen C. White Hall
flock@wisc.edu

ENGLISH 100 TUTORIAL PROGRAM

6101 Helen C. White Hall
100tutorial@english.wisc.edu

Approaches to Rhetoric, Writing, and Revision in English 100

INTRODUCTION TO RHETORIC

In common usage, "rhetoric" is typically associated with a lack of substance and even with deceitful intentions. We hear this in common claims made by pundits and politicians when they say things like "Let's cut the rhetoric and get down to the facts" or "That's just rhetoric." In reality, rhetoric has a long and esteemed history. In the West, it developed from a Greco-Roman tradition that prepared men for public leadership (at that time women were largely discouraged from public life). Although this tradition focused on speech (orality), today it informs our understanding of wider communicative practices, including writing.

Over time and across cultures, rhetoric has taken on a variety of definitions. One of the best-known conceptions of rhetoric was that of the Greek philosopher Aristotle, who suggested that rhetoric entails identifying the "available means of persuasion" in any given situation. More recently, composition scholar Andrea Lunsford defined rhetoric as "the art, practice, and study of communication." Both conceptions of rhetoric link persuasion and communication, a link that transcends a multitude of rhetorical traditions.

English 100 offers a space for developing rhetorical awareness and for understanding how rhetoric informs writing practices. If we typically understand communication as an exchange of ideas, information, or experiences among people, rhetorical awareness asks us to pay attention to how and why that communication happens in the first place.

RHETORIC AND NARRATIVE

Sequence 1 in English 100 focuses on narrative modes of communication and persuasion. A **narrative** is a story with a beginning, middle, and end that describes a sequence of events.

Narratives can be heard and read everywhere, from conversations to newscasts to books. People constantly use narratives in speech and writing to entertain, to teach, to bond with one another, or simply to share information. We also use narratives to help us think. We understand identity, personal history, and life goals through narratives. For example, they help us understand how we got through the toughest years of high school, or why we excel at a particular skill. Narratives can also be very broad and shared by millions of people. Think of familiar childhood stories such as "Chicken Little" or "The Three Little Pigs" or a narrative about an event such as the "I Have a Dream" speech delivered by Martin Luther King, Jr. These shared narratives communicate an idea, belief, or lesson beyond just telling a good story or providing an historical account.

Many scholars have argued that much of our thought and communication takes the form of narrative. Consequently, knowing how narratives work and how to analyze them are fundamental skills for any writer. Perhaps the most important aspect of narrative is **memory.** Many narratives that people tell are based on their own experiences, and therefore memory provides a critical tool—as well as the source material—for a writer or storyteller to turn an experience into a narrative. To tell stories about the past, writers need to be able to draw upon remembrances, facts, events, and other pertinent information.

Memory helps a writer to be inventive and creative. Using memory, a writer draws upon what he or she knows, has heard, has read in books, or has spoken. Memory allows a writer to remember the links between concepts and ideas, to connect one narrative to another, and to draw various elements together to form a complete idea. For example, in writing an essay about love, a writer could draw from personal experience, the story of Romeo and Juliet (and its many versions), or the film *Titanic.*

Additionally, memory can be a form of **research.** Scrapbooks, yearbooks, diaries, letters, photo albums, old school essays, and drawings are some of the places where memories are stored. Analyzing these objects can allow a writer to access memories that have been archived and to learn about the people who saved them.

Another kind of memory is cultural or **collective memory,** the practice of keeping alive culturally specific histories to teach a culture's current and future generations about themselves. Books, museums, songs, traditions, and rituals are all ways that cultures actively remember and reconstruct their pasts to teach the next generation what it means to belong. The Wisconsin Historical Society's collections and the television show *Band of Brothers* are examples of ways in which a culture is preserved for future generations.

14

For English 100 students, an important aspect of narrative to understand is that memories are not yet narratives; for a memory to become a narrative, it needs to be *told*. In being told, a memory changes from sensation, image, or other vestige of sensory or thought experience into a crafted narrative. That is, the narrative reflects the writer's choices, omissions, emphasis, and so on. In other words, once a memory is transformed into a narrative, it has the ability to influence people to think about themselves or the world in specific ways—it becomes **rhetorical**. Consider a criminal trial in which two lawyers are arguing about whether a defendant is innocent or guilty. The defense lawyer constructs a story that claims the defendant's innocence, while the prosecution constructs a story that demonstrates the defendant's guilt. Both narratives are argumentative; they try to persuade a jury to think a certain way about the defendant. Because narratives can omit, rearrange, or amplify details in order to achieve a specific effect, they can be used rhetorically.

The philosopher Paul Ricoeur takes this conception of narrative to an even deeper level. He argues that narratives are *all* inherently persuasive by virtue of their composition. First, narratives draw various elements, memories, or sundry details together *in time*. When you tell a story, you link events, some related, some not, into a chronology. This chronology functions to suggest that all of the elements of your story have a natural unity or relationship. For example, when you tell a story about taking a nap and being awakened by the doorbell, your story implies an inherent relationship between these two events. Second, when you tell a story, every event that is recounted appears as if it were necessary, as if it *had* to happen. For example, someone who won the lottery might begin telling the story from the moment he bought the ticket, connecting events in a way that implies winning the lottery was the most natural thing that could have happened. In truth, the outcome of winning the lottery was incredibly unlikely. Third, narratives usually involve people, real or fictional, who share relationships with others and who act, react, and are framed in particular ways. Any time a real person becomes a character in a story, that person is re-created by the teller. In essence, the person becomes a narrative device for the storyteller. With all of these aspects, Ricoeur suggests that we can never regard narrative as a perfect representation of reality, for it is *always* distorted in its translation into language.

These complex ideas suggest some important things about narrative. First, a narrative, whether based on memory or not, can never be completely "true," even when the writer is upholding high ethical standards, such as those required in college writing. What we mean when we say that a narrative cannot be absolutely true is that it cannot be a perfect representation of memory or reality. After all, words are symbols, and a narrative is always the product of choices, conscious or otherwise, that shape a story or an argument. Second, understanding that narratives can be a form of argument allows us to read narratives for their rhetorical content. Because narratives reflect their writers' choices, we can analyze the decisions made by a writer, along with our own responses to the text, in order to discover how narratives persuade us. Understood this way, narratives are not only stories but also complex forms of interaction that represent details in order to influence the reader or listener in specific ways.

RHETORIC AND WRITING TO INFORM

In Sequence 1, memory and invention are considered in relation to narrative. You construct a narrative to express a concept of your own. Sequence 3 requires you to craft your own researched inquiry, usually as an argument or persuasive project. Sequence 2 serves as a bridge between these tasks and asks you to explore a conversation surrounding a given issue, text, or event.

The informational (expository) writing required in Sequence 2 asks you to use memory and invention again, but in a different way. In Sequence 1, when we considered memory it was largely in terms of personal experience, and you were invited to use your own memories as sources for invention and inquiry through narrative. In Sequence 2, we'll begin to draw on a conception of research as cultural memory. That is, we can say that memory not only exists in individual consciousness but also is recorded by members of a culture in written documents and other materials. Members of a culture might hold certain values, ideas, places, histories, or languages in common. At the same time, no culture is monolithic. There are always competing and complementary versions and values. The resources of cultural memory can help us understand the conversations that are generated around any topic you may choose to explore.

Sequence 2 asks you to engage with others' ideas and with data or other raw material through research. Specifically, you will practice the process of selecting, summarizing, analyzing, and synthesizing information and ideas from sources. Completing these four activities effectively requires you to make decisions in response to the components of the rhetorical situation: your role as a writer as well as your audience, your purpose, and the context in which you are writing. "Selecting" means strategically choosing sources from a range that will be appropriate for your audience, purpose, and context. "Summarizing" has to do with accurately conveying and representing another writer's argument or purpose to your audience. "Analyzing" requires you to consider the structure, strengths, and

16

weaknesses of a text. Finally, "synthesizing" entails interpreting for your audience how multiple sources convey meaning in relationship to one another. Completing these tasks will help you to engage in an ongoing conversation and to begin crafting your own project for Sequence 3.

RHETORIC AND DEVELOPING A CRITICAL APPROACH OR CRITIQUE THROUGH RESEARCH

In Sequence 3, you will bring together the thinking and writing you have done throughout the semester to create a self-designed project that identifies, researches, and makes an argument about an idea or issue you want to explore. Thus far the rhetorical situation has been discussed in relation to specific practices and purposes such as composing a narrative or analyzing and presenting information. For Sequence 3 you will need to consider the rhetorical situation in a more comprehensive manner in order to map your research, develop your line of inquiry, and make an argument. After all, communication is effective based on how well it negotiates the elements of any given situation.

The writing and work you do in Sequence 3 will require you to be particularly mindful of the rhetorical situation as you negotiate and consider many different ideas, sift through research and information, and begin to formulate a new idea, an argument, or a call to action. The rhetorical situation focuses on how any communicative act occurs within a context, with various actors such as writer/speaker and reader/audience, and the writer/speaker's purpose in communicating.

- **Context:** Thinking about contexts—whether social, cultural, historical, political, or some other framework—directs attention to how writers enter into an ongoing conversation, and that their writing places them in relation to other writers and audience members. Context also highlights that people always write for a reason. That is, writing does not just happen but most often is a response to some form of exigency, question, or disagreement.
- **Writer:** Responding to an exigency (an event, happening, or action that creates a purpose for communication), the writer establishes an ethos (credibility, personality) with his or her readers through the writing. This ethos may be informed by the writer's background, expertise, and the way he or she creates an identity through the writing.
- **Purpose:** In public writing, a writer always has some purpose he or she would like to achieve with readers. A writer may

17

want to persuade his or her audience to take a certain course of action or to inform them of new and compelling perspectives on the issue-at-hand.

- **Audience:** College writing is always done for an audience (readers). Through the text, a writer creates a relationship with this audience. Writers base their decisions at least in part on assumptions about this audience and the communicative expectations this audience may have.

Successfully negotiating the rhetorical situation is largely what leads to effective writing. That is, the effectiveness of writing is not based on how it follows certain rules but on its ability to achieve a writer's purpose with an audience.

WRITING WORKSHOPS

Workshops can be useful at any stage of the writing process. In English 100, you might be in a workshop group to brainstorm ideas for a writing project, generate or answer questions related to research, respond to partial or entire drafts, or help one another review nearly finished work.

A writing workshop is, simply speaking, a place to borrow someone else's eyes to help you see your ideas and writing from a different perspective. Often you are too invested in or exhausted from your own writing to see it clearly, and a writing workshop helps you see what you can't see yourself. Workshops are not places for evaluation. Instead, they provide a low-stakes venue for responses and feedback to your work.

When working with other writers to provide feedback, be sure to balance appreciation and useful criticism. If your aim as a reader is to respond to the text, then you need to draw attention to the writer's effective strategies as well as to places in the text that still need work. Workshops can be open-ended interactions that help both the writer and the reader. They can help the writer by generating new ideas, letting him or her hear a response from an actual reader, or by providing specific suggestions that will help the process of revision. At the same time, they can help the reader to develop analytical and critical skills for both reading and writing. Workshops are a chance to go public and test your work without worrying about a grade or losing face.

A writing workshop is an activity that gets better with time, practice, and training. The most productive writing workshops consider both the writer's concerns and the reader's attention to higher order points. Those higher order points include:

18

- **Information:** How interesting, specific, accurate, or relevant is the information?
- **Meaning:** How are the writer's key claims significant? What consequences might they hold: in terms of logic, readers' likely reactions, or clarity?
- **Audience:** What might readers want and need to know? What relationship does the writer want to create?
- **Form:** Are the genres and language/discourse conventions an effective choice for communicating the text's intended meaning?
- **Structure:** What is the logic of the organization, arrangement (global and local levels), and development of the text?
- **Voice:** How does the writer seek to develop a sense of authority and style, and demonstrate a connection or concern for the topic?

In a typical workshop session to review a draft, smaller order concerns such as spelling, punctuation, and grammar would not be the major focus. Rather, global concerns take precedence, because at this stage you would want to see how effectively the draft considers its audience and fulfills its purpose, participating in a broader conversation and ultimately answering the "so what" or "why does this matter" questions. Possible questions could be:

- What sort of information do you assume your audience already knows?
- How formal does the language need to be for your audience?
- How does the central claim you make change the way other researchers might approach a similar problem?
- How can you justify why your research question is important? In other words, how does it answer the question "so what"?
- Can you explain the logic of your structure? Why does the organization have to be the way it is?
- Can you show me where you're supporting your claims with evidence?

A workshop might begin with a brief conversation in which the writer clearly identifies his or her main concerns and asks for specific feedback. Readers might want to jot those topics down and ask the writer to explain the context for the draft. Then, after listening to the writer read the draft out loud or reading the draft yourself, you can begin to tackle the higher order concerns of the paper.

Since a writing workshop is a place for dialogue, you should listen carefully to the writer's intentions, ask open-ended questions, make suggestions that lead to learning and new ideas rather than to simple solutions, and be responsive rather than judgmental. For example, when looking at information, consider whether the information is interesting, accurate, relevant, and specific. Ask the writer to explain his or her choices and then consider how that information serves the paper's purpose.

REVISION

English 100 is a class that emphasizes that composition requires practice. Learning how to write well is like learning to play a sport or a musical instrument. You have to practice to develop good habits and skills, and like shooting free throws in basketball or playing scales on the piano, practice makes perfect. Revision is like working on your free-throw shooting form. When you practice free throws, you go over the same thing multiple times, improving as you find out and preserve what works and change or discard what doesn't. Revising your writing involves the same kind of self-assessment. This is why revision plays such a prominent role in the English 100 program: becoming a better writer is about developing good habits of writing through practice, drafting, and redrafting to see what works and what doesn't.

Writing is a process that includes at least four major steps. These steps are recursive—that is, the process does not necessarily move in one direction in a straight line. Generally, though, we think of the steps in this order: prewriting (invention), when you come up with your initial plan for what you're going to write; drafting, when you put down on paper your ideas; revision, when you look at your draft and consider all the ways you can strengthen it; and editing and proofreading, when you put the finishing touches on the spelling, grammar, and overall presentation of your writing.

When we think about writing, we often think primarily of the prewriting and drafting stages of the process. Sometimes, too, we procrastinate and only have time for one draft. But this results in weaker writing, because the best way (some might say the only way) to improve our writing is to keep focusing on it over time. When we spend time revising, which literally means "looking back" or "looking again" we give ourselves a new perspective on what we initially did, and it is much easier to see ways of improving our work.

Revision does not mean simply correcting mistakes in grammar, punctuation, or formatting. These are "lower order concerns," sentence-level problems which are easily fixed with the help of a good style guide during the editing stage of the writing process. In contrast, revision focuses on "higher order concerns," such as the organization of an argument, the point of a narrative, the assumptions we make about our audience and so forth. Unlike editing, or even prewriting and drafting, revision takes much time. In fact many writers spend much more time revising than they do writing a first draft or polishing a final one. The emphasis on revision in English 100 underscores the fact that good writing need not rest on 'natural' talent but requires the development of good habits. This understanding of writing as a process is built into the English 100 grading system, which relies on portfolios. Papers are not drafted and turned in for an immediate grade. Instead, major assignments go through a process of drafting, feedback, and revision. Grades come at the end of the process when you turn in a portfolio (or collection) of your work according to guidelines your instructor will give you.

DIGITAL MEDIA AND MULTIMODAL COMPOSING IN ENGLISH 100

The term "media" encompasses any format for communication. "Media" is actually the plural form of "medium," which is a Latin (and now English) word meaning "middle" or "intermediary." A "medium" is the "middle" part of communication—the means by which a message travels from one person to another. Different "middles" exist for oral, written, printed, and digital communication. For example, a musician uses a voice to share tunes and lyrics with listeners, or you might handwrite a postcard to communicate with your grandparents or a friend who is far away. In the first case, the voice is the medium; in the second, it is the postcard (or the writing on the postcard). Often, media are used in combination. Digital media, such as Web sites and blogs, are especially integrated. And YouTube videos, for example, combine oral and written media and then transmit them to an audience using a digital medium.

One of the central goals of English 100 is to teach students critical and effective ways to engage in the four modes of literacy: speaking, reading, listening, and especially writing. But these modes of literacy aren't static: as the media or texts we encounter change, our literacy must also adapt. Think about the way you read today. A typical Web page displays a complex arrangement of text, hyperlinks, images, advertisements, even videos and sound. Reading a Web page requires a different literacy than reading a book: you must learn how to navigate all the elements of the digital page. Digital literacy might be something you've grown up with, something you use every day when you text or contact friends through social media sites. Digital literacy is also an important tool in the classroom. Improving digital literacy can help you become a more discerning researcher, capable of analyzing the reliability of sources. In addition, learning to create and assess your own digital writing can strengthen your critical thinking skills by promoting rhetorical awareness across different media. In other words, the skills of synthesis and analysis that you learn with one kind of text are transportable to other modes of communication. The rhetorical approach you take to analyzing a digital film can inform the way you construct a podcast or write a paper. Exploring digital media in English 100 provides the opportunity for you to understand how communication is changing in our culture and, more broadly, how you can most effectively communicate ideas within this changing context.

So far we have touched upon many examples of digital media: Web sites, blogs, YouTube videos, and the like. But as technology changes, the types of digital media we use will evolve as well. How, then, can you recognize digital media?

Digital media share three common elements: they integrate various forms of media, are social, and are user generated. Let's take a blog as an example. A blog includes text and usually pictures and video or audio content; each of these elements engages with different rhetorical modes, enhancing audience interaction. Blogs also participate in and stimulate conversations: links connect one blog to additional sources, and comments create a space for readers to agree with or challenge a blogger's argument. Finally, anyone with an Internet connection can start a blog. Unlike traditional media, no one vets or publishes — or refuses to publish — a blogger's post. While everyone has a voice, you still must scrutinize sources for yourself to determine their ultimate reliability or legitimacy. Digital media transcend the boundaries between content producers and content readers, between static texts and dynamic discourses, and between official and nonofficial sources. When you use digital media in the classroom, you create dynamic texts that participate in real-world conversations.

Multimedia work often involves prohibitively expensive equipment and software. Fortunately, UW-Madison offers a wide variety of multimedia tools for rent to students, TAs, and faculty. Laptops, projectors, still cameras, video cameras, audio recorders, and even iPads are available across campus. Generally speaking, renting equipment is free with a Wisconsin ID card. The easiest way to find out what can be rented where—and what's available at any given time—is the UW InfoLabs Equipment Checkout System, accessible at **ecs.library.wisc.edu**. On this page, you can search by equipment type, find all the locations that carry what you want, see where the buildings are located on a map, and get in touch with the location to arrange your rental. And some of these locations—College Library, for example—have computers with multimedia software like Photoshop and Final Cut Pro installed on them. Just call or e-mail the location to find out if they have what you need.

To help you maximize your time and the efficacy of your multimedia work, UW-Madison also provides training for both equipment and software. DoIT offers a huge range of training services, including personal and class sessions through a program called Software Training for Students (STS), and extensive video training. Information on DoIT training is available at **www.doit.wisc.edu/training/**. And if your equipment ever malfunctions or breaks, DoIT has a staff of trained technicians to help you get back up and running. You may also find help at DesignLab located in College Library (**designlab.wisc.edu**).

STUART GREENE

Argument as Conversation: The Role of Inquiry in Writing a Researched Argument

Argument is very much a part of what we do every day: We confront a public issue, something that is open to dispute, and we take a stand and support what we think and feel with what we believe are good reasons. Seen in this way, argument is very much like a conversation. By this, I mean that making an argument entails providing good reasons to support your viewpoint, as well as counterarguments, and recognizing how and why readers might object to your ideas. The metaphor of conversation emphasizes the social nature of writing. Thus inquiry, research, and writing arguments are intimately related. If, for example, you are to understand the different ways others have approached your subject, then you will need to do your "homework." This is what Doug Brent (1996) means when he says that research consists of "the looking-up of facts in the context of other worldviews, other ways of seeing" (78).

In learning to argue within an academic setting, such as the one you probably find yourself in now, it is useful to think about writing as a form of inquiry in which you convey your understanding of the claims people make, the questions they raise, and the conflicts they address. As a form of inquiry, then, writing begins with problems, conflicts, and questions that you identify as important. The questions that your teacher raises and that you raise should be questions that are open to dispute and for which there are not prepackaged answers. Readers within an academic setting expect that you will advance a scholarly conversation and not reproduce

Greene, Stuart. "Argument as Conversation: The Role of Inquiry in Writing a Researched Argument." *The Subject Is Research*. Ed. Wendy Bishop and Pavel Zemliansky. Portsmouth, NH: Boynton/Cook, 2001. 145–64. Reprinted by permission of the author.

others' ideas. Therefore, it is important to find out who else has confronted these problems, conflicts, and questions in order to take a stand within some ongoing scholarly conversation. You will want to read with an eye toward the claims writers make, claims that they are making with respect to you, in the sense that writers want you to think and feel in a certain way. You will want to read others' work critically, seeing if the reasons writers use to support their arguments are what you would consider good reasons. And finally, you will want to consider the possible counterarguments to the claims writers make and the views that call your own ideas into question.

Like the verbal conversations you have with others, effective arguments never take place in a vacuum; they take into account previous conversations that have taken place about the subject under discussion. Seeing research as a means for advancing a conversation makes the research process more *real*, especially if you recognize that you will need to support your claims with evidence in order to persuade readers to agree with you. The concept and practice of research arises out of the specific social context of your readers' questions and skepticism.

Reading necessarily plays a prominent role in the many forms of writing that you do, but not simply as a process of gathering information. This is true whether you write personal essays, editorials, or original research based on library research. Instead, as James Crosswhite suggests in his book *The Rhetoric of Reason*, reading "means making judgments about which of the many voices one encounters can be brought together into productive conversation" (131).

When we sit down to write an argument intended to persuade someone to do or to believe something, we are never really the first to broach the topic about which we are writing. Thus, learning how to write a researched argument is a process of learning how to enter conversations that are already going on in written form. This idea of writing as dialogue—not only between author and reader but between the text and everything that has been said or written beforehand—is important. Writing is a process of balancing our goals with the history of similar kinds of communication, particularly others' arguments that have been made on the same subject. The conversations that have already been going on about a topic are the topic's historical context.

Perhaps the most eloquent statement of writing as conversation comes from Kenneth Burke (1941) in an oft-quoted passage:

Imagine that you enter a parlor. You come late. When you arrive, others have long preceded you, and they are engaged in a heated discussion, a discussion too heated for them to pause and tell you exactly what it is about. In fact the discussion had already begun long before any of them got there, so that no one present is qualified to retrace for you all the steps that had gone before. You listen for a while, until you decide that you have caught the tenor of the argument; then you put in your oar. Someone answers; you answer him; another comes to your defense; another aligns himself against you, to either the embarrassment or gratification of your opponent, depending on the quality of your ally's assistance. However, the discussion is interminable. The hour grows late, you must depart, with the discussion still vigorously in progress. (110–111)

As this passage describes, every argument you make is connected to other arguments. Every time you write an argument, the way you position yourself will depend on three things: which previously stated arguments you share, which previously stated arguments you want to refute, and what new opinions and supporting information you are going to bring to the conversation. You may, for example, affirm others for raising important issues, but assert that they have not given those issues the thought or emphasis that they deserve. Or you may raise a related issue that has been ignored entirely.

ENTERING THE CONVERSATION

To develop an argument that is akin to a conversation, it is helpful to think of writing as a process of understanding conflicts, the claims others make, and the important questions to ask, not simply as the ability to tell a story that influences readers' ways of looking at the world or to find good reasons to support our own beliefs. The real work of writing a researched argument occurs when you try to figure out the answers to the following:

- What topics have people been talking about?
- What is a relevant problem?
- What kinds of evidence might persuade readers?
- What objections might readers have?
- What is at stake in this argument? (What if things change? What if things stay the same?)

26

In answering these questions, you will want to read with an eye toward identifying an *issue*, the *situation* that calls for some response in writing, and framing a *question*.

Identify an Issue

An issue is a fundamental tension that exists between two or more conflicting points of view. For example, imagine that I believe that the best approach to educational reform is to change the curriculum in schools. Another person might suggest that we need to address reform by considering social and economic concerns. One way to argue the point is for each writer to consider the goals of education that they share, how to best reach those goals, and the reasons why their approach might be the best one to follow. One part of the issue is (*a*) that some people believe that educational reform should occur through changes in the curriculum; the second part is (*b*) that some people believe that reform should occur at the socioeconomic level. Notice that in defining different parts of an issue, the conflicting claims may not necessarily invalidate each other. In fact, one could argue that reform at the levels of curriculum and socioeconomic change may both be effective measures.

Keep in mind that issues are dynamic and arguments are always evolving. One of my students felt that a book he was reading placed too much emphasis on school-based learning and not enough on real-world experience. He framed the issue in this way: "We are not just educated by concepts and facts that we learn in school. We are educated by the people around us and the environments that we live in every day." In writing his essay, he read a great deal in order to support his claims and did so in light of a position he was writing against: "that education in school is the most important type of education."

Identify the Situation

It is important to frame an issue in the context of some specific situation. Whether curricular changes make sense depends on how people view the problem. One kind of problem that E. D. Hirsch identified in his book *Cultural Literacy* is that students do not have sufficient knowledge of history and literature to communicate well. If that is true in a particular school, perhaps the curriculum might be changed. But there might be other factors involved that call for a different emphasis. Moreover, there are often many different ways to define an issue or frame a question. For example, we might observe that at a local high school, scores on standardized tests have steadily decreased during the past five years. This trend contrasts with scores during the ten years prior to any noticeable decline. Growing out of this situation is the broad question, "What factors have influenced the decline in standardized scores at this school?" Or one could ask this in a different way: "To what extent have scores declined as a result of the curriculum?"

The same principle applies to Anna Quindlen's argument about the homeless in her commentary "No Place Like Home," which illustrates the kinds of connections an author tries to make with readers. Writing her piece as an editorial in the *New York Times*, Quindlen addresses an issue that appears to plague New Yorkers. And yet many people have come to live with the presence of homelessness in New York and other cities. This is the situation that motivates Quindlen to write her editorial: People study the problem of homelessness, yet nothing gets done. Homelessness has become a way of life, a situation that seems to say to observers that officials have declared defeat when it comes to this problem.

Frame a Good Question

A good question can help you think through what you might be interested in writing; it is specific enough to guide inquiry and meets the following criteria:

- It can be answered with the tools you have.
- It conveys a clear idea of who you are answering the question for.
- It is organized around an issue.
- It explores "how," "why," or "whether," and the "extent to which."

A good question, then, is one that can be answered given the access we have to certain kinds of information. The tools we have at hand can be people or other texts. A good question also grows out of an issue, some fundamental tension that you identify within a conversation. Through identifying what is at issue, you should begin to understand for whom it is an issue—who you are answering the question for.

FRAMING AS A CRITICAL STRATEGY FOR WRITING, READING, AND DOING RESEARCH

Thus far, I have presented a conversational model of argument, describing writing as a form of dialogue, with writers responding to the ways others have defined problems and anticipating possible counterarguments. In this section, I want to add another element that some people call framing. This is a strategy that can help you orchestrate different and conflicting voices in advancing your argument.

Framing is a metaphor for describing the lens, or perspective, from which writers present their arguments. Writers want us to see the world in one way as opposed to another, not unlike the way a photographer manipulates a camera lens to frame a picture. For example, if you were taking a picture of friends in front of the football stadium on campus, you would focus on what you would most like to remember, blurring the images of people in the background. How you set up the picture, or frame it, might entail using light and shade to make some images stand out more than others. Writers do the same with language.

For instance, in writing about education in the United States, E. D. Hirsch uses the term *cultural literacy* as a way to understand a problem, in this case the decline of literacy. To say that there is a decline, Hirsch has to establish the criteria against which to measure whether some people are literate and some are not. Hirsch uses *cultural literacy* as a lens through which to discriminate between those who fulfill his criteria for literacy and those who do not. He defines *cultural literacy* as possessing certain kinds of information. Not all educators agree. Some oppose equating literacy and information, describing literacy as an *event* or as a *practice* to argue that literacy is not confined to acquiring bits of information; instead, the notion of literacy as an *event* or *practice* says something about how people use what they know to accomplish the work of a community. As you can see, any perspective or lens can limit readers' range of vision: readers will see some things and not others.

In my work as a writer, I have identified four reasons to use framing as a strategy for developing an argument. First, framing encourages you to name your position, distinguishing the way you think about the world from the ways others do. Naming also makes what you say memorable through key terms and theories. Readers may not remember every detail of Hirsch's argument, but they recall the principle—cultural literacy—around which he organizes his details. Second, framing forces you to offer both a definition and description of the principle around which your argument develops.

For example, Hirsch defines *cultural literacy* as "the possession of basic information needed to thrive in the modern world." By defining your argument, you give readers something substantive to respond to. Third, framing specifies your argument, enabling others to respond to your argument and to generate counterarguments that you will want to engage in the spirit of conversation. Fourth, framing helps you organize your thoughts, and readers', in the same way that a title for an essay, a song, or a painting does.

To extend this argument, I would like you to think about framing as a strategy of critical inquiry when you read. By critical inquiry, I mean that reading entails understanding the framing strategies that writers use and using framing concepts in order to shed light on our own ideas or the ideas of others. Here I distinguish *reading as inquiry* from *reading as a search for information*. For example, you might consider your experiences as readers and writers through the lens of Hirsch's conception of cultural literacy. You might recognize that schooling for you was really about accumulating information and that such an approach to education served you well. It is also possible that it has not. Whatever you decide, you may begin to reflect upon your experiences in new ways in developing an argument about what the purpose of education might be.

Alternatively, you might think about your educational experiences through a very different conceptual frame in reading the following excerpt from Richard Rodriguez's memoir, *Hunger of Memory*. In this book, Rodriguez explains the conflicts he experienced as a nonnative speaker of English who desperately sought to enter mainstream culture, even if this meant sacrificing his identity as the son of Mexican immigrants. Notice how Rodriguez recalls his experience as a student through the framing concept of "scholarship boy" that he reads in Richard Hoggart's 1957 book, *The Uses of Literacy*. Using this notion of "scholarship boy" enables him to revisit his experience from a new perspective.

As you read this passage, consider what the notion of "scholarship boy" helps Rodriguez to understand about his life as a student. In turn, what does such a concept help you understand about your own experience as a student?

For weeks I read, speed-read, books by modern educational theorists, only to find infrequent and slight mention of students like me. . . . Then one day, leafing through Richard Hoggart's *The Uses of Literacy*, I found, in his description of the scholarship boy, myself. For the first time I realized that there were

Motivated to reflect upon his life as a student, Rodriguez comes across Richard Hoggart's book and a description of "the scholarship boy."

other students like me, and so I was able to frame the meaning of my academic success, its consequent price—the loss.

Hoggart's description is distinguished, at least initially, by deep understanding. What he grasps very well is that the scholarship boy must move between environments, his home and the classroom, which are at cultural extremes, opposed. With his family, the boy has the intense pleasure of intimacy, the family's consolation in feeling public alienation. Lavish emotions texture home life. *Then*, at school, the instruction bids him to trust lonely reason primarily. Immediate needs set the pace of his parents' lives. From his mother and father the boy learns to trust spontaneity and nonrational ways of knowing. *Then*, at school, there is mental calm. Teachers emphasize the value of a reflectiveness that opens a space between thinking and immediate action.

Years of schooling must pass before the boy will be able to sketch the cultural differences in his day as abstractly as this. But he senses those differences early. Perhaps as early as the night he brings home an assignment from school and finds the house too noisy for study.

He has to be more and more alone, if he is going to 'get on.' He will have, probably unconsciously, to oppose the ethos of the health, the intense gregariousness of the working-class family group. . . . The boy has to cut himself off mentally, so as to do his homework, as well as he can. (47)

His initial response is to identify with Hoggart's description. Notice that Rodriguez says he used what he read to "frame the meaning of my academic success."

The scholarship boy moves between school and home, between moments of spontaneity and reflectiveness.

Rodriguez uses Hoggart's words and idea to advance his own understanding of the problem he identifies in his life: that he was unable to find solace at home and within his working-class roots.

31

In this excerpt, the idea of framing highlights the fact that other people's texts can serve as tools for helping you say more about your own ideas. If you were writing an essay using Hoggart's term *scholarship boy* as a lens through which to say something about education, you might ask how Hoggart's term illuminates new aspects of another writer's examples or your own—as opposed to asking, "How well does Hoggart's term *scholarship boy* apply to my experience?" (to which you could answer, "Not very well"). Further, you might ask, "To what extent does Hirsch's concept throw a more positive light on what Rodriguez and Hoggart describe?" or "Do my experiences challenge, extend, or complicate such a term as *scholarship boy?*"

Now that you have a sense of how framing works, let's look at an excerpt from a researched argument a first-year composition student wrote, titled "Learning 'American' in Spanish." The assignment to which she responded asked her to do the following:

> Draw on your life experiences in developing an argument about education and what it has meant to you in your life. In writing your essay, use two of the four authors (Freire, Hirsch, Ladson-Billings, Pratt) included in this unit to frame your argument or any of the reading you may have done on your own. What key terms, phrases, or ideas from these texts help you teach your readers what you want them to learn from your experiences? How do your experiences extend or complicate your critical frames?
>
> In the past, in responding to this assignment, some people have offered an overview of almost their entire lives, some have focused on a pivotal experience, and others have used descriptions of people who have influenced them. The important thing is that you use those experiences to argue a position: for example, that even the most well-meaning attempts to support students can actually hinder learning. This means going beyond narrating a simple list of experiences, or simply asserting an opinion. Instead you must use— and analyze—your experiences, determining which will most effectively convince your audience that your argument has a solid basis.

As you read the excerpt from this student's essay, ask yourself how the writer uses two framing concepts—"transculturation" and "contact zone"—from Mary Louise Pratt's article "Arts of the Contact Zone." What do these ideas help the writer bring into focus? What experience do these frames help her to name, define, and describe?

Exactly one week after graduating from high school, with thirteen years of American education behind me, I boarded a plane and headed for a	The writer has not yet named her framing concept; but notice that the concrete details she

Caribbean island. I had fifteen days to spend on an island surrounded with crystal blue waters, white sandy shores, and luxurious ocean resorts. With beaches to play on by day and casinos to play in during the night. I was told that this country was an exciting new tourist destination. My days in the Dominican Republic, however, were not filled with snorkeling lessons and my nights were not spent at the blackjack table. Instead of visiting the ritzy East Coast, I traveled inland to a mountain community with no running water and no electricity. The bus ride to this town, called Guayabal, was long, hot, and uncomfortable. The mountain roads were not paved and the bus had no air-conditioning. Surprisingly, the four-hour ride flew by. I had plenty to think about as my mind raced with thoughts of the next two weeks. I wondered if my host family would be welcoming, if the teenagers would be friendly, and if my work would be hard. I mentally prepared myself for life without the everyday luxuries of a flushing toilet, a hot shower, and a comfortable bed. Because Guayabal was without such basic commodities, I did not expect to see many reminders of home. I thought I was going to leave behind my American ways and immerse myself into another culture. These thoughts filled my head as the bus climbed the rocky hill toward Guayabal. When I finally got off the bus and stepped into the town square, I realized that I had thought wrong: There was no escaping the influence of the American culture.

In a way, Guayabal was an example of what author Mary Louise Pratt refers to as a contact zone. Pratt defines a contact zone as "a place where cultures meet, clash, and grapple with each other, often in

gathers here set readers up to expect that she will juxtapose the culture of Guayabal and the Dominican Republic with that of the United States.

The writer names her experience as an example

33

contexts of highly asymmetrical relations of power" (76). In Guayabal, American culture and American consumerism were clashing with the Hispanic and Caribbean culture of the Dominican Republic. The clash came from the Dominicans' desire to be American in every sense, and especially to be consumers of American products. This is nearly impossible for Dominicans to achieve due to their extreme poverty. Their poverty provided the "asymmetrical relation of power" found in contact zones, because it impeded not only the Dominican's ability to be consumers, but also their ability to learn, to work, and to live healthily. The effects of their poverty could be seen in the eyes of the seven-year-old boy who couldn't concentrate in school because all he had to eat the day before was an underripe mango. It could be seen in the brown, leathered hands of the tired old man who was still picking coffee beans at age seventy.

The moment I got off the bus I noticed the clash between the American culture, the Dominican culture, and the community's poverty. It was apparent in the Dominicans' fragmented representation of American pop culture. Everywhere I looked in Guayabal I saw little glimpses of America. I saw Coca-Cola ads painted on raggedy fences. I saw knockoff Tommy Hilfiger shirts. I heard little boys say, "I wanna be like Mike" in their best English, while playing basketball. I listened to merengue house, the American version of the traditional Dominican merengue music. In each instance the Dominicans had adopted an aspect of American culture, but with an added Dominican twist. Pratt calls this transculturation. This term is used to "describe processes whereby mem-

of Pratt's conception of a "contact zone." Further, the writer expands on Pratt's quote by relating it to her own observations. And finally, she uses this frame as a way to organize the narrative (as opposed to ordering her narrative chronologically).

The writer provides concrete evidence to support her point.

The writer offers an illustration of what she experienced, clarifying how this experience is similar to what Pratt describes. Note that Pratt's verb *clash*, used in the defi nition of *contact zone*, reappears here as part of the author's observation.

34

bers of subordinated or marginal groups select and invent from materials transmitted by a dominant or metropolitan culture" (80). She claims that transculturation is an identifying feature of contact zones. In the contact zone of Guayabal, the marginal group, made up of impoverished Dominicans, selected aspects of the dominant American culture, and invented a unique expression of a culture combining both Dominican and American styles. My most vivid memory of this transculturalization was on a hot afternoon when I heard some children yelling, "Helado! Helado!" or "Ice cream! Ice cream!" I looked outside just in time to see a man ride by on a bicycle, ringing a hand bell and balancing a cooler full of ice cream in the front bicycle basket. The Dominican children eagerly chased after him, just as American children chase after the ice-cream truck.

The author adds another layer to her description, introducing Pratt's framing concept of "transculturation." Here again she quotes Pratt in order to bring into focus her own context here. The writer offers another example of transculturation.

Although you will notice that the writer does not challenge the framing terms she uses in this paper, it is clear that rather than simply reproducing Pratt's ideas and using her as the Voice of Authority, she incorporates Pratt's understandings to enable her to say more about her own experiences and ideas. Moreover, she uses this frame to advance an argument in order to affect her readers' views of culture. In turn, when she mentions others' ideas, she does so in the service of what she wants to say.

CONCLUSION: WRITING RESEARCHED ARGUMENTS

I want to conclude this chapter by making a distinction between two different views of research. On the one hand, research is often taught as a process of collecting information for its own sake. On the other hand, research can also be conceived as the discovery and purposeful use of information. The emphasis here is upon *use* and the ways you can shape information in ways that enable you to enter conversations. To do so, you need to demonstrate to readers that you understand the conversation: what others have said in the past, what the context is, and what you anticipate is the direction this conversation might take. Keep in mind, however, that contexts are neither found nor located. Rather, context, derived from the Latin *contexere*, denotes a process of weaving together. Thus your attempt to understand context is an active process of making connections among the different and conflicting views people present within a conversation. Your version of the context will vary from others' interpretations.

Your attempts to understand a given conversation may prompt you to do research, as will your attempts to define what is at issue. Your reading and inquiry can help you construct a question that is rooted in some issue that is open to dispute. In turn, you need to ask yourself what is at stake for you and your reader other than the fact that you might be interested in educational reform, homelessness, affirmative action, or any other subject. Finally, your research can provide a means for framing an argument in order to move a conversation along and to say something new.

If you see inquiry as a means of entering conversations, then you will understand research as a social process. It need not be the tedious task of collecting information for its own sake. Rather, research has the potential to change readers' worldviews and your own.

[2001]

Works Cited

Bartholomae, David, and Anthony Petrosky. 1996. *Ways of Reading: An Anthology for Writers*. New York: Bedford Books.

Brent, Doug. 1996. "Rogerian Rhetoric: Ethical Growth Through Alternative Forms of Argumentation." In *Argument Revisited; Argument Redefi ned: Negotiating Meaning in a Composition Classroom*, 73–96. Edited by Barbara Emmel, Paula Resch, and Deborah Tenney. Thousand Oaks, CA: Sage Publications.

Burke, Kenneth. 1941. *The Philosophy of Literary Form*. Berkeley: University of California Press.

Crosswhite, James. 1996. *The Rhetoric of Reason: Writing and the Attractions of Argument*. Madison, WI: University of Wisconsin Press.

Freire, Paulo. 1970. *Pedagogy of the Oppressed*. New York: Continuum.

Hirsch, E. D. 1987. *Cultural Literacy*. New York: Vintage Books.

Ladson-Billings, Gloria. 1994. *The Dreamkeepers: Successful Teachers of African American Children*. New York: Teachers College Press.

Pratt, Mary Louise. "Arts of the Contact Zone." *Profession* 91 (1991): 33–40.

Quindlen, Anna. 1993. "No Place Like Home." In *Thinking Out Loud: On the Personal, the Public, and the Private*, 42–44. New York: Random House.

Rodriguez, Richard. 1983. *Hunger of Memory: The Education of Richard Rodriguez*. New York: Bantam Books.

Acknowledgment

I wish to thank Robert Kachur and April Lidinsky for helping me think through the notions of argument as conversation and framing.

Reading Processes

What's so special about college reading? Don't you pick up the book, start on the first page, and keep going, just as you have ever since you met *The Cat in the Hat*? Reading from beginning to end works especially well when you are eager to find out what happens next, as in a thriller, or what to do next, as in a cookbook. On the other hand, much of what you read in college—textbooks, scholarly articles, research reports, your peers' papers—is complicated and challenging. Dense material like this often requires closer reading and deeper thinking—in short, a process for reading critically.

Reading critically is a useful skill. For assignments in this course alone, you probably will need to evaluate the strengths and weaknesses of essays by professionals and students. If you research any topic, you will need to figure out what your sources say, whether they are reliable, and how you might use their information. Critical reading is important in other courses too. For example, you might analyze a sociology report on violent children for its assumptions and implications as well as the soundness of its argument. When your writing relies on critical reading, you generally need to explain what is going on in the reading material and then go further, making your own point based on what you have read.

A PROCESS OF CRITICAL READING

Reading critically means approaching whatever you read in an active, questioning manner. This essential college-level skill changes reading from a spectator sport to a contact sport. You no longer sit in the stands, watching figure skaters glide by. Instead, you charge right into a rough-and-tumble hockey game, gripping your stick and watching out for your teeth.

X. J. Kennedy, Dorothy M. Kennedy, and Marcia F. Muth, *Writing and Revising: A Portable Guide*, pages 11–21. Copyright © 2007 by Bedford/St. Martin's.

38

Critical reading, like critical thinking, is not an isolated activity. It is a continuum of strategies that thoughtful people use every day to grapple with new information, to integrate it with existing knowledge, and to apply it to problems in daily life and in academic courses. Many readers use similar strategies:

• They get ready to do their reading.
• They respond as they read.
• They read on literal and analytical levels.

■ **ACTIVITY: Describing Your Own Reading Process**

How do you read a magazine, newspaper, or popular novel? What are your goals when you do this kind of reading? What's different about reading the material assigned in college? What techniques do you use for reading assignments? Which of your strategies might help your classmates, especially in classes with a lot of reading? How might you read more effectively?

Preparing to Read

College reading is active reading. Before you read, think ahead about how to approach the reading process, how to make the most of the time you spend reading.

Thinking about Your Purpose. Naturally, your overall goal for doing most college reading is to succeed in your courses. When you begin to read, ask questions like these about your immediate purpose:

• What are you reading?
• Why are you reading?
• What do you want to do with the reading?
• What does your instructor expect you to learn from the reading?
• Do you need to memorize details, find main points, or connect ideas?
• How does this reading build on, add to, contrast with, or otherwise relate to other reading assignments in the course?

Planning Your Follow-up. When you are assigned a specific essay, chapter, or article or are required to choose a reading about a certain topic, ask yourself what your instructor probably expects to follow the reading:

- Do you need to be ready to discuss the reading during class?
- Will you need to mention it or analyze it during an examination?
- Will you need to write about it or its topic?
- Do you need to find its main points? Sum it up? Compare it? Question it? Discuss its strengths and weaknesses? Draw useful details from it?

Skimming the Text. Before you actively read a text, begin by skimming it, quickly reading only enough to introduce yourself to its content and organization. If the reading has a table of contents or subheadings, read those first to figure out what the material covers and how it is organized. Read the first paragraph and then the first (or first and last) sentence of each paragraph that follows. If the material has any illustrations or diagrams, read the captions.

Responding to Reading

Encourage yourself to read energetically by monitoring both what you read and how you respond to it.

Reading Deeply. The books and articles assigned in college often require more concentration from you as a reader than simpler readings do. Use the following questions to help you understand the complexities below the surface of a reading:

- Are difficult or technical terms defined in specific ways? How might you highlight, list, or record those terms so that you can master them?
- How might you record or recall the details in the reading? How might you track or diagram interrelated ideas to grasp the connections?
- How does word choice, tone, or style alert you to the complex purpose of a reading that is layered or indirect rather than straightforward?
- How might you trace the progression of ideas in the reading? Where do you spot headings, previews of what's coming up, summaries of what's gone before, transitions, and other clues to the reading's organization?
- Does the reading include figurative or descriptive language, allusions to other works, or recurring themes? How do these elements enrich the reading?

Keeping a Reading Journal. A reading journal helps you read actively and build a reservoir of ideas for follow-up writing. You can use a special notebook or computer file to address questions like these:

- What is the subject of the reading? What is the writer's stand?
- What does the writer take for granted? What assumptions does he or she begin with? Where are these assumptions stated or suggested?
- What evidence supports the writer's main points?
- Do you agree with what the writer is saying? Do his or her ideas clash with your ideas or call into question something you take for granted?
- Has the writer taken account of other views, opinions, or interpretations of evidence?
- What conclusions can you draw from the reading?
- Has the reading opened your eyes to new ways of viewing the subject?

Annotating the Text. Writing notes on the page (or on a photocopy if the material is not your own) is a useful way to trace the author's points and to respond to them with questions or comments. You can underline key points, mark checks and stars by ideas when you agree or disagree, and jot questions in the margins. (A Critical Reading Checklist appears later in this chapter.) When one student investigated the history of women's professional sports, she annotated a key passage from an article called "Why Men Fear Women's Teams" by Kate Rounds from the January–February 1991 issue of *Ms.*

different case from individual sports

By contrast, women's professional (team) sports have failed — *key point*

spectacular. Since the mid-seventies, every professional

✓ league — softball, basketball, and volleyball — has gone belly-up.

bitter tone

In 1981, after a four-year struggle, the Women's Basketball

1st example backs up point

League (WBL), backed by sports promoter Bill Byrne, folded. The

league was drawing fans in a number of cities, but the sponsors — *What women's teams have gotten these?*

✓ weren't there, TV wasn't there, and nobody seemed to miss the

spectacle of a few good women fighting for a basketball.

Something I know about!

Or a (volleyball,) for that matter. Despite the success of (bikini) — *Why does she call it this?*

volleyball, an organization called MLV (Major League Volleyball)

bit the dust in March of 1989 after nearly three years of — *2nd example*

41

struggling for sponsorship, fan support, and television exposure.
[As with pro basketball, there was a man behind women's

She's suspicious of men

professional volleyball,] real estate investor Robert (Bat)
Batinovich. Batinovich admits that, unlike court volleyball,

oh, great

beach volleyball has a lot of "visual T&A mixed into it."

What court volleyball does have, according to former

seems like these are only two options

credential MLV executive director Lindy Vivas, is strong women athletes.
Vivas is assistant volleyball coach at San Jose State University.

Why do guys always think we're weak and prissy?

"The United States in general," she says, "has problems
dealing with women athletes and strong, aggressive females.

good quote

The perception is you have to be more aggressive in team sports
than in golf and tennis, which aren't contact sports. Women
athletes are looked at as masculine and get the stigma
of being gay."

This student's annotations helped her deepen her reading of the article
and generate ideas for her writing.

■ ACTIVITY: Annotating a Passage

Annotate the following passage from the middle of Ellen Goodman's
essay "Kids, Divorce, and the Myth" from the *Boston Globe Online*
(September 28, 2000).

Not that long ago, when the divorce statistics first began to rise, many
Americans comforted themselves with the belief that parents and children
shared the same perspective. A child in an unhappy home would surely
know it, surely suffer from it. What was right for parents—including
divorce—was right for children.

But today that seems like a soothing or perhaps self-serving myth.

One of the myth-busters is Judith Wallerstein, who has been studying
the children of divorce for over twenty-five years. Her latest book about
The Unexpected Legacy of Divorce is written about and for the offspring
of splintered families, children who carry the family rupture into their
adulthood.

This psychologist has followed 131 children of 80 California families,
a small and not-so-random sample of the one million children whose
parents divorce each year. Today a quarter of all adults under forty-four
come from divorced homes, and Wallerstein takes a handful of these

children to show in rich detail the way divorce was and remains a life-transforming event.

Her book echoes with the laments of their tribe. These are adults who spent childhood negotiating between two parents and two homes. Some were emotionally abandoned, others were subject to the crazy postdivorce years. Some still wait for disaster, and others are stronger for the struggle.

But as the elder to their tribe, Wallerstein makes one central and challenging point: "The myth that if the parents have a poor marriage the children are going to be unhappy is not true."

A SPOTLIGHT ON READING LEVELS

Educational expert Benjamin Bloom identified six levels of cognitive activity: knowledge, comprehension, application, analysis, synthesis, and evaluation.[1] Each level acts as a foundation for the next. Each also becomes more complex and demands higher thinking skills than the previous one. (See Fig. 1.) Experienced readers, however, may jump among these levels, gathering information and insight as they occur.

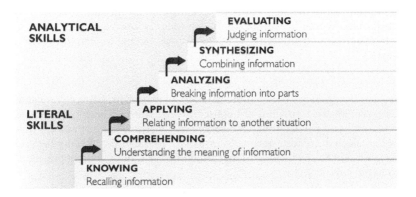

Figure 1. Using Literal and Analytical Reading Skills.
SOURCE: The information in this figure is adapted from Benjamin S. Bloom et al., *Taxonomy of Educational Objectives, Handbook 1: Cognitive Domain* (New York: McKay, 1956).

[1]Benjamin S. Bloom et al., *Taxonomy of Educational Objectives, Handbook 1: Cognitive Domain.* Copyright © 1956 by David McKay, Inc.

The first three levels are literal skills. When you show that you know a fact, comprehend its meaning, and can apply it to a new situation, you demonstrate your mastery over building blocks of thought. The last three levels—analysis, synthesis, and evaluation—are critical skills. These skills take you beyond the literal level: you break apart the building blocks to see what makes them work, recombine them in new and useful ways, and judge their worth or significance. To read critically, you must engage with a piece on both literal and analytical levels.

Reading on Literal Levels

As you first tackle an unfamiliar reading, you may struggle simply to discover what—exactly—it presents to readers. When you read literally, you decode the words in the passage, figure out the meaning, and connect the information to what you already know. For example, suppose you read in your history book a passage about Franklin Delano Roosevelt (FDR), the only American president elected to four consecutive terms of office.

Becoming Aware of the Information. Once you read the passage, even if you have little background in American history, you know and can recall the information it presents about FDR and his four terms in office.

Comprehending the Information. To comprehend the information, you need to know that a term for a U.S. president is four years and that *consecutive* means "continuous." Thus, FDR was elected to serve for sixteen years.

Applying the Information. To apply this knowledge, you think of other presidents—George Washington, who served two terms; Grover Cleveland, who served two terms but not consecutively; Jimmy Carter, who served one term; and Bill Clinton, who served two terms. Then you realize that being elected to four terms is unusual. In fact, the Twenty-Second Amendment to the Constitution, ratified in 1951, now limits a president to two terms.

Reading on Analytical Levels

After mastering a passage on the literal levels, you need to read on the analytical levels, probing the meaning beneath the surface. First, you analyze the information, considering its parts and implications from various angles. Then you gather related material and synthesize all of it, combining it to achieve new insights. Finally, you evaluate the significance of the information.

Analyzing the Information. To return to FDR's four terms as president, you can ask questions to scrutinize this information from various angles, selecting a principle that suits your purpose to break the information into its components or parts. For example, you might analyze FDR's tenure in office in relation to the political longevity of other presidents. Why has FDR been the only president elected to serve four terms? What circumstances during his terms contributed to three reelections? How is FDR different from other presidents?

Synthesizing the Information. To answer your questions, you may have to read more or review material you have read in the past. Then you begin synthesizing—combining information, pulling together the facts and opinions, identifying the evidence accepted by all or most sources, examining any controversial evidence, and drawing whatever conclusions reliable evidence seems to support. For example, it would be logical to conclude that the special circumstances of the Great Depression and World War II contributed to FDR's four terms. On the other hand, it would not be logical to conclude that Americans reelected FDR out of pity because he was a victim of polio.

Evaluating the Information. Finally, you evaluate your new knowledge to determine its significance, both to your understanding of Depression-era politics and to your assessment of your history book's approach. For instance, you might ask yourself why the book's author has chosen to make this point. How does it affect the rest of the discussion? Does this author seem reliable? And you may also have formed your own opinion about FDR's reelections, perhaps concluding that FDR's four-term presidency is understandable in light of the events of the 1930s and 1940s, that the author has mentioned this fact to highlight the unique political atmosphere of that era, and that, in your opinion, it is evidence neither for nor against FDR's excellence as a president.

■ ACTIVITY: Reading Analytically

Think back to something you have read recently that helped you make a decision, perhaps a newspaper or magazine article, an electronic posting, or a college brochure. How did you analyze what you read, breaking the information into parts? How did you synthesize it, combining it with what you already knew? How did you evaluate it, judging its contribution to your decision making?

GENERATING IDEAS FROM READING

Like flints that strike each other and cause sparks, writers and readers provoke one another. For example, when your class discusses an essay, you may be surprised by the range of insights your classmates report. If you missed some of their insights during your reading, remember that they may be equally surprised by what you see.

Often you look to other writers—in books or articles—to suggest a topic, provide information about it, or help you explain it or back it up with evidence. You may read because you want to understand ideas, test them, or debate with the writer, but reading is a dynamic process. You may find that it changes your ideas instead of supporting them. Here are suggestions for unlocking the potential hidden in a good text.

Looking for Meaty Pieces. Stimulate your thinking about current topics that intrigue you by browsing through essay collections or magazines in the library or online. Try *The Atlantic, Harper's, The New Republic, Commentary*, or a special-interest magazine like *Architectural Digest* or *Scientific American*. Check the editorials and op-ed columns in your local newspaper, the *New York Times*, or the *Wall Street Journal*. Also search the Internet on interesting subjects that challenge you to think seriously (for example, film classics or the effects of poverty on children). Look for articles that are meaty, not superficial, and that are written to inform and convince, not to entertain or amuse.

Logging Your Reading. For several days keep a log of the articles that you find. Record the author, title, and source for each promising piece so that you can easily find it again. Briefly note the subject and point of view in order to identify a range of possibilities.

Recalling Something You Have Already Read. What have you read lately that started you thinking? Return to a recent reading—a chapter in a humanities textbook, an article assigned in a sociology course, a research study for a biology course.

Capturing Complex Ideas. When you find a challenging reading, do you sometimes feel too overwhelmed to develop ideas from it? If so, read it slowly and carefully. Then consider two common methods of recording and integrating ideas from sources into papers. First, try *paraphrasing*, restating the author's ideas fully but in your own words. Then try *summarizing*, reducing the author's main point to essentials. Accurately restating what a reading says can help you grasp its ideas, especially on literal levels. Once you understand what it says, you are better equipped to agree with, disagree with, or question its points.

Reading Critically. Read first literally and then analytically. Instead of just soaking up what the reading says, engage in a dialogue or conversation with the writer. Criticize. Wonder. Argue back. Demand convincing evidence. Use the following checklist to get you started as a critical reader.

CRITICAL READING CHECKLIST

☐ What problems and issues does the author raise?

☐ What is the author's purpose? Is it to explain or inform? To persuade? To amuse? In addition to this overall purpose, is the author trying to accomplish some other agenda?

☐ How does the author appeal to readers? Where do you agree, and where do you disagree? Where do you want to say "Yeah, right!" or "I don't think so!"?

☐ How does this piece relate to your own experiences or thoughts? Have you encountered anything similar? Does the topic or approach intrigue you?

☐ Are there any important words or ideas that you don't understand? If so, do you need to reread or turn to a dictionary or reference book?

☐ What is the author's point of view? What does the author assume or take for granted? Where does the author reveal these assumptions? Do they make the selection seem weak or biased?

☐ Which statements are facts that can be verified by observation, firsthand testimony, or research? Which are opinions? Does one or the other dominate the piece?

☐ Is the writer's evidence accurate, relevant, and sufficient? Do you find it persuasive?

Analyzing Writing Strategies. Reading widely and deeply can reveal not only what others say but also how they say it and how they shape such key features as the introduction, thesis statement or main idea, major points, and supporting evidence. Ask questions like those in the following Writing Strategies Checklist to help you identify writing strategies.

WRITING STRATEGIES CHECKLIST

☐ How does the author introduce the reading? In what ways does the author try to engage readers?

☐ Where does the author state or imply the main idea or thesis?

☐ How is the text organized? What are the main points used to develop the thesis? What does the selection of these points suggest about the author's approach?

☐ How does the author supply support—facts, data, statistics, expert opinions, personal experiences, observations, explanations, examples, or other information?

☐ How does the author connect or emphasize ideas for readers?

☐ How does the author conclude the reading?

☐ What is the author's tone? How do the words and examples reveal the author's attitude, biases, or assumptions?

DAVE EGGERS [b. 1971]

Serve or Fail

In 1998, **Dave Eggers** founded the literary magazine *Timothy McSweeney's Quarterly Concern*. Three years later, *A Heartbreaking Work of Staggering Genius*, his best-selling memoir about raising his younger brother after the deaths of their parents, was a finalist for the Pulitzer Prize. Since then, he has written several books including *You Shall Know Our Velocity!* (2002) and *What Is the What* (2006). He also edits the *Best American Nonrequired Reading*, a yearly anthology, in addition to being the founding publisher of McSweeney's Press. In 2005, he coauthored *Teachers Have It Easy: The Big Sacrifices and Small Salaries of America's Teachers*.

In "Serve or Fail," a 2004 Op-Ed piece in the *New York Times*, Eggers argues that students required to do community service in college are more likely to become lifelong volunteers. Though he describes his collegiate self as a community service dropout, Eggers later founded 826 National, a network of nonprofit learning centers dedicated to teaching writing to children, and currently teaches at 826 Valencia in San Francisco.

About now, most recent college graduates, a mere week or two beyond their last final, are giving themselves a nice respite. Maybe they're on a beach, maybe they're on a road trip, maybe they're in their rooms, painting their toenails black with a Q-tip and shoe polish. Does it matter? What's important is that they have some time off.

Do they deserve the time off? Well, yes and no. Yes, because finals week is stressful and sleep-deprived and possibly involves trucker-style stimulants. No, because a good deal of the four years of college is spent playing foosball.

I went to a large state school—the University of Illinois—and during my time there, I became one of the best two or three foosball players in the Land of Lincoln. I learned to pass deftly between my rigid players, to play the corners, to strike the ball like a cobra would strike something a cobra would want to strike. I also mastered the dart game called Cricket, and the billiards contest called Nine-ball. I became expert at whiffle ball,

Dave Eggers, "Serve or Fail" from *The New York Times*, June 13, 2004. Copyright © 2004 by The New York Times Company, Inc. Reprinted by permission of the publisher.

at backyard archery, and at a sport we invented that involved one person tossing roasted chickens from a balcony to a group of us waiting below. We got to eat the parts that didn't land on the patio.

The point is that college is too long—it should be three years—and that even with a full course load and part-time jobs (I had my share) there are many hours in the days and weeks that need killing. And because most of us, as students, saw our hours as in need of killing—as opposed to thinking about giving a few of these hours to our communities in one way or another—colleges should consider instituting a service requirement for graduation.

I volunteered a few times in Urbana-Champaign—at a Y.M.C.A. and   5
at a home for senior citizens—and in both cases it was much too easy to quit. I thought the senior home smelled odd, so I left, and though the Y.M.C.A. was a perfect fit, I could have used nudging to continue— nudging the university might have provided. Just as parents and schools need to foster in young people a "reading habit"—a love of reading that becomes a need, almost an addiction—colleges are best-poised to create in their students a lifelong commitment to volunteering even a few hours a month.

Some colleges, and many high schools, have such a thing in place, and last year Michael R. Veon, a Democratic member of Pennsylvania's House of Representatives, introduced a bill that would require the more than 90,000 students at 14 state-run universities to perform 25 hours of community service annually. That comes out to more than two million volunteer hours a year.

College students are, for the most part, uniquely suited to have time for and to benefit from getting involved and addressing the needs of those around them. Unlike high school students, they're less programmed, less boxed-in by family and after-school obligations. They're also more mature, and better able to handle a wide range of tasks. Finally, they're at a stage where exposure to service—and to the people whose lives non-profit service organizations touch—would have a profound effect on them. Meeting a World War II veteran who needs meals brought to him would be educational for the deliverer of that meal, I would think. A college history major might learn something by tutoring a local middle school class that's studying the Underground Railroad. A connection would be forged; a potential career might be discovered.

A service requirement won't work everywhere. It probably wouldn't be feasible, for example, for community college students, who tend to be transient and who generally have considerable family and work demands. But exempt community colleges and you would still have almost 10 million college students enrolled in four-year colleges in the United States. If you exempted a third of them for various reasons, that would leave more than

50

6 million able-bodied young people at the ready. Even with a modest 10-hour-a-year requirement (the equivalent of two mornings a year) America would gain 60 million volunteer hours to invigorate the nation's nonprofit organizations, churches, job corps, conservation groups and college outreach programs.

And with some flexibility, it wouldn't have to be too onerous. Colleges could give credit for service. That is, at the beginning of each year, a student could opt for service, and in return he or she might get credits equal to one class period. Perhaps every 25 hours of service could be traded for one class credit, with a maximum of three credits a year. What a student would learn from working in a shelter for the victims of domestic abuse would surely equal or surpass his or her time spent in racquetball class — at my college worth one full unit.

Alternatively, colleges could limit the service requirement to a student's 10 junior year — a time when the students are settled and have more hours and stability in their schedules. Turning the junior year into a year when volunteering figures prominently could also help colleges bridge the chasm that usually stands between the academic world and the one that lies beyond it.

When Gov. Gray Davis of California proposed a service requirement in 1999, an editorial in *The Daily Californian*, the student newspaper at the University of California at Berkeley, opposed the plan: "Forced philanthropy will be as much an oxymoron in action as it is in terms. Who would want to receive community service from someone who is forced to serve? Is forced community service in California not generally reserved for criminals and delinquents?"

First of all, that's putting forth a pretty dim view of the soul of the average student. What, is the unwilling college volunteer going to *throw food* at visitors to the soup kitchen? Volunteering is by nature transformative — reluctant participants become quick converts every day, once they meet those who need their help.

Second, college is largely about fulfilling requirements, isn't it? Students have to complete this much work in the sciences, that much work in the arts. Incoming freshmen accept a tacit contract, submitting to the wisdom of the college's founders and shapers, who decide which experiences are necessary to create a well-rounded scholar, one ready to make a contribution to the world. But while colleges give their students the intellectual tools for life beyond campus, they largely ignore the part about how they might contribute to the world. That is, until the commencement speech, at which time all the "go forth's" and "be helpful's" happen.

But what if such a sentiment happened on the student's first day? What if graduating seniors already knew full well how to balance jobs, studies, family, and volunteer work in the surrounding community? What if campuses were full of underserved high school students meeting with their college tutors? What if the tired and clogged veins of thousands of towns and cities had the energy of millions of college students coursing through them? What if the student who might have become a foosball power—and I say this knowing how much those skills have enhanced my life and those who had the good fortune to have watched me—became instead a lifelong volunteer? That might be pretty good for everybody.

[2004]

JIB FOWLES [b. 1940]

Advertising's Fifteen Basic Appeals

Born in Hartford, Connecticut, **Jib Fowles** was educated at Wesleyan University (B.A.), Columbia University (M.A.), and New York University (Ph.D.). After completing his doctorate, Fowles was a Fulbright scholar in India from 1963 to 1964. His distinguished academic career includes teaching positions at New York University and the University of Houston, where he presently chairs the program in Studies of the Future. As a researcher and writer, Fowles has studied aspects of American popular culture, focusing on the intersections of media, advertising, and celebrity. He has published several books related to his specialization, including *Mass Advertising as Social Forecast* (1976), *Television Viewers and Media Snobs: What TV Does for People* (1989), and *The Case for Television* (1999). Of his work, Fowles states: "My chief preoccupation is with an appreciative analysis of industrial culture—its past, present and future."

In his essay "Advertising's Fifteen Basic Appeals," Fowles examines the human psychology behind the attractive power of elemental advertising strategies.

EMOTIONAL APPEALS

The nature of effective advertisements was recognized full well by the late media philosopher Marshall McLuhan. In his *Understanding Media*, the first sentence of the section on advertising reads, "The continuous pressure is to create ads more and more in the image of audience motives and desires."

By giving form to people's deep-lying desires, and picturing states of being that individuals privately yearn for, advertisers have the best chance of arresting attention and affecting communication. And that is the immediate goal of advertising: to tug at our psychological shirt sleeves and slow us down long enough for a word or two about whatever

Jib Fowles, "Advertising's Fifteen Basic Appeals," from *Etc.* 39, No. 3. Reprinted with permission of the International Society for General Semantics, Concord, California.

is being sold. We glance at a picture of a solitary rancher at work, and "Marlboro" slips into our minds.

Advertisers (I'm using the term as a shorthand for both the products' manufacturers, who bring the ambition and money to the process, and the advertising agencies, who supply the know-how) are ever more compelled to invoke consumers' drives and longings; this is the "continuous pressure" McLuhan refers to. Over the past century, the American marketplace has grown increasingly congested as more and more products have entered into the frenzied competition after the public's dollars. The economies of other nations are quieter than ours since the volume of goods being hawked does not so greatly exceed demand. In some economies, consumer wares are scarce enough that no advertising at all is necessary. But in the United States, we go to the other extreme. In order to stay in business, an advertiser must strive to cut through the considerable commercial hub-bub by any means available—including the emotional appeals that some observers have held to be abhorrent and underhanded.

The use of subconscious appeals is a comment not only on conditions among sellers. As time has gone by, buyers have become stoutly resistant to advertisements. We live in a blizzard of these messages and have learned to turn up our collars and ward off most of them. A study done a few years ago at Harvard University's Graduate School of Business Administration ventured that the average American is exposed to some 500 ads daily from television, newspapers, magazines, radio, billboards, direct mail, and so on. If for no other reason than to preserve one's sanity, a filter must be developed in every mind to lower the number of ads a person is actually aware of—a number this particular study estimated at about seventy-five ads per day. (Of these, only twelve typically produced a reaction—nine positive and three negative, on the average.) To be among the few messages that do manage to gain access to minds, advertisers must be strategic, perhaps even a little underhanded at times.

There are assumptions about personality underlying advertisers' efforts 5 to communicate via emotional appeals, and while these assumptions have stood the test of time, they still deserve to be aired. Human beings, it is presumed, walk around with a variety of unfulfilled urges and motives swirling in the bottom half of their minds. Lusts, ambitions, tendernesses, vulnerabilities—they are constantly bubbling up, seeking resolution. These mental forces energize people, but they are too crude and irregular to be given excessive play in the real world. They must be capped with the competent, sensible behavior that permits individuals to get along well in society. However, this upper layer of mental activity, shot through with caution and rationality, is not receptive to advertising's pitches. Advertisers want to circumvent this shell of consciousness if they can, and latch on to one of the lurching, subconscious drives.

In effect, advertisers over the years have blindly felt their way around the underside of the American psyche, and by trial and error have discovered the softest points of entree, the places where their messages have the greatest likelihood of getting by consumers' defenses. As McLuhan says elsewhere, "Gouging away at the surface of public sales resistance, the ad men are constantly breaking through into the *Alice in Wonderland* territory behind the looking glass, which is the world of subrational impulses and appetites."

An advertisement communicates by making use of a specially selected image (of a supine female, say, or a curly-haired child, or a celebrity) which is designed to stimulate "subrational impulses and desires" even when they are at ebb, even if they are unacknowledged by their possessor. Some few ads have their emotional appeal in the text, but for the greater number by far the appeal is contained in the artwork. This makes sense, since visual communication better suits more primal levels of the brain. If the viewer of an advertisement actually has the importuned motive, and if the appeal is sufficiently well fashioned to call it up, then the person can be hooked. The product in the ad may then appear to take on the semblance of gratification for the summoned motive. Many ads seem to be saying, "If you have this need, then this product will help satisfy it." It is a primitive equation, but not an ineffective one for selling.

Thus, most advertisements appearing in national media can be understood as having two orders of content. The first is the appeal to deep-running drives in the minds of consumers. The second is information regarding the good[s] or service being sold: its name, its manufacturer, its picture, its packaging, its objective attributes, its functions. For example, the reader of a brassiere advertisement sees a partially undraped but blandly unperturbed woman standing in an otherwise commonplace public setting, and may experience certain sensations; the reader also sees the name "Maidenform," a particular brassiere style, and, in tiny print, words about the material, colors, price. Or, the viewer of a television commercial sees a demonstration with four small boxes labelled 650, 650, 650, and 800; something in the viewer's mind catches hold of this, as trivial as thoughtful consideration might reveal it to be. The viewer is also exposed to the name "Anacin," its bottle, and its purpose.

Sometimes there is an apparently logical link between an ad's emotional appeal and its product information. It does not violate common sense that Cadillac automobiles be photographed at country clubs, or that Japan Air Lines be associated with Orientalia. But there is no real need for the linkage to have a bit of reason behind it. Is there anything inherent to the connection between Salem cigarettes and mountains, Coke and a smile, Miller Beer and comradeship? The link being forged in minds between product and appeal is a pre-logical one.

People involved in the advertising industry do not necessarily talk in 10 the terms being used here. They are stationed at the sending end of this communications channel, and may think they are up to any number of things—Unique Selling Propositions, explosive copywriting, the optimal use of demographics or psychographics, ideal media buys, high recall ratings, or whatever. But when attention shifts to the receiving end of the channel, and focuses on the instant of reception, then commentary becomes much more elemental: an advertising message contains something primary and primitive, an emotional appeal, that in effect is the thin end of the wedge, trying to find its way into a mind. Should this occur, the product information comes along behind.

When enough advertisements are examined in this light, it becomes clear that the emotional appeals fall into several distinguishable categories, and that every ad is a variation on one of a limited number of basic appeals. While there may be several ways of classifying these appeals, one particular list of fifteen has proven to be especially valuable. Advertisements can appeal to:

1. The need for sex
2. The need for affiliation
3. The need to nurture
4. The need for guidance
5. The need to aggress
6. The need to achieve
7. The need to dominate
8. The need for prominence
9. The need for attention
10. The need for autonomy
11. The need to escape
12. The need to feel safe
13. The need for aesthetic sensations
14. The need to satisfy curiosity
15. Physiological needs: food, drink, sleep, etc.

MURRAY'S LIST

Where does this list of advertising's fifteen basic appeals come from? Several years ago, I was involved in a research project which was to have as one segment an objective analysis of the changing appeals made in post–World War II American advertising. A sample of magazine ads would have their appeals coded into the categories of psychological needs they seemed aimed at. For this content analysis to happen, a complete roster of human motives would have to be found. The first thing that came to mind was Abraham Maslow's famous four-part hierarchy of needs. But the briefest look at the range of appeals made in advertising was enough to reveal that they are more varied, and more profane, than Maslow had cared to account for. The search led on to the work of psychologist Henry A. Murray, who together with his colleagues at the Harvard Psychological Clinic has constructed a full taxonomy of needs. As described in *Explorations in Personality*, Murray's team had conducted a lengthy series of in-depth interviews with a number of subjects in order to derive from scratch what they felt to be the essential variables of personality. Forty-four variables were distinguished by the Harvard group, of which twenty were motives. The need for achievement ("to overcome obstacles and obtain a high standard") was one, for instance; the need to defer was another; the need to aggress was a third; and so forth.

Murray's list had served as the groundwork for a number of subsequent projects. Perhaps the best-known of these was David C. McClelland's extensive study of the need for achievement, reported in his *The Achieving Society*. In the process of demonstrating that a people's high need for achievement is predictive of later economic growth, McClelland coded achievement imagery and references out of a nation's folklore, songs, legends, and children's tales.

Following McClelland, I too wanted to cull the motivational appeals 15 from a culture's imaginative product—in this case, advertising. To develop categories expressly for this purpose, I took Murray's twenty motives and added to them others he had mentioned in passing in *Explorations in Personality* but not included on the final list. The extended list was tried out on a sample of advertisements, and motives which never seemed to be invoked were dropped. I ended up with eighteen of Murrays' motives, into which 770 print ads were coded. The resulting distribution is included in the 1976 book *Mass Advertising as Social Forecast*.

Since that time, the list of appeals has undergone refinements as a result of using it to analyze television commercials. A few more adjustments stemmed from the efforts of students in my advertising classes to decode appeals; tens of term papers surveying thousands of advertisements have caused some inconsistencies in the list to be hammered out. Fundamentally, though, the list remains the creation of Henry Murray. In developing a comprehensive, parsimonious inventory of human motives, he pinpointed the subsurface mental forces that are the least quiescent and most susceptible to advertising's entreaties.

FIFTEEN APPEALS

1. *Need for sex.* Let's start with sex, because this is the appeal which seems to pop up first whenever the topic of advertising is raised. Whole books have been written about this one alone, to find a large audience of mildly titillated readers. Lately, due to campaigns to sell blue jeans, concern with sex in ads has redoubled.

The fascinating thing is not how much sex there is in advertising, but how little. Contrary to impressions, unambiguous sex is rare in these messages. Some of this surprising observation may be a matter of definition: the Jordache ads with the lithe, blouse-less female astride a similarly clad male is clearly an appeal to the audience's sexual drives, but the same cannot be said about Brooke Shields in the Calvin Klein commercials. Directed at young women and their credit-card carrying mothers, the image of Miss Shields instead invokes the need to be looked at. Buy Calvins and you'll be the center of much attention, just as Brooke is, the ads imply; they do not primarily inveigle their target audience's need for sexual intercourse.

In the content analysis reported in *Mass Advertising as Social Forecast* only two percent of ads were found to pander to this motive. Even *Playboy* ads shy away from sexual appeals: a recent issue contained eighty-three full-page ads, and just four of them (or less than five percent) could be said to have sex on their minds.

The reason this appeal is so little used is that it is too blaring and 20 tends to obliterate the product information. Nudity in advertising has the effect of reducing brand recall. The people who do remember the product may do so because they have been made indignant by the ad; this is not the response most advertisers seek.

To the extent that sexual imagery is used, it conventionally works better on men than women; typically a female figure is offered up to the male reader. A Black Velvet liquor advertisement displays an attractive woman wearing a tight black outfit, recumbent under the legend, "Feel the Velvet." The figure does not have to be horizontal, however, for the appeal to be present as National Airlines revealed in its "Fly me" campaign. Indeed, there does not even have to be a female in the ad; "Flick my Bic" was sufficient to convey the idea to many.

As a rule, though, advertisers have found sex to be a tricky appeal, to be used sparingly. Less controversial and equally fetching are the appeals to our need for affectionate human contact.

2. *Need for affiliation.* American mythology upholds autonomous individuals, and social statistics suggest that people are ever more going it alone in their lives, yet the high frequency of affiliative appeals in ads

belies this. Or maybe it does not: maybe all the images of companionship are compensation for what Americans privately lack. In any case, the need to associate with others is widely invoked in advertising and is probably the most prevalent appeal. All sorts of goods and services are sold by linking them to our unfulfilled desires to be in good company.

According to Henry Murray, the need for affiliation consists of desires "to draw near and enjoyably cooperate or reciprocate with another; to please and win affection of another; to adhere and remain loyal to a friend." The manifestations of this motive can be segmented into several different types of affiliation, beginning with romance.

Courtship may be swifter nowadays, but the desire for pair-bonding is 25 far from satiated. Ads reaching for this need commonly depict a youngish male and female engrossed in each other. The head of the male is usually higher than the female's, even at this late date; she may be sitting or leaning while he is standing. They are not touching in the Smirnoff vodka ads, but obviously there is an intimacy, sometimes frolicsome, between them. The couple does touch for Martell Cognac when "The moment was Martell." For Wind Song perfume they have touched, and "Your Wind Song stays on his mind."

Depending on the audience, the pair does not absolutely have to be young—just together. He gives her a DeBeers diamond, and there is a tear in her laugh lines. She takes Geritol and preserves herself for him. And numbers of consumers, wanting affection too, follow suit.

Warm family feelings are fanned in ads when another generation is added to the pair. Hallmark Cards brings grandparents into the picture, and Johnson and Johnson Baby Powder has Dad, Mom, and baby, all fresh from the bath, encircled in arms and emblazoned with "Share the Feeling." A talc has been fused to familial love.

Friendship is yet another form of affiliation pursued by advertisers. Two women confide and drink Maxwell House coffee together; two men walk through the woods smoking Salem cigarettes. Miller Beer promises that afternoon "Miller Time" will be staffed with three or four good buddies. Drink Dr. Pepper, as Mickey Rooney is coaxed to do, and join in with all the other Peppers. Coca-Cola does not even need to portray the friendliness; it has reduced this appeal to "a Coke and a smile."

The warmth can be toned down and disguised, but it is the same affiliative need that is being fished for. The blonde has a direct gaze and her friends are firm businessmen in appearance, but with a glass of Old Bushmill you can sit down and fit right in. Or, for something more upbeat, sing along with the Pontiac choirboys.

As well as presenting positive images, advertisers can play to the need 30 for affiliation in negative ways, by invoking the fear of rejection. If we don't use Scope, we'll have the "Ugh! Morning Breath" that causes the male and female models to avert their faces. Unless we apply Ultra Brite or Close-Up to our teeth, it's good-bye romance. Our family will be cursed with "House-a-tosis" if we don't take care. Without Dr. Scholl's antiperspirant foot spray, the bowling team will keel over. There go all the guests when the supply of Dorito's nacho cheese chips is exhausted. Still more rejection if our shirts have ring-around-the-collar, if our car needs to be Midasized. But make a few purchases, and we are back in the bosom of human contact.

As self-directed as Americans pretend to be, in the last analysis we remain social animals, hungering for the positive, endorsing feelings that only those around us can supply. Advertisers respond, urging us to "Reach out and touch someone," in the hopes our monthly bills will rise.

3. *Need to nurture.* Akin to affiliative needs is the need to take care of small, defenseless creatures—children and pets, largely. Reciprocity is of less consequence here, though; it is the giving that counts. Murray uses synonyms like "to feed, help, support, console, protect, comfort, nurse, heal." A strong need it is, woven deep into our genetic fabric, for if it did not exist we could not successfully raise up our replacements. When advertisers put forth the image of something diminutive and furry, something that elicits the word "cute" or "precious," then they are trying to trigger this motive. We listen to the childish voice singing the Oscar Mayer weiner song, and our next hot-dog purchase is prescribed. Aren't those darling kittens something, and how did this Meow Mix get into our shopping cart?

This pitch is often directed at women, as Mother Nature's chief nurturers. "Make me some Kraft macaroni and cheese, please," says the elfin preschooler just in from the snowstorm, and mothers' hearts go out, and Kraft's sales go up. "We're cold, wet, and hungry," whine the husband and kids, and the little woman gets the Manwiches ready. A facsimile of this need can be hit without children or pets: the husband is ill and sleepless in the television commercial, and the wife grudgingly fetches the NyQuil.

But it is not women alone who can be touched by this appeal. The father nurses his son Eddie through adolescence while the John Deere lawn tractor survives the years. Another father counts pennies with his young son as the subject of New York Life Insurance comes up. And all over America are businessmen who don't know why they dial Qantas Airlines when they have to take a trans-Pacific trip; the koala bear knows.

4. *Need for guidance.* The opposite of the need to nurture is the need 35 to be nurtured: to be protected, shielded, guided. We may be loath to admit it, but the child lingers on inside every adult—and a good thing it

does, or we would not be instructable in our advancing years. Who wants a nation of nothing but flinty personalities? Parent-like figures can successfully call up this need. Robert Young recommends Sanka coffee, and since we have experienced him for twenty-five years as television father and doctor, we take his word for it. Florence Henderson as the expert mom knows a lot about the advantages of Wesson oil.

The parent-ness of the spokesperson need not be so salient; sometimes pure authoritativeness is better. When Orson Welles scowls and intones, "Paul Masson will sell no wine before its time," we may not know exactly what he means, but we still take direction from him. There is little maternal about Brenda Vaccaro when she speaks up for Tampax, but there is a certainty to her that many accept.

A celebrity is not a necessity in making a pitch to the need for guidance, since a fantasy figure can serve just as well. People accede to the Green Giant, or Betty Crocker, or Mr. Goodwrench. Some advertisers can get by with no figure at all: "When E.F. Hutton talks, people listen."

Often it is tradition or custom that advertisers point to and consumers take guidance from. Bits and pieces of American history are used to sell whiskeys like Old Crow, Southern Comfort, Jack Daniel's. We conform to traditional male/female roles and age-old social norms when we purchase Barclay cigarettes, which informs us "The pleasure is back."

The product itself, if it has been around for a long time, can constitute 40 a tradition. All those old labels in the ad for Morton salt convince us that we should continue to buy it. Kool-Aid says "You loved it as a kid. You trust it as a mother," hoping to get yet more consumers to go along.

Even when the product has no history at all, our need to conform to tradition and to be guided are strong enough that they can be invoked through bogus nostalgia and older actors. Country-Time lemonade sells because consumers want to believe it has a past they can defer to.

So far the needs and the ways they can be invoked which have been looked at are largely warm and affiliative; they stand in contrast to the next set of needs, which are much more egoistic and assertive.

5. *Need to aggress.* The pressures of the real world create strong retaliatory feelings in every functioning human being. Since these impulses can come forth as bursts of anger and violence, their display is normally tabooed. Existing as harbored energy, aggressive drives present a large, tempting target for advertisers. It is not a target to be aimed at thoughtlessly, though, for few manufacturers want their products associated with destructive motives. There is always the danger that, as in the case of sex, if the appeal is too blatant, public opinion will turn against what is being sold.

61

Jack-in-the-Box sought to abruptly alter its marketing by going after older customers and forgetting the younger ones. Their television commercials had a seventy-ish lady command, "Waste him," and the Jack-in-the-Box clown exploded before our eyes. So did public reaction until the commercials were toned down. Print ads for Club cocktails carried the faces of octogenarians under the headline, "Hit me with a Club"; response was contrary enough to bring the campaign to a stop.

Better disguised aggressive appeals are less likely to backfire: Triumph 45 cigarettes has models making a lewd gesture with their uplifted cigarettes, but the individuals are often laughing and usually in close company of others. When Exxon said, "There's a Tiger in your tank," the implausibility of it concealed the invocation of aggressive feelings.

Depicted arguments are a common way for advertisers to tap the audience's needs to aggress. Don Rickles and Lynda Carter trade gibes, and consumers take sides as the name of Seven-Up is stitched on minds. The Parkay tub has a difference of opinion with the user; who can forget it, or who (or what) got the last word in?

6. *Need to achieve.* This is the drive that energizes people, causing them to strive in their lives and careers. According to Murray, the need for achievement is signalled by the desires "to accomplish something difficult. To overcome obstacles and attain a high standard. To excel one's self. To rival and surpass others." A prominent American trait, it is one that advertisers like to hook on to because it identifies their product with winning and success.

The Cutty Sark ad does not disclose that Ted Turner failed at his latest attempt at yachting's America Cup; here he is represented as a champion on the water as well as off in his television enterprises. If we drink this whiskey, we will be victorious alongside Turner. We can also succeed with O.J. Simpson by renting Hertz cars, or with Reggie Jackson by bringing home some Panasonic equipment. Cathy Rigby and Stayfree Maxipads will put people out front.

Sports heroes are the most convenient means to snare consumers' needs to achieve, but they are not the only one. Role models can be established, ones which invite emulation, as with the profiles put forth by Dewar's scotch. Successful, tweedy individuals relate they have "graduated to the flavor of Myer's rum." Or the advertiser can establish a prize: two neighbors play one-on-one basketball for a Michelob beer in a television commercial, while in a print ad a bottle of Johnnie Walker Black Label has been gilded like a trophy.

Any product that advertises itself in superlatives—the best, the first, 50 the finest—is trying to make contact with our needs to succeed. For many consumers, sales and bargains belong in this category of appeals, too; the person who manages to buy something at fifty percent off is seizing an opportunity and coming out ahead of others.

7. *Need to dominate.* This fundamental need is the craving to be powerful—perhaps omnipotent, as in the Xerox ad where Brother Dominic exhibits heavenly powers and creates miraculous copies. Most of us will settle for being just a regular potentate, though. We drink Budweiser because it is the King of Beers, and here comes the powerful Clydesdales to prove it. A taste of Wolfschmidt vodka and "The spirit of the Czar lives on."

The need to dominate and control one's environment is often thought of as being masculine, but as close students of human nature advertisers know, it is not so circumscribed. Women's aspirations for control are suggested in the campaign theme, "I like my men in English Leather, or nothing at all." The females in the Chanel No. 19 ads are "outspoken" and wrestle their men around.

Male and female, what we long for is clout; what we get in its place is Mastercard.

8. *Need for prominence.* Here comes the need to be admired and respected, to enjoy prestige and high social status. These times, it appears, are not so egalitarian after all. Many ads picture the trappings of high position; the Oldsmobile stands before a manorial doorway, the Volvo is parked beside a steeplechase. A book-lined study is the setting for Dewar's 12, and Lenox China is displayed in a dining room chock full of antiques. Beefeater gin represents itself as "The Crown Jewel of England" and uses no illustrations of jewels or things British, for the words are sufficient indicators of distinction. Buy that gin and you will rise up the prestige hierarchy, or achieve the same effect on yourself with Seagram's 7 Crown, which ambiguously describes itself as "classy." ⁵⁵

Being respected does not have to entail the usual accoutrements of wealth: "Do you know who I am?" the commercials ask, and we learn that the prominent person is not so prominent without his American Express card.

9. *Need for attention.* The previous need involved being *looked up to,* while this is the need to be *looked at.* The desire to exhibit ourselves in such a way as to make others look at us is a primitive, insuppressible instinct. The clothing and cosmetic industries exist just to serve this need, and this is the way they pitch their wares. Some of this effort is aimed at males, as the ads for Hathaway shirts and Jockey underclothes. But the greater bulk of such appeals is targeted singlemindedly at women.

To come back to Brooke Shields: this is where she fits into American marketing. If I buy Calvin Klein jeans, consumers infer, I'll be the object of fascination. The desire for exhibition has been most strikingly played to in a print campaign of many years' duration, that of Maidenform lingerie. The woman exposes herself, and sales surge. "Gentlemen prefer Hanes" the ads dissemble, and women who want eyes upon them know what they should do. Peggy Fleming flutters her legs for L'eggs, encouraging females who want to be the star in their own lives to purchase this product. The same appeal works for cosmetics and lotions. For years, the little girl with the exposed backside sold gobs of Coppertone, but now the company has picked up the pace a little: as a female, you are supposed to "Flash 'em a Coppertone tan." Food can be sold the same way, especially to the diet-conscious; Angie Dickinson poses for California avocados and says, "Would this body lie to you?" Our eyes are too fixed on her for us to think to ask if she got that way by eating mounds of guacomole.

10. *Need for autonomy.* There are several ways to sell credit card ser- 60 vices, as has been noted: Mastercard appeals to the need to dominate, and American Express to the need for prominence. When Visa claims, "You can have it the way you want it," yet another primary motive is being beckoned forward—the need to endorse the self. The focus here is upon the independence and integrity of the individual; this need is the antithesis of the need for guidance and is unlike any of the social needs. "If running with the herd isn't your style, try ours," says Rotan-Mosle, and many Americans feel they have finally found the right brokerage firm.

The photo is of a red-coated Mountie on his horse, posed on a snow-covered ledge; the copy reads, "Windsor—One Canadian stands alone." This epitome of the solitary and proud individual may work best with male customers, as may Winston's man in the red cap. But one-figure advertisements also strike the strong need for autonomy among American women. As Shelly Hack strides for Charlie perfume, females respond to her obvious pride and flair; she is her own person. The Virginia Slims tale is of people who have come a long way from subservience to independence. Cachet perfume feels it does not need a solo figure to work this appeal, and uses three different faces in its ads; it insists, though, "It's different on every woman who wears it."

Like many psychological needs, this one can also be appealed to in a negative fashion, by invoking the loss of independence or self-regard. Guilt and regrets can be stimulated: "Gee, I could have had a V-8." Next time, get one and be good to yourself.

11. *Need to escape.* An appeal to the need for autonomy often co-occurs with one for the need to escape, since the desire to duck out of our social obligations, to seek rest or adventure, frequently takes the form of one-person flight. The dashing image of a pilot, in fact, is a standard way of quickening this need to get away from it all.

Freedom is the pitch here, the freedom that every individual yearns for whenever life becomes too oppressive. Many advertisers like appealing to the need for escape because the sensation of pleasure often accompanies escape, and what nicer emotional nimbus could there be for a product? "You deserve a break today," says McDonald's, and Stouffer's frozen foods chime in, "Set yourself free."

For decades men have imaginatively bonded themselves to the 65 Marlboro cowboy who dwells untarnished and unencumbered in Marlboro Country some distance from modern life; smokers' aching needs for autonomy and escape are personified by that cowpoke. Many women can identify with the lady ambling through the woods behind the words, "Benson and Hedges and mornings and me."

But escape does not have to be solitary. Other Benson and Hedges ads, part of the same campaign, contain two strolling figures. In Salem cigarette advertisements, it can be several people who escape together into the mountaintops. A commercial for Levi's pictured a cloudbank above a city through which ran a whole chain of young people.

There are varieties of escape, some wistful like the Boeing "Some day" campaign of dream vacations, some kinetic like the play and parties in soft drink ads. But in every instance, the consumer exposed to the advertisement is invited to momentarily depart his everyday life for a more carefree experience, preferably with the product in hand.

12. *Need to feel safe.* Nobody in their right mind wants to be intimidated, menaced, battered, poisoned. We naturally want to do whatever it takes to stave off threats to our well-being, and to our families'. It is the instinct of self-preservation that makes us responsive to the ad of the St. Bernard with the keg of Chivas Regal. We pay attention to the stern talk of Karl Malden and the plight of the vacationing couples who have lost all their funds in the American Express travelers cheques commercials. We want the omnipresent stag from Hartford Insurance to watch over us too.

In the interest of keeping failure and calamity from our lives, we like to see the durability of products demonstrated. Can we ever forget that Timex takes a licking and keeps on ticking? When the American Tourister suitcase bounces all over the highway and the egg inside doesn't break, the need to feel safe has been adroitly plucked.

We take precautions to diminish future threats. We buy Volkswagen 70 Rabbits for the extraordinary mileage, and MONY insurance policies to avoid the tragedies depicted in their black-and-white ads of widows and orphans.

We are careful about our health. We consume Mazola margarine because it has "corn goodness" backed by the natural food traditions of the American Indians. In the medicine cabinet is Alka-Seltzer, the "home remedy"; having it, we are snug in our little cottage.

We want to be safe and secure; buy these products, advertisers are saying, and you'll be safer than you are without them.

13. *Need for aesthetic sensations.* There is an undeniable aesthetic component to virtually every ad run in the national media: the photography or filming or drawing is near-perfect, the type style is well chosen, the layout could scarcely be improved upon. Advertisers know there is little chance of good communication occurring if an ad is not visually pleasing. Consumers may not be aware of the extent of their own sensitivity to artwork, but it is undeniably large.

Sometimes the aesthetic element is expanded and made into an ad's primary appeal. Charles Jordan shoes may or may not appear in the accompanying avant-grade photographs; Kohler plumbing fixtures catch attention through the high style of their desert settings. Beneath the slightly out of focus photograph, languid and sensuous in tone, General Electric feels called upon to explain, "This is an ad for the hair dryer."

This appeal is not limited to female consumers: J&B scotch says "It 75 whispers" and shows a bucolic scene of lake and castle.

14. *Need to satisfy curiosity.* It may seem odd to list a need for information among basic motives, but this need can be as primal and compelling as any of the others. Human beings are curious by nature, interested in the world around them, and intrigued by tidbits of knowledge and new developments. Trivia, percentages, observations counter to conventional wisdom—these items all help sell products. Any advertisement in a question-and-answer format is strumming this need.

A dog groomer has a question about long distance rates, and Bell Telephone has a chart with all the figures. An ad for Porsche 911 is replete with diagrams and schematics, numbers and arrows. Lo and behold, Anacin pills have 150 more milligrams than its competitors; should we wonder if this is better or worse for us?

15. *Physiological needs.* To the extent that sex is solely a biological need, we are now coming around full circle, back toward the start of the list. In this final category are clustered appeals to sleeping, eating, drinking. The art of photographing food and drink is so advanced, sometimes these temptations are wondrously caught in the camera's lens: the crab meat in the Red Lobster restaurant ads can start us salivating, the Quarterpounder can almost be smelled, the liquor in the glass glows invitingly. Imbibe, these ads scream.

STYLES

Some common ingredients of advertisements were not singled out for separate mention in the list of fifteen because they are not appeals in and of themselves. They are stylistic features, influencing the way a basic appeal is presented. The use of humor is one, and the use of celebrities is another. A third is time imagery, past and future, which goes to several purposes.

For all of its employment in advertising, humor can be treacherous, 80 because it can get out of hand and smother the product information. Supposedly, this is what Alka-Seltzer discovered with its comic commercials of the late sixties; "I can't believe I ate the whole thing," the sad-faced husband lamented, and the audience cackled so much it forgot the antacid. Or, did not take it seriously.

But used carefully, humor can punctuate some of the softer appeals and soften some of the harsher ones. When Emma says to the Fruit-of-the-Loom fruits, "Hi, cuties. Whatcha doing in my laundry basket?" we smile as our curiosity is assuaged along with hers. Bill Cosby gets consumers tickled about the children in his Jell-O commercials, and strokes the need to nurture.

An insurance company wants to invoke the need to feel safe, but does not want to leave readers with an unpleasant aftertaste; cartoonist Rowland Wilson creates an avalanche about to crush a gentleman who is saying to another, "My insurance company? New England Life, of course. Why?" The same tactic of humor undercutting threat is used in the cartoon commercials for Safeco when the Pink Panther wanders from one disaster to another. Often humor masks aggression: comedian Bob Hope in the outfit of a boxer promises to knock out the knock-knocks with Texaco; Rodney Dangerfield, who "can't get no respect," invites aggression as the comic relief in Miller Lite commercials.

Roughly fifteen percent of all advertisements incorporate a celebrity, almost always from the fields of entertainment or sports. The approach can also prove troublesome for advertisers, for celebrities are human beings too, and fully capable of the most remarkable behavior. If anything distasteful about them emerges, it is likely to reflect on the product. The advertisers making use of Anita Bryant and Billy Jean King suffered several anxious moments. An untimely death can also react poorly on a product. But advertisers are willing to take risks because celebrities can be such a good link between producers and consumers, performing the social role of introducer.

There are several psychological needs these middlemen can play upon. Let's take the product class of cameras and see how different celebrities can hit different needs. The need for guidance can be invoked by Michael

67

Landon, who plays such a wonderful dad on "Little House on the Prairie"; when he says to buy Kodak equipment, many people listen. James Garner for Polaroid cameras is put in a similar authoritative role, so defined by a mocking spouse. The need to achieve is summoned up by Tracy Austin and other tennis stars for Canon AE-1; the advertiser first makes sure we see these athletes playing to win. When Cheryl Tiegs speaks up for Olympus cameras, it is the need for attention that is being targeted.

The past and future, being outside our grasp, are exploited by adver- 85 tisers as locales for the projection of needs. History can offer up heroes (and call up the need to achieve) or traditions (need for guidance) as well as art objects (need for aesthetic sensations). Nostalgia is a kindly version of personal history and is deployed by advertisers to rouse needs for affiliation and for guidance; the need to escape can come in here, too. The same need to escape is sometimes the point of futuristic appeals but picturing the avant-garde can also be a way to get at the need to achieve.

ANALYZING ADVERTISEMENTS

When analyzing ads yourself for their emotional appeals, it takes a bit of practice to learn to ignore the product information (as well as one's own experience and feelings about the product). But that skill comes soon enough, as does the ability to quickly sort out from all the non-product aspects of an ad the chief element which is the most striking, the most likely to snag attention first and penetrate brains farthest. The key to the appeal, this element usually presents itself centrally and forwardly to the reader or viewer.

Another clue: the viewing angle which the audience has on the ad's subjects is informative. If the subjects are photographed or filmed from below and thus are looking down at you much as the Green Giant does, then the need to be guided is a good candidate for the ad's emotional appeal. If, on the other hand, the subjects are shot from above and appear deferential, as is often the case with children or female models, then other needs are being appealed to.

To figure out an ad's emotional appeal, it is wise to know (or have a good hunch about) who the targeted consumers are; this can often be inferred from the magazine or television show it appears in. This piece of information is a great help in determining the appeal and in deciding between two different interpretations. For example, if an ad features a partially undressed female, this would typically signal one appeal for readers of *Penthouse* (need for sex) and another for readers of *Cosmopolitan* (need for attention).

It would be convenient if every ad made just one appeal, were aimed at just one need. Unfortunately, things are often not that simple. A cigarette ad with a couple at the edge of a polo field is trying to hit both the need for affiliation and the need for prominence; depending on the attitude of the male, dominance could also be an ingredient in this. An ad for Chimere perfume incorporates two photos: in the top one the lady is being commanding at a business luncheon (need to dominate), but in the lower one she is being bussed (need for affiliation). Better ads, however, seem to avoid being too diffused; in the study of post–World War II advertising described earlier, appeals grew more focused as the decades passed. As a rule of thumb, about sixty percent have two conspicuous appeals; the last twenty percent have three or more. Rather than looking for the greatest number of appeals, decoding ads is most productive when the loudest one or two appeals are discerned, since those are the appeals with the best chance of grabbing people's attention.

Finally, analyzing ads does not have to be a solo activity and probably 90 should not be. The greater number of people there are involved, the better chance there is of transcending individual biases and discerning the essential emotional lure built into an advertisement.

DO THEY OR DON'T THEY?

Do the emotional appeals made in advertisements add up to the sinister manipulation of consumers?

It is clear that these ads work. Attention is caught, communication occurs between producers and consumers, and sales result. It turns out to be difficult to detail the exact relationship between a specific ad and a specific purchase, or even between a campaign and subsequent sales figures, because advertising is only one of a host of influences upon consumption. Yet no one is fooled by this lack of perfect proof; everyone knows that advertising sells. If this were not the case, then tight-fisted American businesses would not spend a total of fifty billion dollars annually on these messages.

But before anyone despairs that advertisers have our number to the extent that they can marshal us at will and march us like automatons to the check-out counters, we should recall the resiliency and obduracy of the American consumer. Advertisers may have uncovered the softest spots in minds, but that does not mean they have found truly gaping apertures. There is no evidence that advertising can get people to do things contrary to their self-interests. Despite all the finesse of advertisements, and all the subtle emotional tugs, the public resists the vast majority of the petitions.

According to the marketing division of the A.C Nielsen Company, a whopping seventy-five percent of all new products die within a year in the marketplace, the victims of consumer disinterest which no amount of advertising could overcome. The appeals in advertising may be the most captivating there are to be had, but they are not enough to entrap the wiley consumer.

The key to understanding the discrepancy between, on the one hand, the fact that advertising truly works, and, on the other, the fact that it hardly works, is to take into account the enormous numbers of people exposed to an ad. Modern-day communications permit an ad to be displayed to millions upon millions of individuals; if the smallest fraction of that audience can be moved to buy the product, then the ad has been successful. When one percent of the people exposed to a television advertising campaign reach for their wallets, that could be one million sales, which may be enough to keep the product in production and the advertisements coming.

In arriving at an evenhanded judgment about advertisements and their emotional appeals, it is good to keep in mind that many of the purchases which might be credited to these ads are experienced as genuinely gratifying to the consumer. We sincerely like the goods or service we have bought, and we may even like some of the emotional drapery that an ad suggests comes with it. It has sometimes been noted that the most avid students of advertisements are the people who have just bought the product; they want to steep themselves in the associated imagery. This may be the reason that Americans, when polled, are not negative about advertising and do not disclose any sense of being misused. The volume of advertising may be an irritant, but the product information as well as the imaginative material in ads are partial compensation.

A productive understanding is that advertising messages involve costs and benefits at both ends of the communications channel. For those few ads which do make contact, the consumer surrenders a moment of time, has the lower brain curried, and receives notice of a product; the advertiser has given up money and has increased the chance of sales. In this sort of communications activity, neither party can be said to be the loser.

MALCOLM GLADWELL   [b. 1963]

Something Borrowed

Malcolm Gladwell was born in the United Kingdom, earned a degree in history in Canada, and now lives and works as a writer in New York. He has served as a science reporter for the *Washington Post* and as a staff writer for the *New Yorker*. Gladwell's profile of inventor and marketer Ron Popeil garnered a National Magazine Award in 2001; in 2005, Gladwell was named one of *Time* magazine's 100 Most Influential People. As a writer, he links topics relating to psychology, sociology, politics, human communication, and consumer behavior. His books include *The Tipping Point: How Little Things Can Make a Big Difference* (2000), *Blink: The Power of Thinking without Thinking* (2005), and *Outliers: The Story of Success* (2008).

In "Something Borrowed," Gladwell describes the plagiarism case of the Broadway play *Frozen*, which contained verbatim excerpts from a profile written by Gladwell. For this reason, the case was personal and inspired him to pose the question of whether or not plagiarism charges should ruin one's life. In the essay, this question and Gladwell's answer is exposed.

One day this spring, a psychiatrist named Dorothy Lewis got a call from her friend Betty, who works in New York City. Betty had just seen a Broadway play called "Frozen," written by the British playwright Bryony Lavery. "She said, 'Somehow it reminded me of you. You really ought to see it,'" Lewis recalled. Lewis asked Betty what the play was about, and Betty said that one of the characters was a psychiatrist who studied serial killers. "And I told her, 'I need to see that as much as I need to go to the moon.'"

Lewis has studied serial killers for the past twenty-five years. With her collaborator, the neurologist Jonathan Pincus, she has published a great many research papers, showing that serial killers tend to suffer from predictable patterns of psychological, physical, and neurological dysfunction: that they were almost all the victims of harrowing physical and sexual abuse as children, and that almost all of them have suffered some kind of brain injury or mental illness. In 1998, she published a memoir

Malcolm Gladwell, "Something Borrowed" from *The New Yorker*, November 22, 2004. Reprinted by permission of the author.

of her life and work entitled "Guilty by Reason of Insanity." She was the last person to visit Ted Bundy before he went to the electric chair. Few people in the world have spent as much time thinking about serial killers as Dorothy Lewis, so when her friend Betty told her that she needed to see "Frozen" it struck her as a busman's holiday.

But the calls kept coming. "Frozen" was winning raves on Broadway, and it had been nominated for a Tony. Whenever someone who knew Dorothy Lewis saw it, they would tell her that she really ought to see it, too. In June, she got a call from a woman at the theatre where "Frozen" was playing. "She said she'd heard that I work in this field, and that I see murderers, and she was wondering if I would do a talk-back after the show," Lewis said. "I had done that once before, and it was a delight, so I said sure. And I said, would you please send me the script, because I wanted to read the play."

The script came, and Lewis sat down to read it. Early in the play, something caught her eye, a phrase: "it was one of those days." One of the murderers Lewis had written about in her book had used that same expression. But she thought it was just a coincidence. "Then, there's a scene of a woman on an airplane, typing away to her friend. Her name is Agnetha Gottmundsdottir. I read that she's writing to her colleague, a neurologist called David Nabkus. And with that I realized that more was going on, and I realized as well why all these people had been telling me to see the play."

Lewis began underlining line after line. She had worked at New York 5 University School of Medicine. The psychiatrist in "Frozen" worked at New York School of Medicine. Lewis and Pincus did a study of brain injuries among fifteen death-row inmates. Gottmundsdottir and Nabkus did a study of brain injuries among fifteen death-row inmates. Once, while Lewis was examining the serial killer Joseph Franklin, he sniffed her, in a grotesque, sexual way. Gottmundsdottir is sniffed by the play's serial killer, Ralph. Once, while Lewis was examining Ted Bundy, she kissed him on the cheek. Gottmundsdottir, in some productions of "Frozen," kisses Ralph. "The whole thing was right there," Lewis went on. "I was sitting at home reading the play, and I realized that it was I. I felt robbed and violated in some peculiar way. It was as if someone had stolen—I don't believe in the soul, but, if there was such a thing, it was as if someone had stolen my essence."

Lewis never did the talk-back. She hired a lawyer. And she came down from New Haven to see "Frozen." "In my book," she said, "I talk about where I rush out of the house with my black carry-on, and I have two black pocket-books, and the play opens with her"—Agnetha—"with one big black bag and a carry-on, rushing out to do a lecture." Lewis had written about biting her sister on the stomach as a child. Onstage, Agnetha fantasized out loud about attacking a stewardess on an airplane and "biting out her throat." After the play was over, the cast came onstage and took questions from the audience. "Somebody in the audience said, 'Where did Bryony Lavery get the idea for the psychiatrist?' " Lewis recounted. "And one of the cast members, the male lead, said, 'Oh, she said that she read it in an English medical magazine.' " Lewis is a tiny woman, with enormous, childlike eyes, and they were wide open now with the memory. "I wouldn't have cared if she did a play about a shrink who's interested in the frontal lobe and the limbic system. That's out there to do. I see things week after week on television, on 'Law & Order' or 'C.S.I.,' and I see that they are using material that Jonathan and I brought to light. And it's wonderful. That would have been acceptable. But she did more than that. She took things about my own life, and that is the part that made me feel violated."

At the request of her lawyer, Lewis sat down and made up a chart detailing what she felt were the questionable parts of Lavery's play. The chart was fifteen pages long. The first part was devoted to thematic similarities between "Frozen" and Lewis's book "Guilty by Reason of Insanity." The other, more damning section listed twelve instances of almost verbatim similarities—totalling perhaps six hundred and seventy-five words—between passages from "Frozen" and passages from a 1997 magazine profile of Lewis. The profile was called "Damaged." It appeared in the February 24, 1997, issue of *The New Yorker*. It was written by me.

Words belong to the person who wrote them. There are few simpler ethical notions than this one, particularly as society directs more and more energy and resources toward the creation of intellectual property. In the past thirty years, copyright laws have been strengthened. Courts have become more willing to grant intellectual-property protections. Fighting piracy has become an obsession with Hollywood and the recording industry, and, in the worlds of academia and publishing, plagiarism has gone from being bad literary manners to something much closer to a crime. When, two years ago, Doris Kearns Goodwin was found to have lifted passages from several other historians, she was asked to resign from the board of the Pulitzer Prize committee. And why not? If she had robbed a bank, she would have been fired the next day.

I'd worked on "Damaged" through the fall of 1996. I would visit Dorothy Lewis in her office at Bellevue Hospital, and watch the videotapes of her interviews with serial killers. At one point, I met up with her in Missouri. Lewis was testifying at the trial of Joseph Franklin, who claims responsibility for shooting, among others, the civil-rights leader Vernon Jordan and the pornographer Larry Flynt. In the trial, a videotape was shown of an interview that Franklin once gave to a television station. He was asked whether he felt any remorse. I wrote:

> "I can't say that I do," he said. He paused again, then added, "The only thing I'm sorry about is that it's not legal."
> "What's not legal?"
> Franklin answered as if he'd been asked the time of day: "Killing Jews."

That exchange, almost to the word, was reproduced in "Frozen." 10 Lewis, the article continued, didn't feel that Franklin was fully responsible for his actions. She viewed him as a victim of neurological dysfunction and childhood physical abuse. "The difference between a crime of evil and a crime of illness," I wrote, "is the difference between a sin and a symptom." That line was in "Frozen," too—not once but twice. I faxed Bryony Lavery a letter:

> I am happy to be the source of inspiration for other writers, and had you asked for my permission to quote—even liberally—from my piece, I would have been delighted to oblige. But to lift material, without my approval, is theft.

Almost as soon as I'd sent the letter, though, I began to have second thoughts. The truth was that, although I said I'd been robbed, I didn't feel that way. Nor did I feel particularly angry. One of the first things I had said to a friend after hearing about the echoes of my article in "Frozen" was that this was the only way I was ever going to get to Broadway—and I was only half joking. On some level, I considered Lavery's borrowing to be a compliment. A savvier writer would have changed all those references to Lewis, and rewritten the quotes from me, so that their origin was no longer recognizable. But how would I have been better off if Lavery had disguised the source of her inspiration?

Dorothy Lewis, for her part, was understandably upset. She was considering a lawsuit. And, to increase her odds of success, she asked me to assign her the copyright to my article. I agreed, but then I changed my mind. Lewis had told me that she "wanted her life back." Yet in order to get her life back, it appeared, she first had to acquire it from me. That seemed a little strange.

Then I got a copy of the script for "Frozen." I found it breathtaking, I realize that this isn't supposed to be a relevant consideration. And yet it was: instead of feeling that my words had been taken from me, I felt that they had become part of some grander cause. In late September the story broke. The *Times*, the *Observer* in England, and the Associated Press all

74

ran stories about Lavery's alleged plagiarism, and the articles were picked up by newspapers around the world. Bryony Lavery had seen one of my articles, responded to what she read, and used it as she constructed a work of art. And now her reputation was in tatters. Something about that didn't seem right.

In 1992, the Beastie Boys released a song called "Pass the Mic," which begins with a six-second sample taken from the 1976 composition "Choir," by the jazz flutist James Newton. The sample was an exercise in what is called multiphonics, where the flutist "overblows" into the instrument while simultaneously singing in a falsetto. In the case of "Choir," Newton played a C on the flute, then sang C, D-flat, C—and the distortion of the overblown C, combined with his vocalizing, created a surprisingly complex and haunting sound. In "Pass the Mic," the Beastie Boys repeated the Newton sample more than forty times. The effect was riveting.

In the world of music, copyrighted works fall into two categories—the recorded performance and the composition underlying that performance. If you write a rap song, and want to sample the chorus from Billy Joel's "Piano Man," you first have to get permission from the record label to use the "Piano Man" recording, and then get permission from Billy Joel (or whoever owns his music) to use the underlying composition. In the case of "Pass the Mic," the Beastie Boys got the first kind of permission—the rights to use the recording of "Choir"—but not the second. Newton sued, and he lost—and the reason he lost serves as a useful introduction to how to think about intellectual property.

At issue in the case wasn't the distinctiveness of Newton's performance. The Beastie Boys, everyone agreed, had properly licensed Newton's performance when they paid the copyright recording fee. And there was no question about whether they had copied the underlying music to the sample. At issue was simply whether the Beastie Boys were required to ask for that secondary permission: was the composition underneath those six seconds so distinctive and original that Newton could be said to own it? The court said that it wasn't.

The chief expert witness for the Beastie Boys in the "Choir" case was Lawrence Ferrara, who is a professor of music at New York University, and when I asked him to explain the court's ruling he walked over to the piano in the corner of his office and played those three notes: C, D-flat, C. "That's it!" he shouted. "There ain't nothing else! That's what was used. You know what this is? It's no more than a mordent, a turn. It's been done thousands upon thousands of times. No one can say they own that."

Ferrara then played the most famous four-note sequence in classical music, the opening of Beethoven's Fifth: G, G, G, E-flat. This was unmistakably Beethoven. But was it original? "That's a harder case," Ferrara

15

75

said. "Actually, though, other composers wrote that. Beethoven himself wrote that in a piano sonata, and you can find figures like that in composers who predate Beethoven. It's one thing if you're talking about *da-da-da dummm, da-da-da dummm* — those notes, with those durations. But just the four pitches, G, G, G, E-flat? Nobody owns those."

Ferrara once served as an expert witness for Andrew Lloyd Webber, 20 who was being sued by Ray Repp, a composer of Catholic folk music. Repp said that the opening few bars of Lloyd Webber's 1984 "Phantom Song," from "The Phantom of the Opera," bore an overwhelming resemblance to his composition "Till You," written six years earlier, in 1978. As Ferrara told the story, he sat down at the piano again and played the beginning of both songs, one after the other; sure enough, they sounded strikingly similar. "Here's Lloyd Webber," he said, calling out each note as he played it. "Here's Repp. Same sequence. The only difference is that Andrew writes a perfect fourth and Repp writes a sixth."

But Ferrara wasn't quite finished. "I said, let me have everything Andrew Lloyd Webber wrote prior to 1978 — 'Jesus Christ Superstar,' 'Joseph,' 'Evita.' " He combed through every score, and in "Joseph and the Amazing Technicolor Dreamcoat" he found what he was looking for. "It's the song 'Benjamin Calypso.' " Ferrara started playing it. It was immediately familiar. "It's the first phrase of 'Phantom Song.' It's even using the same notes. But wait — it gets better. Here's 'Close Every Door,' from a 1969 concert performance of 'Joseph.' " Ferrara is a dapper, animated man, with a thin, well-manicured mustache, and thinking about the Lloyd Webber case was almost enough to make him jump up and down. He began to play again. It was the second phrase of "Phantom." "The first half of 'Phantom' is in 'Benjamin Calypso.' The second half is in 'Close Every Door.' They are identical. On the button. In the case of the first theme, in fact, 'Benjamin Calypso' is closer to the first half of the theme at issue than the plaintiff's song. Lloyd Webber writes something in 1984, and he borrows from himself."

In the "Choir" case, the Beastie Boys' copying didn't amount to theft because it was too trivial. In the "Phantom" case, what Lloyd Webber was alleged to have copied didn't amount to theft because the material in question wasn't original to his accuser. Under copyright law, what matters is not that you copied someone else's work. What matters is *what* you copied, and *how much* you copied. Intellectual-property doctrine isn't a straightforward application of the ethical principle "Thou shalt not steal." At its core is the notion that there are certain situations where you *can* steal. The protections of copyright, for instance, are time-limited; once something passes into the public domain, anyone can copy it without restriction. Or suppose that you invented a cure for breast cancer in your basement lab. Any patent you received would protect your intellectual property for twenty years, but after that anyone could take your invention. You get an initial monopoly on your creation because we want to provide economic incentives for people to invent things like cancer drugs. But everyone gets to steal your breast-cancer cure—after a decent interval—because it is also in society's interest to let as many people as possible copy your invention; only then can others learn from it, and build on it, and come up with better and cheaper alternatives. This balance between the protecting and the limiting of intellectual property is, in fact, enshrined in the Constitution: "Congress shall have the power to promote the Progress of Science and useful Arts, by securing for limited"—note that specification, *limited*—"Times to Authors and Inventors the exclusive Right to their respective Writings and Discoveries."

So is it true that words belong to the person who wrote them, just as other kinds of property belong to their owners? Actually, no. As the Stanford law professor Lawrence Lessig argues in his new book "Free Culture":

> In ordinary language, to call a copyright a "property" right is a bit misleading, for the property of copyright is an odd kind of property. . . . I understand what I am taking when I take the picnic table you put in your backyard. I am taking a thing, the picnic table, and after I take it, you don't have it. But what am I taking when I take the good idea you had to put a picnic table in the backyard—by, for example, going to Sears, buying a table, and putting it in my backyard? What is the thing that I am taking then?
>
> The point is not just about the thingness of picnic tables versus ideas, though that is an important difference. The point instead is that in the ordinary case—indeed, in practically every case except for a narrow range of exceptions—ideas released to the world are free. I don't take anything from you when I copy the way you dress—though I might seem weird if I do it every day. . . . Instead, as Thomas Jefferson said (and this is especially true when I copy the way someone dresses), "He who receives an idea from me, receives instruction himself without lessening mine; as he who lights his taper at mine, receives light without darkening me."

Lessig argues that, when it comes to drawing this line between private interests and public interests in intellectual property, the courts and Congress have, in recent years, swung much too far in the direction of private interests. He writes, for instance, about the fight by some developing countries to get access to inexpensive versions of Western drugs through what is called "parallel importation"—buying drugs from another developing country that has been licensed to produce patented medicines.

The move would save countless lives. But it has been opposed by the United States not on the ground that it would cut into the profits of Western pharmaceutical companies (they don't sell that many patented drugs in developing countries anyway) but on the ground that it violates the sanctity of intellectual property. "We as a culture have lost this sense of balance," Lessig writes. "A certain property fundamentalism, having no connection to our tradition, now reigns in this culture."

Even what Lessig decries as intellectual-property extremism, however, 25 acknowledges that intellectual property has its limits. The United States didn't say that developing countries could never get access to cheap versions of American drugs. It said only that they would have to wait until the patents on those drugs expired. The arguments that Lessig has with the hard-core proponents of intellectual property are almost all arguments about *where* and *when* the line should be drawn between the right to copy and the right to protection from copying, not *whether* a line should be drawn.

But plagiarism is different, and that's what's so strange about it. The ethical rules that govern when it's acceptable for one writer to copy another are even more extreme than the most extreme position of the intellectual-property crowd: when it comes to literature, we have somehow decided that copying is *never* acceptable. Not long ago, the Harvard law professor Laurence Tribe was accused of lifting material from the historian Henry Abraham for his 1985 book, *God Save This Honorable Court*. What did the charge amount to? In an exposé that appeared in the conservative publication *The Weekly Standard*, Joseph Bottum produced a number of examples of close paraphrasing, but his smoking gun was this one borrowed sentence: "Taft publicly pronounced Pitney to be a 'weak member' of the Court to whom he could not assign cases." That's it. Nineteen words.

Not long after I learned about "Frozen," I went to see a friend of mine who works in the music industry. We sat in his living room on the Upper East Side, facing each other in easy chairs, as he worked his way through a mountain of CDs. He played "Angel," by the reggae singer Shaggy, and then "The Joker," by the Steve Miller Band, and told me to listen very carefully to the similarity in bass lines. He played Led Zeppelin's "Whole Lotta Love" and then Muddy Waters's "You Need Love," to show the extent to which Led Zeppelin had mined the blues for inspiration. He played "Twice My Age," by Shabba Ranks and Krystal, and then the saccharine seventies pop standard "Seasons in the Sun," until I could hear the echoes of the second song in the first. He played "Last Christmas," by Wham!, followed by Barry Manilow's "Can't Smile Without You" to explain why Manilow might have been startled when he first heard that song, and then "Joanna," by Kool and the Gang, because, in a different way, "Last Christmas" was an homage to Kool and the Gang as well. "That sound you hear in Nirvana," my friend said at one point, "that soft and then loud, kind of exploding thing, a lot of that was inspired by the Pixies. Yet Kurt Cobain"—Nirvana's lead singer and songwriter—"was such a genius that he managed to make it his own. And 'Smells Like Teen Spirit'?"—here he was referring to perhaps the best-known Nirvana song. "That's Boston's 'More Than a Feeling.' " He began to hum the riff of the Boston hit, and said, "The first time I heard 'Teen Spirit,' I said, 'That guitar lick is from "More Than a Feeling.' " But it was different—it was urgent and brilliant and new."

He played another CD. It was Rod Stewart's "Do Ya Think I'm Sexy," a huge hit from the nineteen-seventies. The chorus has a distinctive, catchy hook—the kind of tune that millions of Americans probably hummed in the shower the year it came out. Then he put on "Taj Mahal," by the Brazilian artist Jorge Ben Jor, which was recorded several years before the Rod Stewart song. In his twenties, my friend was a d.j. at various downtown clubs, and at some point he'd become interested in world music. "I caught it back then," he said. A small, sly smile spread across his face. The opening bars of "Taj Mahal" were very South American, a world away from what we had just listened to. And then I heard it. It was so obvious and unambiguous that I laughed out loud; virtually note for note, it was the hook from "Do Ya Think I'm Sexy." It was possible that Rod Stewart had independently come up with that riff, because resemblance is not proof of influence. It was also possible that he'd been in Brazil, listened to some local music, and liked what he heard.

My friend had hundreds of these examples. We could have sat in his living room playing at musical genealogy for hours. Did the examples upset him? Of course not, because he knew enough about music to know that these patterns of influence—cribbing, tweaking, transforming— were at the very heart of the creative process. True, copying could go too far. There were tunes when one artist was simply replicating the work of another, and to let that pass inhibited true creativity. But it was equally dangerous to be overly vigilant in policing creative expression, because if Led Zeppelin hadn't been free to mine the blues for inspiration we wouldn't have got "Whole Lotta Love," and if Kurt Cobain couldn't listen to "More Than a Feeling" and pick out and transform the part he really liked we wouldn't have "Smells Like Teen Spirit"—and, in the evolution of rock, "Smells Like Teen Spirit" was a real step forward from "More Than a Feeling." A successful music executive has to understand the distinction between borrowing that is transformative and borrowing that is merely derivative, and that distinction, I realized, was what was missing from the discussion of Bryony Lavery's borrowings. Yes, she had copied my work. But no one was asking why she had copied it, or what she had copied, or whether her copying served some larger purpose.

Bryony Lavery came to see me in early October. It was a beautiful Satur-   30 day afternoon, and we met at my apartment. She is in her fifties, with short tousled blond hair and pale-blue eyes, and was wearing jeans and a loose green shirt and clogs. There was something rugged and raw about her. In the *Times* the previous day, the theatre critic Ben Brantley had not been kind to her new play, "Last Easter." This was supposed to be her moment of triumph. "Frozen" had been nominated for a Tony. "Last Easter" had opened Off Broadway. And now? She sat down heavily at my kitchen table. "I've had the absolute gamut of emotions," she said, playing nervously with her hands as she spoke, as if she needed a cigarette. "I think when one's working, one works between absolute confidence and absolute doubt, and I got a huge dollop of each. I was terribly confident that I could write well after 'Frozen,' and then this opened a chasm of doubt." She looked up at me. "I'm terribly sorry," she said.

Lavery began to explain: "What happens when I write is that I find that I'm somehow zoning on a number of things. I find that I've cut things out of newspapers because the story or something in them is interesting to me, and seems to me to have a place onstage. Then it starts coagulating. It's like the soup starts thickening. And then a story, which is also a structure, starts emerging. I'd been reading thrillers like 'The Silence of the Lambs,' about fiendishly clever serial killers. I'd also seen a documentary of the victims of the Yorkshire killers, Myra Hindley and Ian Brady, who were called the Moors Murderers. They spirited away several children. It seemed to me that killing somehow wasn't fiendishly clever. It was the opposite of clever. It was as banal and stupid and destructive as it could be. There are these interviews with the survivors, and what struck me was that they appeared to be frozen in time. And one of them said, 'If that man was out now, I'm a forgiving man but I couldn't forgive him. I'd kill him.' That's in 'Frozen.' I was thinking about that. Then my mother went into hospital for a very simple operation, and the surgeon punctured her womb, and therefore her intestine, and she got peritonitis and died."

When Lavery started talking about her mother, she stopped, and had to collect herself. "She was seventy-four, and what occurred to me is that I utterly forgave him. I thought it was an honest mistake. I'm very sorry it happened to my mother, but it's an honest mistake." Lavery's feelings confused her, though, because she could think of people in her own life whom she had held grudges against for years, for the most trivial of reasons. "In a lot of ways, 'Frozen' was an attempt to understand the nature of forgiveness," she said.

Lavery settled, in the end, on a play with three characters. The first is a serial killer named Ralph, who kidnaps and murders a young girl. The second is the murdered girl's mother, Nancy. The third is a psychiatrist from New York, Agnetha, who goes to England to examine Ralph. In the course of the play, the three lives slowly intersect—and the characters gradually change and become "unfrozen" as they come to terms with the idea of forgiveness. For the character of Ralph, Lavery says that she drew on a book about a serial killer titled "The Murder of Childhood," by Ray Wyre and Tim Tate. For the character of Nancy, she drew on an article written in the *Guardian* by a woman named Marian Partington, whose sister had been murdered by the serial killers Frederick and Rosemary West. And, for the character of Agnetha, Lavery drew on a reprint of my article that she had read in a British publication. "I wanted a scientist who would understand," Lavery said—a scientist who could explain how it was possible to forgive a man who had killed your daughter, who could explain that a serial killing was not a crime of evil but a crime of illness. "I wanted it to be *accurate*," she added.

So why didn't she credit me and Lewis? How could she have been so meticulous about accuracy but not about attribution? Lavery didn't have an answer. "I thought it was O.K. to use it," she said with an embarrassed shrug. "It never occurred to me to ask you. I thought it was *news*."

She was aware of how hopelessly inadequate that sounded, and when   35
she went on to say that my article had been in a big folder of source material that she had used in the writing of the play, and that the folder had got lost during the play's initial run, in Birmingham, she was aware of how inadequate that sounded, too.

But then Lavery began to talk about Marian Partington, her other important inspiration, and her story became more complicated. While she was writing "Frozen," Lavery said, she wrote to Partington to inform her of how much she was relying on Partington's experiences. And when "Frozen" opened in London she and Partington met and talked. In reading through articles on Lavery in the British press, I found this, from the *Guardian* two years ago, long before the accusations of plagiarism surfaced:

> Lavery is aware of the debt she owes to Partington's writing and is eager to acknowledge it.
> "I always mention it, because I am aware of the enormous debt that I owe to the generosity of Marian Partington's piece. . . . You have to be hugely careful when writing something like this, because it touches on people's shattered lives and you wouldn't want them to come across it unawares."

Lavery wasn't indifferent to other people's intellectual property, then; she was just indifferent to my intellectual property. That's because, in her eyes, what she took from me was different. It was, as she put it, "news." She copied my description of Dorothy Lewis's collaborator, Jonathan Pincus, conducting a neurological examination. She copied the description of the disruptive neurological effects of prolonged periods of high stress. She copied my transcription of the television interview with Franklin. She reproduced a quote that I had taken from a study of abused children, and she copied a quotation from Lewis on the nature of evil. She didn't copy my musings, or conclusions, or structure. She lifted sentences like "It is the function of the cortex—and, in particular, those parts of the cortex beneath the forehead, known as the frontal lobes—to modify the impulses that surge up from within the brain, to provide judgment, to organize behavior and decision-making, to learn and adhere to rules of everyday life." It is difficult to have pride of authorship in a sentence like that. My guess is that it's a reworked version of something I read in a textbook. Lavery knew that failing to credit Partington would have been wrong. Borrowing the personal story of a woman whose sister was murdered by a serial killer matters because that story has real emotional value to its owner. As Lavery put it, it touches on someone's shattered life. Are boilerplate descriptions of physiological functions in the same league?

It also matters *how* Lavery chose to use my words. Borrowing crosses the line when it is used for a derivative work. It's one thing if you're writing a history of the Kennedys, like Doris Kearns Goodwin, and borrow, without attribution, from another history of the Kennedys. But Lavery wasn't writing another profile of Dorothy Lewis. She was writing a play about something entirely new—about what would happen if a mother met the man who killed her daughter. And she used my descriptions of Lewis's work and the outline of Lewis's life as a building block in making that confrontation plausible. Isn't that the way creativity is supposed to work? Old words in the service of a new idea aren't the problem. What inhibits creativity is new words in the service of an old idea.

And this is the second problem with plagiarism. It is not merely extremist. It has also become disconnected from the broader question of what does and does not inhibit creativity. We accept the right of one writer to engage in a full-scale knockoff of another—think how many serial-killer novels have been cloned from "The Silence of the Lambs." Yet, when Kathy Acker incorporated parts of a Harold Robbins sex scene verbatim in a satiric novel, she was denounced as a plagiarist (and threatened with a lawsuit). When I worked at a newspaper, we were routinely dispatched to "match" a story from the *Times*: to do a new version of someone else's idea. But had we "matched" any of the *Times'* words—even the most banal of phrases—it could have been a firing offense. The ethics of plagiarism have turned into the narcissism of small differences: because journalism cannot own up to its heavily derivative nature, it must enforce originality on the level of the sentence.

Dorothy Lewis says that one of the things that hurt her most about 40 "Frozen" was that Agnetha turns out to have had an affair with her collaborator, David Nabkus. Lewis feared that people would think she had had an affair with her collaborator, Jonathan Pincus. "That's slander," Lewis told me. "I'm recognizable in that. Enough people have called me and said, 'Dorothy, its about you,' and if everything up to that point is true, then the affair becomes true in the mind. So that is another reason that I feel violated. If you are going to take the life of somebody, and make them absolutely identifiable, you don't create an affair, and you certainly don't have that as a climax of the play."

It is easy to understand how shocking it must have been for Lewis to sit in the audience and see her "character" admit to that indiscretion. But the truth is that Lavery has every right to create an affair for Agnetha, because Agnetha is not Dorothy Lewis. She is a fictional character, drawn from Lewis's life but endowed with a completely imaginary set of circumstances and actions. In real life, Lewis kissed Ted Bundy on the cheek, and in some versions of "Frozen" Agnetha kisses Ralph. But Lewis kissed Bundy only because he kissed her first, and there's a big difference between responding to a kiss from a killer and initiating one. When we first see Agnetha, she's rushing out of the house and thinking murderous thoughts on the airplane. Dorothy Lewis also charges out of her house and thinks murderous thoughts. But the dramatic function of that scene is to make us think, in that moment, that Agnetha is crazy. And the one inescapable fact about Lewis is that she is not crazy: she has helped get people to rethink their notions of criminality because of her unshakable command of herself and her work. Lewis is upset not just about how Lavery copied her life story, in other words, but about how Lavery *changed* her life story. She's not merely upset about plagiarism. She's upset about art—about the use of old words in the service of a new idea—and her feelings are perfectly understandable, because the alterations of art can be every bit as unsettling and hurtful as the thievery of plagiarism. It's just that art is not a breach of ethics.

When I read the original reviews of "Frozen," I noticed that time and again critics would use, without attribution, some version of the sentence "The difference between a crime of evil and a crime of illness is the difference between a sin and a symptom." That's my phrase, of course. I wrote it. Lavery borrowed it from me, and now the critics were borrowing it from her. The plagiarist was being plagiarized. In this case, there is no "art" defense: nothing new was being done with that line. And this was not "news." Yet do I really own "sins and symptoms"? There is a quote by Gandhi, it turns out, using the same two words, and I'm sure that if I were to plow through the body of English literature I would find the path littered with crimes of evil and crimes of illness. The central fact about the "Phantom" case is that Ray Repp, if he was borrowing from Andrew Lloyd Webber, certainly didn't realize it, and Andrew Lloyd Webber didn't realize that he was borrowing from himself. Creative property, Lessig reminds us, has many lives—the newspaper arrives at our door, it becomes part of the archive of human knowledge, then it wraps fish. And, by the time ideas pass into their third and fourth lives, we lose track of where they came from, and we lose control of where they are going. The final dishonesty of the plagiarism fundamentalists is to encourage us to pretend that these chains of influence and evolution do not exist, and that a writer's words have a virgin birth and an eternal life. I suppose that I could get upset about what happened to my words. I could also simply acknowledge that I had a good, long ride with that line—and let it go.

"It's been absolutely bloody, really, because it attacks my own notion of my character," Lavery said, sitting at my kitchen table. A bouquet of flowers she had brought were on the counter behind her. "It feels absolutely terrible. I've had to go through the pain for being careless. I'd like to repair what happened, and I don't know how to do that. I just didn't think I was doing the wrong thing . . . and then the article comes out in the *New York Times* and every continent in the world." There was a long silence. She was heartbroken. But, more than that, she was confused, because she didn't understand how six hundred and seventy-five rather ordinary words could bring the walls tumbling down. "It's been horrible and bloody." She began to cry. "I'm still composting what happened. It will be for a purpose . . . whatever that purpose is."

[2004]

BEVERLY GROSS [b. 1938]

Bitch

Beverly Gross is a professor of English at City University of New York. In 2002 she was awarded a Thirty-Five Year Service Award for her dedication to the university, to teaching, and to her students. Originally published in 1994 in *Salmagundi,* a quarterly magazine in the humanities and social sciences published at Skidmore College, Gross's "Bitch" looks at the usage and effect of that appellation on women. Her investigation of the definition of *bitch* in popular dictionaries of the past four centuries traces the word's evolution from its connotation of carnal looseness to its more recent, and more threatening, association with aggression, competitiveness, and power. Gross recounts uses of the word "bitch" in life and literature to demonstrate that modern women are labeled "bitches" when their power threatens to overturn, or succeeds in overturning, "the female-male nexus." For women Gross sees two choices: Cringe or, like Madonna, continue to "express [yourself]."

We were discussing Mary McCarthy's *The Group* in a course called Women Writers and Literary Tradition. McCarthy's biographer Carol Gelderman, I told the class, had been intrigued by how often critics called Mary McCarthy a bitch. I read a few citations. "Her novels are crammed with cerebration and bitchiness" (John Aldridge). "Her approach to writing [is] reflective of the modern American bitch" (Paul Schlueter). Why McCarthy? a student asked. Her unrelenting standards, I ventured, her tough-minded critical estimates—there was no self-censoring, appeasing Angel in the House of Mary McCarthy's brain. Her combativeness (her marital battles with Edmund Wilson became the stuff of academic legend). Maybe there were other factors. But the discussion opened up to the more inclusive issue of the word bitch itself. What effect does that appellation have on women? What effect might it have had on McCarthy? No one ever called Edmund Wilson a bitch. Do we excuse, even pay respect when a man is critical, combative, assertive? What is the male equivalent of the word bitch, I asked the class.

"Boss," said Sabrina Sims.

Beverly Gross, "Bitch" from *Salmagundi,* Summer 1994 issue. Copyright © 1994 *Salmagundi Magazine.* Reprinted by permission of the author.

This was an evening class at a branch of the City University of New York. Most of the students are older adults trying to fit a college education into otherwise busy lives. Most of them have fulltime jobs during the day. Sabrina Sims works on Wall Street, is a single mother raising a ten year old daughter, is black, and had to take an Incomplete in the course because she underwent a kidney transplant in December.

Her answer gave us all a good laugh. I haven't been able to get it out of my mind. I've been thinking about bitch, watching how it is used by writers and in conversation, and have explored its lexical history. "A name of reproach for a woman" is how Doctor Johnson's Dictionary dealt with the word in the eighteenth century, as though anticipating the great adaptability of this particular execration, a class of words that tends toward early obsolescence. Not bitch, however, which has been around for a millennium, outlasting a succession of definitions. Its longevity is perhaps attributable to its satisfying misogyny. Its meaning matters less than its power to denounce and subjugate. Francis Grose in *A Classical Dictionary of the Vulgar Tongue* (1785) considered bitch "the most offensive appellation that can be given to an English woman, even more provoking than that of whore." He offered as evidence "a low London woman's reply on being called a bitch" in the late eighteenth century: "I may be a whore but can't be a bitch!" The meaning of bitch has changed over the centuries but it remains the word that comes immediately to the tongue, still "the most offensive appellation" the English language provides to hurl at a woman.

The *Oxford English Dictionary* records two main meanings for the 5 noun bitch up through the nineteenth century:

1. The female of the dog

2. Applied opprobriously to a woman; strictly a lewd or sensual woman. Not now in decent use.

It was not until the twentieth century that bitch acquired its opprobrious application in realms irrespective of sensuality. The Supplement to the *OED* (1972) adds:

2a: "In mod. use, esp. a malicious or treacherous woman."

Every current desk dictionary supplies some such meaning:

A spiteful, ill-tempered woman [*World Book Dictionary*]

A malicious, unpleasant, selfish woman, esp. one who stops at nothing to reach her goal. [*Random House Dictionary*]

But malice and treachery only begin to tell the story. The informal questionnaire that I administered to my students and a number of

86

acquaintances elicited ample demonstration of the slippery adaptability of bitch as it might be used these days:

a conceited person, a snob

a self-absorbed woman

a complainer

a competitive woman

a woman who is annoying, pushy, possibly underhanded (in short, a man in a woman's body)

someone rich, thin and free!

"A word used by men who are threatened by women" was one astute response. Threat lurks everywhere: for women the threat is in being called a bitch. "Someone whiny, threatening, crabby, pestering" is what one woman offered as her definition. "Everything I try hard not to be," she added, "though it seeps through." I offer as a preliminary conclusion that bitch means to men whatever they find threatening in a woman and it means to women whatever they particularly dislike about themselves. In either case the word functions as a misogynistic club. I will add that the woman who defined bitch as everything she tries hard not to be when asked to free associate about the word came up immediately with "mother." That woman happens to be my sister. We share the same mother, who was often whiny and crabby, though I would never have applied the word bitch to her, but then again, I don't consider whiny, crabby and pestering to be prominent among my own numerous flaws.

Dictionaries of slang are informative sources, in touch as they are with 10 nascent language and the emotive coloration of words, especially words of abuse. A relatively restrained definition is offered by the only female lexicographer I consulted for whom bitch is "a nasty woman" or "a difficult task" (Anita Pearl, *Dictionary of Popular Slang*). The delineations of bitch by the male lexicographers abound with such cascading hostility that the compilers sometimes seem to be reveling in their task. For example, Howard Wentworth and Stuart Berg Flexner in *Dictionary of American Slang*:

A woman, usu., but not necessarily, a mean, selfish, malicious, deceiving, cruel, or promiscuous woman.

Eugene E. Landy's *The Underground Dictionary* (1971) offers:

1. Female who is mean, selfish, cruel, malicious, deceiving. a.k.a. cunt.

2. Female. See Female.

87

I looked up the entry for "Female" (Landy, by the way, provides no parallel entry for "Male"):

beaver, bird, bitch, broad, bush, cat, chick, crack, cunt, douche, fish, fox, frail, garbage can, heffer, pussy, quail, ruca, scag, snatch, stallion, slave, sweet meat, tail, trick, tuna. See GIRLFRIEND; WIFE.

Richard A. Spear's *Slang and Euphemism* comments on the derivative adjective:

bitchy 1. pertaining to a mood wherein one complains incessantly about anything. Although this applies to men or women, it is usually associated with women, especially when they are menstruating. Cf. DOG DAYS

Robert L. Chapman's definition in *Thesaurus of American Slang* starts off like a feminist analysis:

bitch. 1 n. A woman one dislikes or disapproves of.

Followed, however, by a sobering string of synonyms: "broad, cunt, witch."

And then this most interesting note: 15

Female equivalents of the contemptuous terms for men, listed in this book under "asshole," are relatively rare. Contempt for females, in slang, stresses their putative sexual promiscuity and weakness rather than their moral vileness and general odiousness. Some terms under "asshole," though, are increasingly used of women.

"See ball-buster." Chapman suggests under his second definition for bitch ("anything arduous or very disagreeable"). I looked up "ball-buster":

n. Someone who saps or destroys masculinity.

ball-whacker

bitch

nut-cruncher.

Some*thing* has become some*one*. The ball-buster is not a disagreeable thing but a disagreeable (disagreeing?) person. A female person. "A woman one dislikes or disapproves of." For someone so sensitive to the nuances of hostility and verbal putdown, Chapman certainly takes a circuitous route to get to the underlying idea that no other dictionary even touches: Bitch means ball-buster.

What one learns from the dictionaries: there is no classifiable thing as a bitch, only a label produced by the act of name-calling. The person named is almost always a female. The name-calling refers to alleged faults of ill-temper, selfishness, malice, cruelty, spite, all of them faults in the realm of interpersonal relating—women's faults: it is hard to think of a put-down word encompassing these faults in a man. "Bastard" and even "son of a bitch" have bigger fish to fry. And an asshole is an asshole in and of himself. A bitch is a woman who makes the name-caller feel uncomfortable. Presumably that name-caller is a man whose ideas about how a woman should behave toward him are being violated.

"Women," wrote Virginia Woolf, "have served all these centuries as looking-glasses possessing the magic and delicious power of reflecting the figure of man at twice its natural size." The woman who withholds that mirror is a bitch. Bitchiness is the perversion of womanly sweetness, compliance, pleasantness, ego-building. (Male ego-building, of course, though that is a virtual tautology; women have egos but who builds them?) If a woman is not building ego she is busting balls.

Ball-buster? The word is a nice synecdoche (like asshole) with great 20 powers of revelation. A ball-buster, one gathers, is a demanding bitch who insists on overexertion from a man to satisfy her sexual or material voraciousness. "The bitch is probably his wife." But balls also bust when a disagreeable woman undermines a guy's ego and "saps or destroys masculinity." The bitch could be his wife, but also his boss, Gloria Steinem, the woman at the post office, the woman who spurns his advances. The familiar Freudian delineation of the male-female nexus depicts male sexuality as requiring the admiration, submission and subordination of the female. The ultimate threat of (and to) the back-talking woman is male impotence.

Bitch, the curse and concept, exists to insure male potency and female submissiveness. Men have deployed it to defend their power by attacking and neutralizing the upstart. "Bitch" is admonitory, like "whore," like "dyke." Borrowing something from both words, "bitch" is one of those verbal missiles with the power of shackling women's actions and impulses.

The metamorphosis of bitch from the context of sexuality (a carnal woman, a promiscuous woman) to temperament (an angry woman, a malicious woman) to power (a domineering woman, a competitive woman) is a touchstone to the changing position of women through this century. As women have become more liberated, individually and collectively, the word has taken on connotations of aggressive, hostile, selfish. In the old days a bitch was a harlot; nowadays she is likely to be a woman who won't put out. Female sensuality, even carnality, even infidelity, have been supplanted as what men primarily fear and despise in women. Judging by the contemporary colorations of the word bitch, what men primarily fear and despise in women is power.

Some anecdotes:

1. Barbara Bush's name-calling of Geraldine Ferraro during the 1984 presidential election: "I can't say it but it rhymes with 'rich.'"

How ladylike of the future First Lady to avoid uttering the unmentionable. The slur did its dirty work, particularly among those voters disturbed by the sudden elevation of a woman to such unprecedented political heights. In what possible sense did Barbara Bush mean that Geraldine Ferraro is a bitch? A loose woman? Hardly. A nasty woman? Not likely. A pushy woman? Almost certainly. The unspoken syllable was offered as a response to Ferraro's lofty ambitions, potential power, possibly her widespread support among feminists. Imagine a woman seeking to be vice-president instead of vice-husband.

The ascription of bitchery seems to have nothing to do with Ferraro's 25 bearing and behavior. Certainly not the Ferraro who wrote about the event in her autobiography:

Barbara Bush realized what a gaffe she had made . . .

"I just want to apologize to you for what I said," she told me over the phone while I was in the middle of another debate rehearsal. "I certainly didn't mean anything by it."

"Don't worry about it," I said to her. "We all say things at times we don't mean. It's all right."

"Oh," she said breathlessly. "You're such a lady."

All I could think of when I hung up was: Thank God for my convent school training.

2. Lady Ashley at the end of *The Sun Also Rises*: "It makes one feel rather 30 good, deciding not to be a bitch." The context here is something like this: a bitch is a woman who ruins young heroic bullfighters. A woman who is propelled by her sexual drive, desires and vanity. The fascination of Brett Ashley is that she lives and loves like a man: her sexuality is unrepressed and she doesn't care much for monogamy. (Literary critics until the 1960s commonly called her a nymphomaniac.) She turns her male admirers into women—Mike becomes a self-destructive alcoholic, Robert a moony romantic, Pedro a sacrificial virgin, and Jake a frustrated eunuch. At her entrance in the novel she is surrounded by an entourage of twittering fairies. Lady Ashley is a bitch not because she is nasty, bossy or ill-tempered (she has lovely manners and a terrific personality). And perhaps not even because of her freewheeling, strident sexuality. She is a bitch because

she overturns the male/female nexus. What could be a more threatening infraction in a Hemingway novel?

2a. Speaking of Hemingway: After his falling out with Gertrude Stein who had made unflattering comments about his writing in *The Autobiography of Alice B. Toklas*, Hemingway dropped her off a copy of his newly published *Death in the Afternoon* with the handwritten inscription, "A bitch is a bitch is a bitch."

[Q.] Why was Gertrude Stein a bitch?

[A.] For no longer admiring Hemingway. A bitch is a woman who criticizes.

3. "Ladies and gentlemen. I don't believe Mrs. Helmsley is charged in the indictment with being a tough bitch" is how her defense lawyer Gerald A. Feffer addressed the jury in Leona Helmsley's trial for tax fraud and extortion. He acknowledged that she was "sometimes rude and abrasive," and that she "may have overcompensated for being a woman in a hard-edged men's business world." Recognizing the difficulty of defending what the New York *Post* called "the woman that everyone loves to hate," his tactic was to preempt the prosecution by getting there first with "tough bitch." He lost.

4. *Esquire* awarded a Dubious Achievement of 1990 to Victor Kiam, owner of the New England Patriots football team, for saying "he could never have called Boston *Herald* reporter Lisa Olson 'a classic bitch' because he doesn't use the word classic." Some background on what had been one of that year's most discussed controversies: Olson aroused the ire of the Patriots for showing up in their locker room with the male reporters after a game. Members of the Patriots, as *Esquire* states, surrounded her, "thrusting their genitals in her face and daring her to touch them."

Why is Lisa Olson a bitch? For invading the male domain of sports reportage and the male territory of the locker room? For telling the world, instead of swallowing her degradation, pain and anger? The club owner's use of "bitch" seems meant to conjure up the lurking idea of castrating female. Seen in that light the Patriots' act of "thrusting their genitals in her face" transforms an act of loutishness into a position of innocent vulnerability.

5. Bumper sticker observed on back of pickup truck: 35

Impeach Jane Fonda, American Traitor Bitch

The bumper sticker seemed relatively new and fresh. I observed it a full two decades after Jane Fonda's journey to North Vietnam which is the event that surely inspired this call to impeachment (from what? aerobics class?). Bitch here is an expletive. It originates in and sustains anger. Calling Jane Fonda a "traitor" sounds a bit dated in the 1990s, but adding "bitch" gives the accusation timelessness and does the job of rekindling old indignation.

6. Claude Brown's account in *Manchild in the Promised Land* of how he learned about women from a street-smart older friend:

Johnny was always telling us about bitches. To Johnny, every chick was a bitch. Even mothers were bitches. Of course there were some nice bitches, but they were still bitches. And a man had to be a dog in order to handle a bitch.

Johnny said once, "If a bitch ever tells you she's only got a penny to buy the baby some milk, take it. You take it, 'cause she's gon git some more. Bitches can always git some money." He really knew about bitches. Cats would say, "I saw your sister today, and she is a fine bitch." Nobody was offended by it. That's just the way things were. It was easy to see all women as bitches.

Bitch in black male street parlance seems closer to its original meaning of a female breeder—not a nasty woman and not a powerful woman, but the biological bearer of litters. The word is likely to be used in courting as well as in anger by males seeking the sexual favor of a female, and a black female addressed as bitch by an admirer is expected to feel not insulted but honored by the attention. (Bitch signifies something different when black women use it competitively about other black women.) But even as an endearment, from male to female, there is no mistaking the lurking contempt.

A Dictionary of Afro-American Slang compiled by Clarence Major (under the imprint of the leftist International Publishers) provides only that bitch in black parlance is "a mean, flaunting homosexual," entirely omitting any reference to its rampant use in black street language as the substitute word for woman. A puzzling omission. Perhaps the word is so taken for granted that its primary meaning is not even recognized as black vernacular.

Bitch, mama, motherfucker—how frequently motherhood figures in street language. Mothers are the object of insults when playing the dozens. The ubiquitous motherfucker simultaneously strikes out at one's immediate foe as well as the sanctity of motherhood. Mama, which Clarence Major defines as "a pretty black girl," is an endearment that a man might address to a sexy contemporary. "Hey mama" is tinged with a certain sweetness. "Hey bitch" has more of an edge, more likely to be addressed to a woman the man no longer needs to sweet-talk. It is hard to think of white males coming on by evoking motherhood or of white women going for it. A white male addressing a woman as bitch is not likely to be expecting a sexual reward. She will be a bitch behind her back and after the relationship is over or didn't happen.

The widespread use of bitch by black men talking to black women, its 40 currency in courting, and its routine acceptance by women are suggestive of some powerful alienation in male-female relations and in black self-identity. Although there may be the possibility of ironic inversion, as in calling a loved one nigger, a black man calling a loved one bitch is expressing contempt for the object of his desire with the gratuitous fillip of associative contempt for the woman who gave him life. Bitch, like motherfucker, bespeaks something threatening to the male sense of himself, a furious counter to emasculation in a world where, as the young Claude Brown figured out, mothers have all the power. It is not hard to see that the problem of black men is much more with white racism than it is with black women. Whatever the cause, however, the language sure doesn't benefit the women. Here is still one more saddening instance of the victim finding someone even more hapless to take things out on. (Does this process explain why Clarence Major's only reference for bitch is to the "mean, flaunting homosexual"?)

7. "Do you enjoy playing that role of castrating bitch" is a question put to Madonna by an interviewer for *The Advocate*. Madonna's answer: "I enjoy expressing myself. . . ."

A response to another question about the public's reaction to her movie *Truth or Dare*: "They already think I'm a cunt bitch, they already think I'm Attila the Hun. They already compare me to Adolf Hitler and Saddam Hussein."

Bitch has lost its power to muzzle Madonna. Unlike other female celebrities who have cringed from accusations of bitchiness (Joan Rivers, Imelda Marcos, Margaret Thatcher, Nancy Reagan), Madonna has made her fortune by exploiting criticism. Her career has skyrocketed with the media's charges of obscenity and sacrilege; she seems to embrace the bitch label with the same eager opportunism.

"I enjoy expressing myself" is not merely the explanation for why Madonna gets called bitch; "I enjoy expressing myself" is the key to defusing the power of bitch to fetter and subdue. Madonna has appropriated the word and turned the intended insult to her advantage. This act of appropriation, I predict, will embolden others with what consequences and effects it is impossible to foresee.

WILLIAM LEAST HEAT-MOON [b. 1940]

A List of Nothing
in Particular

William Least Heat-Moon was born William Trogdon in Kansas City, Missouri, in 1940. He is of English-Irish-Osage ancestry, having changed his name in honor of the latter. Educated at the University of Missouri, Columbia, Heat-Moon earned a B.A., M.A., and Ph.D. in English, as well as a B.A. in photojournalism. After losing a teaching position at his alma mater, he took to the road for three months, which resulted in *Blue Highways* (1982), an acclaimed book of topographical travel writing. Two more volumes followed: *PrairyErth: A Deep Map* (1992) focuses on a county in Kansas, and *River Horse* (1999) details Heat-Moon's journey across the United States by water. More recently, he published *Columbus in America: Turning Points in History* (2002).

In "A List of Nothing in Particular," Heat-Moon sets out to disprove the common misconception that there is "nothing" in the West Texas desert. He narrates his encounters with the plants, animals, and people he comes across in this far-from-barren landscape.

Straight as a chief's countenance, the road lay ahead, curves so long and gradual as to be imperceptible except on the map. For nearly a hundred miles due west of Eldorado, not a single town. It was the Texas some people see as barren waste when they cross it, the part they later describe at the motel bar as "nothing." They say, "There's nothing out there."

Driving through the miles of nothing, I decided to test the hypothesis and stopped somewhere in western Crockett County on the top of a broad mesa, just off Texas 29. At a distance, the land looked so rocky and dry, a religious man could believe that the First Hand never got around to the creation in here. Still, somebody had decided to string barbed wire around it.

No plant grew higher than my head. For a while, I heard only miles of wind against the Ghost; but after the ringing in my ears stopped, I heard myself breathing, then a bird note, an answering call, another kind of bird-song, and another: mockingbird, mourning dove, an enigma. I heard the high zizz of flies the color of gray flannel and the deep buzz of a blue bumblebee. I made a list of nothing in particular.

1. mockingbird
2. mourning dove
3. enigma bird (heard not saw)
4. gray flies
5. blue bumblebee
6. two circling buzzards (not yet, boys)
7. orange ants
8. black ants
9. orange-black ants (what's been going on?)
10. three species of spiders
11. opossum skull
12. jackrabbit (chewed on cactus)
13. deer (left scat)
14. coyote (left tracks)
15. small rodent (den full of seed hulls under rock)
16. snake (skin hooked on cactus spine)
17. prickly pear cactus (yellow blossoms)
18. hedgehog cactus (orange blossoms)
19. barrel cactus (red blossoms)
20. devil's pin cushion (no blossoms)
21. catclaw (no better name)
22. two species of grass (neither green, both alive)
23. yellow flowers (blossoms smaller than peppercorns)
24. sage (indicates alkali-free soil)
25. mesquite (three-foot plants with eighty-foot roots to reach water that fell as rain two thousand years ago)
26. greasewood (oh, yes)
27. joint fir (steeped stems make Brigham Young tea)
28. earth
29. sky
30. wind (always)

That was all the nothing I could identify then, but had I waited until dark when the desert really comes to life, I could have done better. To say nothing is out here is incorrect; to say the desert is stingy with everything except space and light, stone and earth is closer to the truth. I drove on. The low sun turned the mesa rimrock to silhouettes, angular and weird and unearthly; had someone said the far side of Saturn looked just like this, I would have believed him. The road dropped to the Pecos River, now dammed to such docility I couldn't imagine it formerly demarking the western edge of a rudimentary white civilization. Even the old wagonmen felt the unease of isolation when they crossed the Pecos, a small but once serious river that has had many names: Rio de las Vacas (River of Cows—perhaps a reference to bison), Rio Salado (Salty River), Rio Puerco (Dirty River).

West of the Pecos, a strangely truncated cone rose from the valley. In 5 the oblique evening light, its silhouette looked like a Mayan temple, so perfect was its symmetry. I stopped again, started climbing, stirring a panic of lizards on the way up. From the top, the rubbled land below— veined with the highway and arroyos, topographical relief absorbed in the dusk—looked like a roadmap.

The desert, more than any other terrain, shows its age, shows time because so little vegetation covers the ancient erosion of wind and storm. What appears is tawny grit once stone and stone crumbling to grit. Everywhere rock, earth's oldest thing. Even desert creatures come from a time older than the woodland animals, and they, in answer to the arduousness, have retained prehistoric coverings of chitin and lapped scale and primitive defenses of spine and stinger, fang and poison, shell and claw.

The night, taking up the shadows and details, wiped the face of the desert into a simple, uncluttered blackness until there were only three things: land, wind, stars. I was there too, but my presence I felt more than saw. It was as if I had been reduced to mind, to an edge of consciousness. Men, ascetics, in all eras have gone into deserts to lose themselves—Jesus, Saint Anthony, Saint Basil, and numberless medicine men—maybe because such a losing happens almost as a matter of course here if you avail yourself. The Sioux once chanted, "All over the sky a sacred voice is calling."

Back to the highway, on with the headlamps, down Six Shooter Draw. In the darkness, deer, just shadows in the lights, began moving toward the desert willows in the wet bottoms. Stephen Vincent Benét:

When Daniel Boone goes by, at night,
The phantom deer arise
And all lost, wild America
Is burning in their eyes.

From the top of another high mesa: twelve miles west in the flat valley floor, the lights of Fort Stockton blinked white, blue, red, and yellow in the heat like a mirage. How is it that desert towns look so fine and big at night? It must be that little is hidden. The glistening ahead could have been a golden city of Cibola. But the reality of Fort Stockton was plywood and concrete block and the plastic signs of Holiday Inn and Mobil Oil.

The desert had given me an appetite that would have made carrion crow 10 stuffed with saltbush taste good. I found a Mexican cafe of adobe, with a whitewashed log ceiling, creekstone fireplace, and jukebox pumping out mariachi music. It was like a bunkhouse. I ate burritos, chile rellenos, and pinto beans, all ladled over with a fine, incendiary sauce the color of sludge from an old steel drum. At the next table sat three big, round men: an Indian wearing a silver headband, a Chicano in a droopy Pancho Villa mustache, and a Negro in faded overalls. I thought what a litany of grievances that table could recite. But the more I looked, the more I believed they were someone's vision of the West, maybe someone making ads for Levy's bread, the ads that used to begin "You don't have to be Jewish."

DARRELL HUFF [1913–2001]

How to Lie with Statistics

Darrell Huff (1913–2001) received his B.A. and M.A. from the University of Iowa. He was the editor of *Better Homes and Gardens* and *Liberty* magazine until becoming a full-time writer in 1946. The author of numerous "How to . . ." articles pertaining to household projects, Huff is best known for his 1954 book *How to Lie with Statistics.*

In "How to Lie with Statistics," originally published as an article in *Harper's* in 1950, Huff delineates the many ways that the news media and corporate America intentionally and unintentionally mislead readers with falsely stated statistics and unreliable graphics. Huff says many statistical analyses are imprecise and sensationalistic, designed to deceive by misrepresenting what seem like incontrovertible facts through a variety of techniques including biased sampling, contrived graphs, and ambiguity regarding means and medians. He calls his pert exposé of quasi-scientific deceptions a "primer" for the honest man.

"The average Yaleman, Class of '24," *Time* magazine reported last year after reading something in the New York *Sun,* a newspaper published in those days, "makes $25,111 a year."

Well, good for him!

But, come to think of it, what does this improbably precise and salubrious figure mean? Is it, as it appears to be, evidence that if you send your boy to Yale you won't have to work in your old age and neither will he? Is this average a mean or is it a median? What kind of sample is it based on? You could lump one Texas oilman with two hundred hungry freelance writers and report *their* average income as $25,000-odd a year. The arithmetic is impeccable, the figure is convincingly precise, and the amount of meaning there is in it you could put in your eye.

In just such ways is the secret language of statistics, so appealing in a fact-minded culture, being used to sensationalize, inflate, confuse, and oversimplify. Statistical terms are necessary in reporting the mass data of social and economic trends, business conditions, "opinion" polls, this year's census. But without writers who use the words with honesty and understanding and readers who know what they mean, the result can only be semantic nonsense.

In popular writing on scientific research, the abused statistic is almost 5 crowding out the picture of the white-jacketed hero laboring overtime without time-and-a-half in an ill-lit laboratory. Like the "little dash of powder, little pot of paint," statistics are making many an important fact "look like what she ain't." Here are some of the ways it is done.

The sample with the built-in bias. Our Yale men—or Yalemen, as they say in the Time-Life building—belong to this flourishing group. The exaggerated estimate of their income is not based on all members of the class nor on a random or representative sample of them. At least two interesting categories of 1924-model Yale men have been excluded.

First there are those whose present addresses are unknown to their classmates. Wouldn't you bet that these lost sheep are earning less than the boys from prominent families and the others who can be handily reached from a Wall Street office?

There are those who chucked the questionnaire into the nearest wastebasket. Maybe they didn't answer because they were not making enough money to brag about. Like the fellow who found a note clipped to his first pay check suggesting that he consider the amount of his salary confidential: "Don't worry," he told the boss. "I'm just as ashamed of it as you are."

Omitted from our sample then are just the two groups most likely to depress the average. The $25,111 figure is beginning to account for itself. It may indeed be a true figure for those of the Class of '24 whose addresses are known and who are willing to stand up and tell how much they earn. But even that requires a possibly dangerous assumption that the gentlemen are telling the truth.

To be dependable to any useful degree at all, a sampling study must 10 use a representative sample (which can lead to trouble too) or a truly random one. If *all* the Class of '24 is included, that's all right. If every tenth name on a complete list is used, that is all right too, and so is drawing an adequate number of names out of a hat. The test is this: Does every name in the group have an equal chance to be in the sample?

You'll recall that ignoring this requirement was what produced the *Literary Digest's* famed fiasco. When names for polling were taken only from telephone books and subscription lists, people who did not have telephones or *Literary Digest* subscriptions had no chance to be in the sample. They possibly did not mind this underprivilege a bit, but their absence was in the end very hard on the magazine that relied on the figures.

This leads to a moral: You can prove about anything you want to by letting your sample bias itself. As a consumer of statistical data—a reader, for example, of a news magazine—remember that no statistical conclusion can rise above the quality of the sample it is based upon. In the absence of information about the procedures behind it, you are not warranted in giving any credence at all to the result.

The truncated, or gee-whiz, graph. If you want to show some statistical information quickly and clearly, draw a picture of it. Graphic presentation is the thing today. If you don't mind misleading the hasty looker, or if you quite clearly *want* to deceive him, you can save some space by chopping the bottom off many kinds of graphs.

Suppose you are showing the upward trend of national income month by month for a year. The total rise, as in one recent year, is 7 per cent. It looks like this:

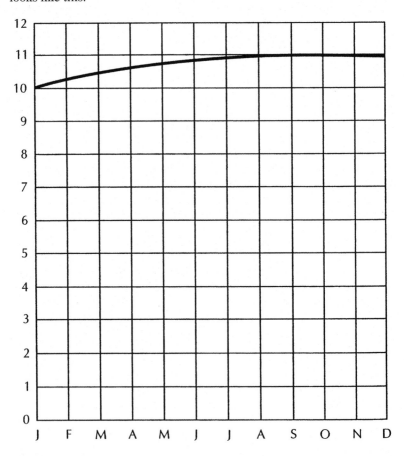

That is clear enough. Anybody can see that the trend is slightly upward. You are showing a 7 per cent increase and that is exactly what it looks like.

But it lacks schmaltz. So you chop off the bottom, this way: 15

The figures are the same. It is the same graph and nothing has been falsified—except the impression that it gives. Anyone looking at it can just feel prosperity throbbing in the arteries of the country. It is a subtler equivalent of editing "National income rose 7 per cent" into ". . . climbed a whopping 7 per cent."

It is vastly more effective, however, because of that illusion of objectivity.

The souped-up graph. Sometimes truncating is not enough. The trifling rise in something or other still looks almost as insignificant as it is. You can make that 7 per cent look livelier than 100 per cent ordinarily does. Simply change the proportion between the ordinate and the abscissa. There's no rule against it, and it does give your graph a prettier shape.

But it exaggerates, to say the least, something awful (see page 2162).

The well-chosen average. I live near a country neighborhood for which I can report an average income of $15,000. I could also report it as $3,500.

If I should want to sell real estate hereabouts to people having a high   20
snobbery content, the first figure would be handy. The second figure, however, is the one to use in an argument against raising taxes, or the local bus fare.

Both are legitimate averages, legally arrived at. Yet it is obvious that at least one of them must be as misleading as an out-and-out lie. The $15,000-figure is a mean, the arithmetic average of the incomes of all the families in the community. The smaller figure is a median; it might be called the income of the average family in the group. It indicates that half the families have less than $3,500 a year and half have more.

Here is where some of the confusion about averages comes from. Many human characteristics have the grace to fall into what is called the "normal" distribution. If you draw a picture of it, you get a curve that is

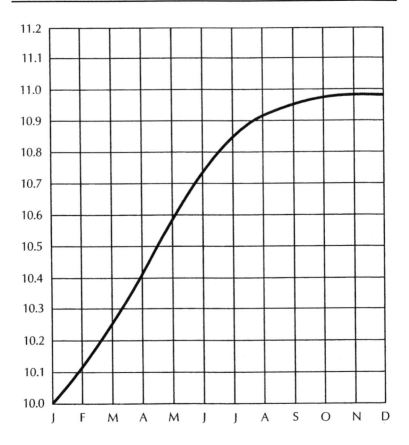

shaped like a bell. Mean and median fall at about the same point, so it doesn't make very much difference which you use.

But some things refuse to follow this neat curve. Income is one of them. Incomes for most large areas will range from under $1,000 a year to upward of $50,000. Almost everybody will be under $10,000, way over on the left-hand side of that curve.

One of the things that made the income figure for the "average Yale-man" meaningless is that we are not told whether it is a mean or a median. It is not that one type of average is invariably better than the other; it depends upon what you are talking about. But neither gives you any real information—and either may be highly misleading—unless you know which of those two kinds of average it is.

In the country neighborhood I mentioned, almost everyone has less 25 than the average—the mean, that is—of $10,500. These people are all small farmers, except for a trio of millionaire week-enders who bring up the mean enormously.

You can be pretty sure that when an income average is given in the form of a mean nearly everybody has less than that.

The insignificant difference or the elusive error. Your two children Peter and Linda (we might as well give them modish names while we're about it) take intelligence tests. Peter's IQ, you learn, is 98 and Linda's is 101. Aha! Linda is your brighter child.

Is she? An intelligence test is, or purports to be, a sampling of intellect. An IQ, like other products of sampling, is a figure with a statistical error, which expresses the precision or reliability of the figure. The size of this probable error can be calculated. For their test the makers of the much-used Revised Stanford-Binet have found it to be about 3 per cent. So Peter's indicated IQ of 98 really means only that there is an even chance that it falls between 95 and 101. There is an equal probability that it falls somewhere else—below 95 or above 101. Similarly, Linda's has no better than a fifty-fifty chance of being within the fairly sizeable range of 98 to 104.

You can work out some comparisons from that. One is that there is rather better than one chance in four that Peter, with his lower IQ rating, is really at least three points smarter than Linda. A statistician doesn't like to consider a difference significant unless you can hand him odds a lot longer than that.

Ignoring the error in a sampling study leads to all kinds of silly conclu- 30 sions. There are magazine editors to whom readership surveys are gospel; with a 40 per cent readership reported for one article and a 35 per cent for another, they demand more like the first. I've seen even smaller differences given tremendous weight, because statistics are a mystery and numbers are impressive. The same thing goes for market surveys and so-called public-opinion polls. The rule is that you cannot make a valid comparison between two such figures unless you know the deviations. And unless the difference between the figures is many times greater than the probable error of each, you have only a guess that the one appearing greater really is.

Otherwise you are like the man choosing a camp site from a report of mean temperature alone. One place in California with a mean annual temperature of 61 is San Nicolas Island on the south coast, where it always stays in the comfortable range between 47 and 87. Another with a mean of 61 is in the inland desert, where the thermometer hops around from 15 to 104. The deviation from the mean marks the difference, and you can freeze or roast if you ignore it.

The one-dimensional picture. Suppose you have just two or three figures to compare—say the average weekly wage of carpenters in the United States and another country. The sums might be $60 and $30. An ordinary bar chart makes the difference graphic:

That is an honest picture. It looks good for American carpenters, but perhaps it does not have quite the oomph you are after. Can't you make that difference appear overwhelming and at the same time give it what I am afraid is known as eye-appeal? Of course you can. Following tradition, you represent these sums by pictures of money bags. If the $30 bag is one inch high, you draw the $60 bag two inches high. That's in proportion, isn't it? The catch is, of course, that the American's money bag, being twice as tall as that of the $30 man, covers an area on your page four times as great. And since your two-dimensional picture represents an object that would in fact have three dimensions, the money bags actually would differ much more than that. The volumes of any two similar solids vary as the cubes of their heights. If the unfortunate foreigner's bag holds $30 worth of dimes, the American's would hold not $60 but a neat $240:

You didn't say that, though, did you? And you can't be blamed, you're only doing it the way practically everybody else does.

The ever-impressive decimal. For a spurious air of precision that will lend all kinds of weight to the most disreputable statistics, consider the decimal.

Ask a hundred citizens how many hours they slept last night. Come out with a total of, say, 781.3. Your data are far from precise to begin with. Most people will miss their guess by fifteen minutes or more and some will recall five sleepless minutes as half a night of tossing insomnia.

But go ahead, do your arithmetic, announce that people sleep an aver- 35 age of 7.813 hours a night. You will sound as if you knew precisely what you are talking about. If you were foolish enough to say 7.8 (or "almost 8") hours it would sound like what it was—an approximation.

The semi-attached figure. If you can't prove what you want to prove, demonstrate something else and pretend that they are the same thing. In the daze that follows the collision of statistics with the human mind, hardly anybody will notice the difference. The semi-attached figure is a durable device guaranteed to stand you in good stead. It always has.

If you can't prove that your nostrum cures colds, publish a sworn laboratory report that the stuff killed 31,108 germs in a test tube in eleven seconds. There may be no connection at all between assorted germs in a test tube and the whatever-it-is that produces colds, but people aren't going to reason that sharply, especially while sniffling.

Maybe that one is too obvious and people are beginning to catch on. Here is a trickier version.

Let us say that in a period when race prejudice is growing it is to your advantage to "prove" otherwise. You will not find it a difficult assignment.

Ask that usual cross section of the population if they think Negroes 40 have as good a chance as white people to get jobs. Ask again a few months later. As Princeton's Office of Public Opinion Research has found out, people who are most unsympathetic to Negroes are the ones most likely to answer yes to this question.

As prejudice increases in a country, the percentage of affirmative answers you will get to this question will become larger. What looks on the face of it like growing opportunity for Negroes actually is mounting prejudice and nothing else. You have achieved something rather remarkable: the worse things get, the better your survey makes them look.

The unwarranted assumption, or post hoc *rides again.* The interrelation of cause and effect, so often obscure anyway, can be most neatly hidden in statistical data.

Somebody once went to a good deal of trouble to find out if cigarette smokers make lower college grades than non-smokers. They did. This naturally pleased many people, and they made much of it.

The unwarranted assumption, of course, was that smoking had produced dull minds. It seemed vaguely reasonable on the face of it, so it was quite widely accepted. But it really proved nothing of the sort, any more than it proved that poor grades drive students to the solace of tobacco. Maybe the relationship worked in one direction, maybe in the other. And maybe all this is only an indication that the sociable sort of fellow who is likely to take his books less than seriously is also likely to sit around and smoke many cigarettes.

Permitting statistical treatment to befog causal relationships is little 45 better than superstition. It is like the conviction among the people of the Hebrides that body lice produce good health. Observation over the centuries had taught them that people in good health had lice and sick people often did not. *Ergo,* lice made a man healthy. Everybody should have them.

Scantier evidence, treated statistically at the expense of common sense, has made many a medical fortune and many a medical article in magazines, including professional ones. More sophisticated observers finally got things straightened out in the Hebrides. As it turned out, almost everybody in those circles had lice most of the time. But when a man took a fever (quite possibly carried to him by those same lice) and his body became hot, the lice left.

Here you have cause and effect not only reversed, but intermingled.

There you have a primer in some ways to use statistics to deceive. A well-wrapped statistic is better than Hitler's "big lie": it misleads, yet it can't be pinned onto you.

Is this little list altogether too much like a manual for swindlers? Perhaps I can justify it in the manner of the retired burglar whose published reminiscences amounted to a graduate course in how to pick a lock and muffle a footfall: The crooks already know these tricks. Honest men must learn them in self-defense.

ANNE LAMOTT   [b. 1954]

Shitty First Drafts

Born in San Francisco in 1954, **Anne Lamott** is the best-selling author of
six novels and several works of nonfiction, including *Operating Instructions*, a brutally honest account of motherhood in her son's first year of
life, *Bird by Bird: Some Instructions on Writing and Life*, a riotous handbook for aspiring writers, and *Traveling Mercies*, a collection of autobio-
graphical essays on living with faith. The recipient of a Guggenheim
fellowship, a one-time food critic for *California* magazine and book
reviewer for *Mademoiselle*, Lamott has taught at the University of California, Davis and at numerous writers' conferences. "Word by Word," her
biweekly personal reflections contributed to the online *Salon Magazine*
from 1996 to 1999, were voted *The Best of the Web* by *Time* magazine.
A self-identified recovering alcoholic and born-again Christian, Lamott's
writing is frank, candid, and utterly sincere. Her sharp words and strong
sense of humor make for a poignantly entertaining read.

"Shitty First Drafts," an excerpt from her book *Bird by Bird: Some
Instructions on Writing and Life*, encourages writers to trust in their writing
processes. Lamott shares her own writing methods and drolly suggests
ways of blocking out even the most annoying distractions.

For me and most of the other writers I know, writing is not rapturous. In
fact, the only way I can get anything written at all is to write really, really
crummy first drafts.

The first draft is the child's draft, where you let it all pour out and then
let it romp all over the place, knowing that no one is going to see it and
that you can shape it later. You just let this childlike part of you channel
whatever voices and visions come through and onto the page. If one of
the characters wants to say "Well, so what, Mr. Poopy Pants?" you let her.
No one is going to see it. If the kid wants to get into really sentimental,
weepy, emotional territory, you let him. Just get it all down on paper,
because there may be something great in those six crazy pages that you
would never have gotten to by more rational, grown-up means. There
may be something in the very last line of the very last paragraph on page
six that you just love, that is so beautiful or wild that you now know what

you're supposed to be writing about, more or less, or in what direction you might go—but there was no way to get to this without first getting through the first five and a half pages. I used to write food reviews for *California* magazine before it folded. (My writing food reviews had nothing to do with the magazine folding, although every single review did cause a couple of canceled subscriptions. Some readers took umbrage at my comparing mounds of vegetable puree with various ex-presidents' brains.) These reviews always took two days to write. First I'd go to a restaurant several times with a few opinionated, articulate friends in tow. I'd sit there writing down everything anyone said that was at all interesting or funny. Then on the following Monday I'd sit down at my desk with my notes, and try to write the review. Even after I'd been doing this for years, panic would set in. I'd try to write a lead, but instead I'd write a couple of dreadful sentences, XX them out, try again, XX everything out, and then feel despair and worry settle on my chest like an x-ray apron. It's over, I'd think, calmly. I'm not going to be able to get the magic to work this time. I'm ruined. I'm through. I'm toast. Maybe, I'd think, I can get my old job back as a clerk-typist. But probably not. I'd get up and study my teeth in the mirror for a while. Then I'd stop, remember to breathe, make a few phone calls, hit the kitchen and chow down. Eventually I'd go back and sit down at my desk, and sigh for the next ten minutes. Finally I would pick up my one-inch picture frame, stare into it as if for the answer, and every time the answer would come: all I had to do was to write a really crummy first draft of, say, the opening paragraph. And no one was going to see it.

So I'd start writing without reining myself in. It was almost just typing, just making my fingers move. And the writing would be *terrible*. I'd write a lead paragraph that was a whole page, even though the entire review could only be three pages long, and then I'd start writing up descriptions of the food, one dish at a time, bird by bird, and the critics would be sitting on my shoulders, commenting like cartoon characters. They'd be pretending to snore, or rolling their eyes at my overwrought descriptions, no matter how hard I tried to tone those descriptions down, no matter how conscious I was of what a friend said to me gently in my early days of restaurant reviewing. "Annie," she said, "it is just a piece of *chicken*. It is just a bit of *cake*."

But because by then I had been writing for so long, I would eventually 5 let myself trust the process—sort of, more or less. I'd write a first draft that was maybe twice as long as it should be, with a self-indulgent and boring beginning, stupefying descriptions of the meal, lots of quotes from my black-humored friends that made them sound more like the

Manson girls° than food lovers, and no ending to speak of. The whole thing would be so long and incoherent and hideous that for the rest of the day I'd obsess about getting creamed by a car before I could write a decent second draft. I'd worry that people would read what I'd written and believe that the accident had really been a suicide, that I had panicked because my talent was waning and my mind was shot.

The next day, though, I'd sit down, go through it all with a colored pen, take out everything I possibly could, find a new lead somewhere on the second page, figure out a kicky place to end it, and then write a second draft. It always turned out fine, sometimes even funny and weird and helpful. I'd go over it one more time and mail it in.

Then, a month later, when it was time for another review, the whole process would start again, complete with the fears that people would find my first draft before I could rewrite it.

Almost all good writing begins with terrible first efforts. You need to start somewhere. Start by getting something—anything—down on paper. A friend of mine says that the first draft is the down draft—you just get it down. The second draft is the up draft—you fix it up. You try to say what you have to say more accurately. And the third draft is the dental draft, where you check every tooth, to see if it's loose or cramped or decayed, or even, God help us, healthy.

What I've learned to do when I sit down to work on a crummy first draft is to quiet the voices in my head. First there's the vinegar-lipped Reader Lady, who says primly, "Well, *that's* not very interesting, is it?" And there's the emaciated German male who writes these Orwellian memos detailing your thought crimes. And there are your parents, agonizing over your lack of loyalty and discretion; and there's William Burroughs, dozing off or shooting up because he finds you as bold and articulate as a houseplant; and so on. And there are also the dogs: let's not forget the dogs, the dogs in their pen who will surely hurtle and snarl their way out if you ever *stop* writing, because writing is, for some of us, the latch that keeps the door of the pen closed, keeps those crazy, ravenous dogs contained. [. . .]

Close your eyes and get quiet for a minute, until the chatter starts up. 10 Then isolate one of the voices and imagine the person speaking as a mouse. Pick it up by the tail and drop it into a mason jar. Then isolate another voice, pick it up by the tail, drop it in the jar. And so on. Drop in any high-maintenance parental units, drop in any contractors, lawyers, colleagues, children, anyone who is whining in your head. Then put the lid on, and watch all these mouse people clawing at the glass, jabbering away, trying to make you feel crummy because you won't do what they

Manson girls: Young, troubled, members of a cult led by Charles Manson (b. 1934). In 1969 Manson and some of his followers were convicted of murder in California.

want—won't give them more money, won't be more successful, won't see them more often. Then imagine that there is a volume-control button on the bottle. Turn it all the way up for a minute, and listen to the stream of angry, neglected, guilt-mongering voices. Then turn it all the way down and watch the frantic mice lunge at the glass, trying to get to you. Leave it down, and get back to your crummy first draft.

A writer friend of mine suggests opening the jar and shooting them all in the head. But I think he's a little angry, and I'm sure nothing like this would ever occur to you.

ALDO LEOPOLD [1887–1948]

The Land Ethic

Born in Burlington, Iowa, **Aldo Leopold** was a powerful force in ecological and conservationist circles for many years and is regarded by
many as the founding father of wildlife ecology. Leopold studied at the
Lawrenceville School in New Jersey, followed by the Yale School of
Forestry and Environmental Studies. After earning his master's degree
in 1909, he began his career working in the Apache National Forest in
Arizona and then Carson National Forest in New Mexico. While living
in New Mexico between 1911 and 1924, Leopold completed the Forest
Service's first *Game and Fish Handbook* and proposed the preservation
of the headwaters of the Gila River, which became the National Forest
System's first wilderness area. He later accepted appointment as a
professor of wildlife management at the University of Wisconsin–
Madison, the first of such positions, in the same year as the publication of *Game Management* (1933), his first important book. Two years
later, in 1935, Leopold was also among the cofounders of the Wilderness Society. He is best known for his proposition of "land ethics" in
A Sand County Almanac, which he finished just prior to his death
in 1948.

In "The Land Ethic," excerpted from *A Sand County Almanac*,
Leopold blames the economic and educational systems for the rupture—both physical and philosophical—between people and the land.
He argues that current education about conservation lacks both an
ethical component, what he calls the "ecological conscience," and a
long-term interest in the community.

When godlike Odysseus returned from the wars in Troy, he hanged all on
one rope a dozen slave girls of his household whom he suspected of mis-
behavior during his absence.

This hanging involved no question of propriety. The girls were property. The disposal of property was then, as now, a matter of expediency,
not of right and wrong.

Concepts of right and wrong were not lacking from Odysseus's Greece: witness the fidelity of his wife through the long years before at last his black-prowed galleys clove the wine-dark seas for home. The ethical structure of that day covered wives, but had not yet been extended to human chattels. During the three thousand years which have since elapsed, ethical criteria have been extended to many fields of conduct, with corresponding shrinkages in those judged by expediency only.

THE ETHICAL SEQUENCE

This extension of ethics, so far studied only by philosophers, is actually a process in ecological evolution. Its sequences may be described in ecological as well as in philosophical terms. An ethic, ecologically, is a limitation on freedom of action in the struggle for existence. An ethic, philosophically, is a differentiation of social from antisocial conduct. These are two definitions of one thing. The thing has its origin in the tendency of interdependent individuals or groups to evolve modes of cooperation. The ecologist calls these symbioses.[1] Politics and economics are advanced symbioses in which the original free-for-all competition has been replaced, in part, by cooperative mechanisms with an ethical content.

The complexity of cooperative mechanisms has increased with population density, and with the efficiency of tools. It was simpler, for example, to define the antisocial uses of sticks and stones in the days of the mastodons than of bullets and billboards in the age of motors.   5

The first ethics dealt with the relation between individuals; the Mosaic Decalogue[2] is an example. Later accretions dealt with the relation between the individual and society. The Golden Rule tries to integrate the individual to society; democracy to integrate social organization to the individual.

There is as yet no ethic dealing with man's relation to land and to the animals and plants which grow upon it. Land, like Odysseus's slave girls, is still property. The land relation is still strictly economic, entailing privileges but not obligations.

The extension of ethics to this third element in human environment is, if I read the evidence correctly, an evolutionary possibility and an ecological necessity. It is the third step in a sequence. The first two have already been taken. Individual thinkers since the days of Ezekiel and Isaiah have

---

[1]**symbioses:** Relationships between interdependent organisms.
[2]**Mosaic Decalogue:** The Ten Commandments.

asserted that the despoliation of land is not only inexpedient but wrong. Society, however, has not yet affirmed their belief. I regard the present conservation movement as the embryo of such an affirmation.

An ethic may be regarded as a mode of guidance for meeting ecological situations so new or intricate, or involving such deferred reactions, that the path of social expediency is not discernible to the average individual. Animal instincts are modes of guidance for the individual in meeting such situations. Ethics are possibly a kind of community instinct in the making.

THE COMMUNITY CONCEPT

All ethics so far evolved rest upon a single premise: that the individual is   10 a member of a community of interdependent parts. His instincts prompt him to compete for his place in the community, but his ethics prompt him also to cooperate (perhaps in order that there may be a place to compete for).

The land ethic simply enlarges the boundaries of the community to include soils, waters, plants, and animals, or collectively: the land.

This sounds simple: Do we not already sing our love for and obligation to the land of the free and the home of the brave? Yes, but just what and whom do we love? Certainly not the soil, which we are sending helter-skelter downriver. Certainly not the waters, which we assume have no function except to turn turbines, float barges, and carry off sewage. Certainly not the plants, of which we exterminate whole communities without batting an eye. Certainly not the animals, of which we have already extirpated many of the largest and most beautiful species. A land ethic of course cannot prevent the alteration, management, and use of these "resources," but it does affirm their right to continued existence, and, at least in spots, their continued existence in a natural state.

In short, a land ethic changes the role of Homo sapiens from conqueror of the land-community to plain member and citizen of it. It implies respect for his fellow members, and also respect for the community as such.

In human history, we have learned (I hope) that the conqueror role is eventually self-defeating. Why? Because it is implicit in such a role that the conqueror knows, ex cathedra,[3] just what makes the community clock tick, and just what and who is valuable, and what and who is

---

[3]**ex cathedra:** Literally, "speaking from the chair," so speaking with great authority.

worthless, in community life. It always turns out that he knows neither, and this is why his conquests eventually defeat themselves.

In the biotic community, a parallel situation exists. Abraham knew exactly what the land was for: it was to drip milk and honey into Abraham's mouth. At the present moment, the assurance with which we regard this assumption is inverse to the degree of our education.

The ordinary citizen today assumes that science knows what makes the community clock tick; the scientist is equally sure that he does not. He knows that the biotic mechanism is so complex that its workings may never be fully understood.

That man is, in fact, only a member of a biotic team is shown by an ecological interpretation of history. Many historical events, hitherto explained solely in terms of human enterprise, were actually biotic interactions between people and land. The characteristics of the land determined the facts quite as potently as the characteristics of the men who lived on it.

Consider, for example, the settlement of the Mississippi Valley. In the years following the Revolution, three groups were contending for its control: the native Indian, the French and English traders, and the American settlers. Historians wonder what would have happened if the English at Detroit had thrown a little more weight into the Indian side of those tipsy scales which decided the outcome of the colonial migration into the cane lands of Kentucky. It is time now to ponder the fact that the cane lands, when subjected to the particular mixture of forces represented by the cow, plow, fire, and ax of the pioneer, became bluegrass. What if the plant succession inherent in this dark and bloody ground had, under the impact of these forces, given us some worthless sedge, shrub, or weed? Would Boone and Kenton[4] have held out? Would there have been any overflow into Ohio, Indiana, Illinois, and Missouri? Any Louisiana Purchase? Any transcontinental union of new states? Any Civil War?

Kentucky was one sentence in the drama of history. We are commonly told what the human actors in this drama tried to do, but we are seldom told that their success, or the lack of it, hung in large degree on the reaction of particular soils to the impact of the particular forces exerted by their occupancy. In the case of Kentucky, we do not even know where the bluegrass came from—whether it is a native species, or a stowaway from Europe.

---

[4]**Daniel Boone (1734–1820) and Simon Kenton (1755–1836):** Boone was an American pioneer remembered for his exploration and settlement of Kentucky. Kenton was a frontiersman and friend of Boone's.

Contrast the cane lands with what hindsight tells us about the South- 20
west, where the pioneers were equally brave, resourceful, and persever-
ing. The impact of occupancy here brought no bluegrass, or other plant
fitted to withstand the bumps and buffetings of hard use. This region,
when grazed by livestock, reverted through a series of more and more
worthless grasses, shrubs, and weeds to a condition of unstable equilib-
rium. Each recession of plant types bred erosion; each increment to erosion bred a further recession of plants. The result today is a progressive
and mutual deterioration, not only of plants and soils, but of the animal
community subsisting thereon. The early settlers did not expect this: on
the ciénegas[5] of New Mexico some even cut ditches to hasten it. So
subtle has been its progress that few residents of the region are aware of
it. It is quite invisible to the tourist who finds this wrecked landscape
colorful and charming (as indeed it is, but it bears scant resemblance to
what it was in 1848).

This same landscape was "developed" once before, but with quite
different results. The Pueblo Indians settled the Southwest in pre-
Columbian times, but they happened *not* to be equipped with range livestock. Their civilization expired, but not because their land expired.

In India, regions devoid of any sod-forming grass have been settled,
apparently without wrecking the land, by the simple expedient of carrying the grass to the cow, rather than vice versa. (Was this the result of
some deep wisdom, or was it just good luck? I do not know.)

In short, the plant succession steered the course of history; the pioneer
simply demonstrated, for good or ill, what successions inhered in the
land. Is history taught in this spirit? It will be, once the concept of land
as a community really penetrates our intellectual life.

THE ECOLOGICAL CONSCIENCE

Conservation is a state of harmony between men and land. Despite
nearly a century of propaganda, conservation still proceeds at a snail's
pace; progress still consists largely of letterhead pieties and convention
oratory. On the back forty we still slip two steps backward for each forward stride.

The usual answer to this dilemma is "more conservation education." 25
No one will debate this, but is it certain that only the *volume* of education needs stepping up? Is something lacking in the *content* as well?

---

[5]**ciénegas:** Wetlands that support the Santa Fe River in New Mexico.

It is difficult to give a fair summary of its content in brief form, but, as I understand it, the content is substantially this: obey the law, vote right, join some organizations, and practice what conservation is profitable on your own land; the government will do the rest. Is not this formula too easy to accomplish anything worthwhile? It defines no right or wrong, assigns no obligation, calls for no sacrifice, implies no change in the current philosophy of values. In respect of land use, it urges only enlightened self-interest. Just how far will such education take us? An example will perhaps yield a partial answer.

By 1930 it had become clear to all except the ecologically blind that southwestern Wisconsin's topsoil was slipping seaward. In 1933 the farmers were told that if they would adopt certain remedial practices for five years, the public would donate CCC[6] labor to install them, plus the necessary machinery and materials. The offer was widely accepted, but the practices were widely forgotten when the five-year contract period was up. The farmers continued only those practices that yielded an immediate and visible economic gain for themselves.

This led to the idea that maybe farmers would learn more quickly if they themselves wrote the rules. Accordingly the Wisconsin legislature in 1937 passed the Soil Conservation District Law. This said to farmers, in effect: *We, the public, will furnish you free technical service and loan you specialized machinery, if you will write your own rules for land use. Each county may write its own rules, and these will have the force of law.* Nearly all the counties promptly organized to accept the proffered help, but after a decade of operation, *no county has yet written a single rule.* There has been visible progress in such practices as strip cropping, pasture renovation, and soil liming, but none in fencing woodlots against grazing, and none in excluding plow and cow from steep slopes. The farmers, in short, have selected those remedial practices which were profitable anyhow, and ignored those which were profitable to the community, but not clearly profitable to themselves.

When one asks why no rules have been written, one is told that the community is not yet ready to support them; education must precede rules. But the education actually in progress makes no mention of obligations to land over and above those dictated by self-interest. The net result is that we have more education but less soil, fewer healthy woods, and as many floods as in 1937.

The puzzling aspect of such situations is that the existence of obligations over and above self-interest is taken for granted in such rural community enterprises as the betterment of roads, schools, churches, and baseball teams. Their existence is not taken for granted, nor as yet

---

[6]CCC: Civilian Conservation Corps.

30

117

seriously discussed, in bettering the behavior of the water that falls on the land, or in the preserving of the beauty or diversity of the farm landscape. Land-use ethics are still governed wholly by economic self-interest, just as social ethics were a century ago.

To sum up: we asked the farmer to do what he conveniently could to save his soil, and he has done just that, and only that. The farmer who clears the woods of a 75-percent slope, turns his cows into the clearing, and dumps its rainfall, rocks, and soil into the community creek, is still (if otherwise decent) a respected member of society. If he puts lime on his fields and plants his crops on contour, he is still entitled to all the privileges and emoluments of his Soil Conservation District. The district is a beautiful piece of social machinery, but it is coughing along on two cylinders because we have been too timid, and too anxious for quick success, to tell the farmer the true magnitude of his obligations. Obligations have no meaning without conscience, and the problem we face is the extension of the social conscience from people to land.

No important change in ethics was ever accomplished without an internal change in our intellectual emphasis, loyalties, affections, and convictions. The proof that conservation has not yet touched these foundations of conduct lies in the fact that philosophy and religion have not yet heard of it. In our attempt to make conservation easy, we have made it trivial.

SUBSTITUTES FOR A LAND ETHIC

When the logic of history hungers for bread and we hand out a stone, we are at pains to explain how much the stone resembles bread. I now describe some of the stones which serve in lieu of a land ethic.

One basic weakness in a conservation system based wholly on economic 35 motives is that most members of the land community have no economic value. Wildflowers and songbirds are examples. Of the 22,000 higher plants and animals native to Wisconsin, it is doubtful whether more than 5 percent can be sold, fed, eaten, or otherwise put to economic use. Yet these creatures are members of the biotic community, and if (as I believe) its stability depends on its integrity, they are entitled to continuance.

When one of these noneconomic categories is threatened, and if we happen to love it, we invent subterfuges to give it economic importance. At the beginning of the century songbirds were supposed to be disappearing. Ornithologists jumped to the rescue with some distinctly shaky evidence to the effect that insects would eat us up if birds failed to control them. The evidence had to be economic in order to be valid.

It is painful to read these circumlocutions today. We have no land ethic yet, but we have at least drawn nearer the point of admitting that birds should continue as a matter of biotic right, regardless of the presence or absence of economic advantage to us.

A parallel situation exists in respect of predatory mammals, raptorial birds, and fish-eating birds. Time was when biologists somewhat overworked the evidence that these creatures preserve the health of game by killing weaklings, or that they control rodents for the farmer, or that they prey only on "worthless" species. Here again, the evidence had to be economic in order to be valid. It is only in recent years that we hear the more honest argument that predators are members of the community, and that no special interest has the right to exterminate them for the sake of a benefit, real or fancied, to itself. Unfortunately this enlightened view is still in the talk stage. In the field the extermination of predators goes merrily on: witness the impending erasure of the timber wolf by fiat of Congress, the Conservation Bureaus, and many state legislatures.

Some species of trees have been "read out of the party" by economics-minded foresters because they grow too slowly, or have too low a sale value to pay as timber crops: white cedar, tamarack, cypress, beech, and hemlock are examples. In Europe, where forestry is ecologically more advanced, the noncommercial tree species are recognized as members of the native forest community, to be preserved as such, within reason. Moreover some (like beech) have been found to have a valuable function in building up soil fertility. The interdependence of the forest and its constituent tree species, ground flora, and fauna is taken for granted.

Lack of economic value is sometimes a character not only of species or groups, but of entire biotic communities: marshes, bogs, dunes, and "deserts" are examples. Our formula in such cases is to relegate their conservation to government as refuges, monuments, or parks. The difficulty is that these communities are usually interspersed with more valuable private lands; the government cannot possibly own or control such scattered parcels. The net effect is that we have relegated some of them to ultimate extinction over large areas. If the private owner were ecologically minded, he would be proud to be the custodian of a reasonable proportion of such areas, which add diversity and beauty to his farm and to his community.

In some instances, the assumed lack of profit in these "waste" areas has proved to be wrong, but only after most of them had been done away with. The present scramble to reflood muskrat marshes is a case in point.

There is a clear tendency in American conservation to relegate to government all necessary jobs that private landowners fail to perform. Government ownership, operation, subsidy, or regulation is now widely prevalent in forestry, range management, soil and watershed management, park

119

and wilderness conservation, fisheries management, and migratory bird management, with more to come. Most of this growth in governmental conservation is proper and logical, some of it is inevitable. That I imply no disapproval of it is implicit in the fact that I have spent most of my life working for it. Nevertheless the question arises: What is the ultimate magnitude of the enterprise? Will the tax base carry its eventual ramifications? At what point will governmental conservation, like the mastodon, become handicapped by its own dimensions? The answer, if there is any, seems to be in a land ethic, or some other force which assigns more obligation to the private landowner.

Industrial landowners and users, especially lumbermen and stockmen, are inclined to wail long and loudly about the extension of government ownership and regulation to land, but (with notable exceptions) they show little disposition to develop the only visible alternative: the voluntary practice of conservation on their own lands.

When the private landowner is asked to perform some unprofitable act for the good of the community, he today assents only with outstretched palm. If the act costs him cash this is fair and proper, but when it costs only forethought, open-mindedness, or time, the issue is at least debatable. The overwhelming growth of land-use subsidies in recent years must be ascribed, in large part, to the government's own agencies for conservation education: the land bureaus, the agricultural colleges, and the extension services. As far as I can detect, no ethical obligation toward land is taught in these institutions.

To sum up: a system of conservation based solely on economic self-interest is hopelessly lopsided. It tends to ignore, and thus eventually to eliminate, many elements in the land community that lack commercial value, but that are (as far as we know) essential to its healthy functioning. It assumes, falsely, I think, that the economic parts of the biotic clock will function without the uneconomic parts. It tends to relegate to government many functions eventually too large, too complex, or too widely dispersed to be performed by government.

An ethical obligation on the part of the private owner is the only visible remedy for these situations.

THE LAND PYRAMID

An ethic to supplement and guide the economic relation to land presupposes the existence of some mental image of land as a biotic mechanism. We can be ethical only in relation to something we can see, feel, understand, love, or otherwise have faith in.

The image commonly employed in conservation education is "the balance of nature." For reasons too lengthy to detail here, this figure of speech fails to describe accurately what little we know about the land mechanism. A much truer image is the one employed in ecology: the biotic pyramid. I shall first sketch the pyramid as a symbol of land, and later develop some of its implications in terms of land use.

Plants absorb energy from the sun. This energy flows through a circuit called the biota, which may be represented by a pyramid consisting of layers. The bottom layer is the soil. A plant layer rests on the soil, an insect layer on the plants, a bird and rodent layer on the insects, and so on up through various animal groups to the apex layer, which consists of the larger carnivores.

The species of a layer are alike not in where they came from, or in 50 what they look like, but rather in what they eat. Each successive layer depends on those below it for food and often for other services, and each in turn furnishes food and services to those above. Proceeding upward, each successive layer decreases in numerical abundance. Thus, for every carnivore there are hundreds of his prey, thousands of their prey, millions of insects, uncountable plants. The pyramidal form of the system reflects this numerical progression from apex to base. Man shares an intermediate layer with the bears, raccoons, and squirrels which eat both meat and vegetables.

The lines of dependency for food and other services are called food chains. Thus soil-oak-deer-Indian is a chain that has now been largely converted to soil-corn-cow-farmer. Each species, including ourselves, is a link in many chains. The deer eats a hundred plants other than oak, and the cow a hundred plants other than corn. Both, then, are links in a hundred chains. The pyramid is a tangle of chains so complex as to seem disorderly, yet the stability of the system proves it to be a highly organized structure. Its functioning depends on the cooperation and competition of its diverse parts.

In the beginning, the pyramid of life was low and squat; the food chains short and simple. Evolution has added layer after layer, link after link. Man is one of thousands of accretions to the height and complexity of the pyramid. Science has given us many doubts, but it has given us at least one certainty: the trend of evolution is to elaborate and diversify the biota.

Land, then, is not merely soil; it is a fountain of energy flowing through a circuit of soils, plants, and animals. Food chains are the living channels which conduct energy upward; death and decay return it to the soil. The circuit is not closed; some energy is dissipated in decay, some is added by absorption from the air, some is stored in soils, peats, and long-lived forests; but it is a sustained circuit, like a slowly augmented revolving fund of life. There is always a net loss by downhill wash, but this is normally small and offset by the decay of rocks. It is deposited in the ocean and, in the course of geological time, raised to form new lands and new pyramids.

The velocity and character of the upward flow of energy depend on the complex structure of the plant and animal community, much as the upward flow of sap in a tree depends on its complex cellular organization. Without this complexity, normal circulation would presumably not occur. Structure means the characteristic numbers, as well as the characteristic kinds and functions, of the component species. This interdependence between the complex structure of the land and its smooth functioning as an energy unit is one of its basic attributes.

When a change occurs in one part of the circuit, many other parts 55 must adjust themselves to it. Change does not necessarily obstruct or divert the flow of energy; evolution is a long series of self-induced changes, the net result of which has been to elaborate the flow mechanism and to lengthen the circuit. Evolutionary changes, however, are usually slow and local. Man's invention of tools has enabled him to make changes of unprecedented violence, rapidity, and scope.

One change is in the composition of floras and faunas. The larger predators are lopped off the apex of the pyramid; food chains, for the first time in history, become shorter rather than longer. Domesticated species from other lands are substituted for wild ones, and wild ones are moved to new habitats. In this worldwide pooling of faunas and floras, some species get out of bounds as pests and diseases, others are extinguished. Such effects are seldom intended or foreseen; they represent unpredicted and often untraceable readjustments in the structure. Agricultural science is largely a race between the emergence of new pests and the emergence of new techniques for their control.

Another change touches the flow of energy through plants and animals and its return to the soil. Fertility is the ability of soil to receive, store, and release energy. Agriculture, by overdrafts on the soil, or by too radical a substitution of domestic for native species in the superstructure, may derange the channels of flow or deplete storage. Soils depleted of their storage, or of the organic matter which anchors it, wash away faster than they form. This is erosion.

Waters, like soil, are part of the energy circuit. Industry, by polluting waters or obstructing them with dams, may exclude the plants and animals necessary to keep energy in circulation.

Transportation brings about another basic change: the plants or animals grown in one region are now consumed and returned to the soil in another. Transportation taps the energy stored in rocks, and in the air, and uses it elsewhere; thus we fertilize the garden with nitrogen gleaned by the guano birds from the fishes of seas on the other side of the equator. Thus the formerly localized and self-contained circuits are pooled on a worldwide scale.

The process of altering the pyramid for human occupation releases 60 stored energy, and this often gives rise, during the pioneering period, to a deceptive exuberance of plant and animal life, both wild and tame. These releases of biotic capital tend to becloud or postpone the penalties of violence.

This thumbnail sketch of land as an energy circuit conveys three basic ideas:

1. That land is not merely soil.
2. That the native plants and animals kept the energy circuit open; others may or may not.
3. That man-made changes are of a different order than evolutionary changes, and have effects more comprehensive than is intended or foreseen.

These ideas, collectively, raise two basic issues: Can the land adjust itself to the new order? Can the desired alterations be accomplished with less violence?

Biotas seem to differ in their capacity to sustain violent conversion. Western Europe, for example, carries a far different pyramid than Caesar found there. Some large animals are lost; swampy forests have become meadows or plowland; many new plants and animals are introduced, some of which escape as pests; the remaining natives are greatly changed in distribution and abundance. Yet the soil is still there and, with the help of imported nutrients, still fertile; the waters flow normally; the new structure seems to function and to persist. There is no visible stoppage or derangement of the circuit.

Western Europe, then, has a resistant biota. Its inner processes are tough, elastic, resistant to strain. No matter how violent the alterations, the pyramid, so far, has developed some new modus vivendi[7] which preserves its habitability for man, and for most of the other natives.

Japan seems to present another instance of radical conversion without 65 disorganization.

Most other civilized regions, and some as yet barely touched by civilization, display various stages of disorganization, varying from initial symptoms to advanced wastage. In Asia Minor and North Africa diagnosis is confused by climatic changes, which may have been either the

[7]modus vivendi: A way of life.

123

cause or the effect of advanced wastage. In the United States the degree of disorganization varies locally; it is worst in the Southwest, the Ozarks, and parts of the South, and least in New England and the Northwest. Better land uses may still arrest it in the less advanced regions. In parts of Mexico, South America, South Africa, and Australia a violent and accelerating wastage is in progress, but I cannot assess the prospects.

This almost worldwide display of disorganization in the land seems to be similar to disease in an animal, except that it never culminates in complete disorganization or death. The land recovers, but at some reduced level of complexity, and with a reduced carrying capacity for people, plants, and animals. Many biotas currently regarded as "lands of opportunity" are in fact already subsisting on exploitative agriculture, i.e., they have already exceeded their sustained carrying capacity. Most of South America is overpopulated in this sense.

In arid regions we attempt to offset the process of wastage by reclamation, but it is only too evident that the prospective longevity of reclamation projects is often short. In our own West, the best of them may not last a century.

The combined evidence of history and ecology seems to support one general deduction: the less violent the man-made changes, the greater the probability of successful readjustment in the pyramid. Violence, in turn, varies with human population density; a dense population requires a more violent conversion. In this respect, North America has a better chance for permanence than Europe, if she can contrive to limit her density.

This deduction runs counter to our current philosophy, which assumes   70 that because a small increase in density enriched human life, than an indefinite increase will enrich it indefinitely. Ecology knows of no density relationship that holds for indefinitely wide limits. All gains from density are subject to a law of diminishing returns.

Whatever may be the equation for men and land, it is improbable that we as yet know all its terms. Recent discoveries in mineral and vitamin nutrition reveal unsuspected dependencies in the up circuit: incredibly minute quantities of certain substances determine the value of soils to plants, of plants to animals. What of the down circuit? What of the vanishing species, the preservation of which we now regard as an esthetic luxury? They helped build the soil; in what unsuspected ways may they be essential to its maintenance? Professor Weaver[8] proposes that we use prairie flowers to reflocculate[9] the wasting soils of the dust bowl; who

[8]**John Ernest Weaver (1884–1966):** Professor at the University of Nebraska and a specialist in prairie studies.
[9]**reflocculate:** To help soil create lumps or masses.

knows for what purpose cranes and condors, otters and grizzlies may some day be used?

LAND HEALTH AND THE A-B CLEAVAGE

A land ethic, then, reflects the existence of an ecological conscience, and this in turn reflects a conviction of individual responsibility for the health of the land. Health is the capacity of the land for self-renewal. Conservation is our effort to understand and preserve this capacity. Conservationists are notorious for their dissensions. Superficially these seem to add up to mere confusion, but a more careful scrutiny reveals a single plane of cleavage common to many specialized fields. In each field one group (A) regards the land as soil, and its function as commodity production; another group (B) regards the land as a biota, and its function as something broader. How much broader is admittedly in a state of doubt and confusion.

In my own field, forestry, Group A is quite content to grow trees like cabbages, with cellulose as the basic forest commodity. It feels no inhibition against violence; its ideology is agronomic. Group B, on the other hand, sees forestry as fundamentally different from agronomy because it employs natural species, and manages a natural environment rather than creating an artificial one. Group B prefers natural reproduction on principle. It worries on biotic as well as economic grounds about the loss of species like chestnut, and the threatened loss of the white pines. It worries about a whole series of secondary forest functions: wildlife, recreation, watersheds, wilderness areas. To my mind, Group B feels the stirrings of an ecological conscience.

In the wildlife field, a parallel cleavage exists. For Group A the basic 75 commodities are sport and meat; the yardsticks of production are ciphers of take in pheasants and trout. Artificial propagation is acceptable as a permanent as well as a temporary recourse—if its unit costs permit. Group B, on the other hand, worries about a whole series of biotic side issues. What is the cost in predators of producing a game crop? Should we have further recourse to exotics? How can management restore the shrinking species, like prairie grouse, already hopeless as shootable game? How can management restore the threatened rarities, like trumpeter swan and whooping crane? Can management principles be extended to wildflowers? Here again it is clear to me that we have the same A-B cleavage as in forestry.

In the larger field of agriculture I am less competent to speak, but there seem to be somewhat parallel cleavages. Scientific agriculture was actively developing before ecology was born, hence a slower penetration of ecological concepts might be expected. Moreover the farmer, by the very nature of his techniques, must modify the biota more radically than the forester or the wildlife manager. Nevertheless, there are many discontents in agriculture which seem to add up to a new vision of "biotic farming."

Perhaps the most important of these is the new evidence that poundage or tonnage is no measure of the food value of farm crops; the products of fertile soil may be qualitatively as well as quantitatively superior. We can bolster poundage from depleted soils by pouring on imported fertility, but we are not necessarily bolstering food value. The possible ultimate ramifications of this idea are so immense that I must leave their exposition to abler pens.

The discontent that labels itself "organic farming," while bearing some of the earmarks of a cult, is nevertheless biotic in its direction, particularly in its insistence on the importance of soil flora and fauna.

The ecological fundamentals of agriculture are just as poorly known to the public as in other fields of land use. For example, few educated people realize that the marvelous advances in technique made during recent decades are improvements in the pump, rather than the well. Acre for acre, they have barely sufficed to offset the sinking level of fertility.

In all of these cleavages, we see repeated the same basic paradoxes: 80 man the conqueror *versus* man the biotic citizen; science the sharpener of his sword *versus* science the searchlight on his universe; land the slave and servant versus land the collective organism. Robinson's[10] injunction to Tristram may well be applied, at this juncture, to Homo sapiens as a species in geological time:

> Whether you will or not
> You are a King, Tristram, for you are one
> Of the time-tested few that leave the world,
> When they are gone, not the same place it was.
> Mark what you leave.

---

[10]**Edwin Arlington Robinson (1869–1935):** New England poet. *Tristram* (1927) was the third volume of a long poem on the Arthurian legends.

THE OUTLOOK

It is inconceivable to me that an ethical relation to land can exist without love, respect, and admiration for land, and a high regard for its value. By value, I of course mean something far broader than mere economic value; I mean value in the philosophical sense.

Perhaps the most serious obstacle impeding the evolution of a land ethic is the fact that our educational and economic system is headed away from, rather than toward, an intense consciousness of land. Your true modern is separated from the land by many middlemen, and by innumerable physical gadgets. He has no vital relation to it; to him it is the space between cities on which crops grow. Turn him loose for a day on the land, and if the spot does not happen to be a golf links or a "scenic" area, he is bored stiff. If crops could be raised by hydroponics instead of farming, it would suit him very well. Synthetic substitutes for wood, leather, wool, and other natural land products suit him better than the originals. In short, land is something he has "outgrown."

Almost equally serious as an obstacle to a land ethic is the attitude of the farmer for whom the land is still an adversary, or a taskmaster that keeps him in slavery. Theoretically, the mechanization of farming ought to cut the farmer's chains, but whether it really does is debatable.

One of the requisites for an ecological comprehension of land is an understanding of ecology, and this is by no means coextensive with "education"; in fact, much higher education seems deliberately to avoid ecological concepts. An understanding of ecology does not necessarily originate in courses bearing ecological labels; it is quite as likely to be labeled geography, botany, agronomy, history, or economics. This is as it should be, but whatever the label, ecological training is scarce.

The case for a land ethic would appear hopeless but for the minority 85 which is in obvious revolt against these "modern" trends.

The "key log" which must be moved to release the evolutionary process for an ethic is simply this: quit thinking about decent land use as solely an economic problem. Examine each question in terms of what is ethically and esthetically right, as well as what is economically expedient. A thing is right when it tends to preserve the integrity, stability, and beauty of the biotic community. It is wrong when it tends otherwise.

It of course goes without saying that economic feasibility limits the tether of what can or cannot be done for land. It always has and it always will. The fallacy the economic determinists have tied around our collective neck, and which we now need to cast off, is the belief that economics determines all land use. This is simply not true. An innumerable host of actions and attitudes, comprising perhaps the bulk of all land

127

relations, is determined by the land users' tastes and predilections, rather than by his purse. The bulk of all land relations hinges on investments of time, forethought, skill, and faith rather than on investments of cash. As a land user thinketh, so is he.

I have purposely presented the land ethic as a product of social evolution because nothing so important as an ethic is ever "written." Only the most superficial student of history supposes that Moses "wrote" the Decalogue; it evolved in the minds of a thinking community, and Moses wrote a tentative summary of it for a "seminar." I say tentative because evolution never stops.

The evolution of a land ethic is an intellectual as well as emotional process. Conservation is paved with good intentions which prove to be futile, or even dangerous, because they are devoid of critical understanding either of the land, or of economic land use. I think it is a truism that as the ethical frontier advances from the individual to the community, its intellectual content increases.

The mechanism of operation is the same for any ethic: social approbation for right actions: social disapproval for wrong actions. 90

By and large, our present problem is one of attitudes and implements. We are remodeling the Alhambra[11] with a steam shovel, and we are proud of our yardage. We shall hardly relinquish the shovel, which after all has many good points, but we are in need of gentler and more objective criteria for its successful use.

[1948]

---

[11]**Alhambra:** Exquisitely detailed citadel built by the Moors in Granada, Spain, in 1248–1354.

MIN-ZHAN LU

From Silence to Words: Writing as Struggle

Having completed graduate work in both the Composition Program and the Cultural and Critical Studies Program at the University of Pittsburgh, **Min-Zhan Lu** is currently a professor of English at the University of Louisville, teaching courses in literature, rhetoric, and composition. Among Lu's research interests is the question of how to best serve the needs of basic, multilingual, and transnational writers in the composition classroom, and in 2005, she received the Richard Braddock Award for her writing on the teaching of English. Lu has published widely in academic journals such as *College English* and *College Composition and Communication*. In collaboration with Bruce Horner, she coedited *Cross-Language Relations in Composition* (2010) and coauthored *Representing the "Other": Basic Writers and the Teaching of Basic Writing* (1999) and *Writing Conventions* (2008). Lu's memoir *Shanghai Quartet: The Crossings of Four Women of China*, in which she relates the story of four generations of women in her family, was published in 2001.

In her literacy narrative "From Silence to Words: Writing as Struggle," crafted following her mother's death and originally published in *College English*, Lu considers her experiences as a child learning English and Marxist ideologies while growing up in China during the Cultural Revolution. She describes the dissonance between her home life and school life, as well as her struggles to reconcile the two. Through her experiences, Lu expresses her concern about conceptions of language as taught in composition classes.

Imagine that you enter a parlor. You come late. When you arrive, others have long preceded you, and they are engaged in a heated discussion. . . . You listen for a while, until you decide that you have caught the tenor of the argument; then you put in your oar. Someone answers; you answer him; another comes to your

Min-Zhan Lu, "From Silence to Words: Writing as Struggle." From *College English*, Volume 49, No. 4, April 1987, pp. 437–77. Copyright © by the National Council of Teachers of English. Reprinted by permission.

defense; another aligns himself against you, to either the embarrassment or gratification of your opponent, depending upon the quality of your ally's assistance. However, the discussion is interminable. The hour grows late, you must depart. And you do depart, with the discussion still vigorously in progress.
—KENNETH BURKE, *The Philosophy of Literary Form*

Men are not built in silence, but in word, in work, in action-reflection. — PAULO FREIRE, *Pedagogy of the Oppressed*

My mother withdrew into silence two months before she died. A few nights before she fell silent, she told me she regretted the way she had raised me and my sisters. I knew she was referring to the way we had been brought up in the midst of two conflicting worlds—the world of home, dominated by the ideology of the Western humanistic tradition, and the world of a society dominated by Mao Tse-tung's Marxism. My mother had devoted her life to our education, an education she knew had made us suffer political persecution during the Cultural Revolution. I wanted to find a way to convince her that, in spite of the persecution, I had benefited from the education she had worked so hard to give me. But I was silent. My understanding of my education was so dominated by memories of confusion and frustration that I was unable to reflect on what I could have gained from it.

This paper is my attempt to fill up that silence with words, words I didn't have then, words that I have since come to by reflecting on my earlier experience as a student in China and on my recent experience as a composition teacher in the United States. For in spite of the frustration and confusion I experienced growing up caught between two conflicting worlds, the conflict ultimately helped me to grow as a reader and writer. Constantly having to switch back and forth between the discourse of home and that of school made me sensitive and self-conscious about the struggle I experienced every time I tried to read, write, or think in either discourse. Eventually, it led me to search for constructive uses for such struggle.

From early childhood, I had identified the differences between home and the outside world by the different languages I used in each. My parents had wanted my sisters and me to get the best education they could conceive of—Cambridge. They had hired a live-in tutor, a Scot, to make us bilingual. I learned to speak English with my parents, my tutor, and my sisters. I was allowed to speak Shanghai dialect only with the servants. When I was four (the year after the Communist Revolution of 1949), my parents sent me to a local private school where I learned to speak, read, and write in a new language—Standard Chinese, the official written language of New China.

In those days I moved from home to school, from English to Standard Chinese to Shanghai dialect, with no apparent friction. I spoke each language with those who spoke the language. All seemed quite "natural"— servants spoke only Shanghai dialect because they were servants; teachers spoke Standard Chinese because they were teachers; languages had different words because they were different languages. I thought of English as my family language, comparable to the many strange dialects I didn't speak but had often heard some of my classmates speak with their families. While I was happy to have a special family language, until second grade I didn't feel that my family language was any different than some of my classmates' family dialects.

My second grade homeroom teacher was a young graduate from a 5 missionary school. When she found out I spoke English, she began to practice her English on me. One day she used English when asking me to run an errand for her. As I turned to close the door behind me, I noticed the puzzled faces of my classmates. I had the same sensation I had often experienced when some stranger in a crowd would turn on hearing me speak English. I was more intensely pleased on this occasion, however, because suddenly I felt that my family language had been singled out from the family languages of my classmates. Since we were not allowed to speak any dialect other than Standard Chinese in the classroom, having my teacher speak English to me in class made English an official language of the classroom. I began to take pride in my ability to speak it.

This incident confirmed in my mind what my parents had always told me about the importance of English to one's life. Time and again they had told me of how my paternal grandfather, who was well versed in classic Chinese, kept losing good-paying jobs because he couldn't speak English. My grandmother reminisced constantly about how she had slaved and saved to send my father to a first-rate missionary school. And we were made to understand that it was my father's fluent English that had opened the door to his success. Even though my family had always stressed the importance of English for my future, I used to complain bitterly about the extra English lessons we had to take after school. It was only after my homeroom teacher had "sanctified" English that I began to connect English with my education. I became a much more eager student in my tutorials.

What I learned from my tutorials seemed to enhance and reinforce what I was learning in my classroom. In those days each word had one meaning. One day I would be making a sentence at school: "The national flag of China is red." The next day I would recite at home, "My love is like

131

a red, red rose." There seemed to be an agreement between the Chinese "red" and the English "red," and both corresponded to the patch of color printed next to the word. "Love" was my love for my mother at home and my love for my "motherland" at school; both "loves" meant how I felt about my mother. Having two loads of homework forced me to develop a quick memory for words and a sensitivity to form and style. What I learned in one language carried over to the other. I made sentences such as, "I saw a red, red rose among the green leaves," with both the English lyric and the classic Chinese lyric—red flower among green leaves—running through my mind, and I was praised by both teacher and tutor for being a good student.

Although my elementary schooling took place during the fifties, I was almost oblivious to the great political and social changes happening around me. Years later, I read in my history and political philosophy textbooks that the fifties were a time when "China was making a transition from a semi-feudal, semi-capitalist, and semi-colonial country into a socialist country," a period in which "the Proletarians were breaking into the educational territory dominated by Bourgeois Intellectuals." While people all over the country were being officially classified into Proletarians, Petty-bourgeois, National-bourgeois, Poor-peasants, and Intellectuals, and were trying to adjust to their new social identities, my parents were allowed to continue the upper middle-class life they had established before the 1949 Revolution because of my father's affiliation with British firms. I had always felt that my family was different from the families of my classmates, but I didn't perceive society's view of my family until the summer vacation before I entered high school.

First, my aunt was caught by her colleagues talking to her husband over the phone in English. Because of it, she was criticized and almost labeled a Rightist. (This was the year of the Anti-Rightist movement, a movement in which the Intellectuals became the target of the "socialist class-struggle.") I had heard others telling my mother that she was foolish to teach us English when Russian had replaced English as the "official" foreign language. I had also learned at school that the American and British Imperialists were the arch-enemies of New China. Yet I had made no connection between the arch-enemies and the English our family spoke. What happened to my aunt forced the connection on me. I began to see my parents' choice of a family language as an anti-Revolutionary act and was alarmed that I had participated in such an act. From then on, I took care not to use English outside home and to conceal my knowledge of English from my new classmates.

Certain words began to play important roles in my new life at the 10 junior high. On the first day of school, we were handed forms to fill out with our parents' class, job, and income. Being one of the few people not employed by the government, my father had never been officially classified. Since he was a medical doctor, he told me to put him down as an Intellectual. My homeroom teacher called me into the office a couple of days afterwards and told me that my father couldn't be an Intellectual if his income far exceeded that of a Capitalist. He also told me that since my father worked for Foreign Imperialists, my father should be classified as an Imperialist Lackey. The teacher looked nonplussed when I told him that my father couldn't be an Imperialist Lackey because he was a medical doctor. But I could tell from the way he took notes on my form that my father's job had put me in an unfavorable position in his eyes.

The Standard Chinese term "class" was not a new word for me. Since first grade, I had been taught sentences such as, "The Working class are the masters of New China." I had always known that it was good to be a worker, but until then, I had never felt threatened for not being one. That fall, "class" began to take on a new meaning for me. I noticed a group of Working-class students and teachers at school. I was made to understand that because of my class background, I was excluded from that group.

Another word that became important was "consciousness." One of the slogans posted in the school building read, "Turn our students into future Proletarians with socialist consciousness and education!" For several weeks we studied this slogan in our political philosophy course, a subject I had never had in elementary school. I still remember the definition of "socialist consciousness" that we were repeatedly tested on through the years: "Socialist consciousness is a person's political soul. It is the consciousness of the Proletarians represented by Marxist Mao Tse-tung thought. It takes expression in one's action, language, and lifestyle. It is the task of every Chinese student to grow up into a Proletarian with a socialist consciousness so that he can serve the people and the motherland." To make the abstract concept accessible to us, our teacher pointed out that the immediate task for students from Working-class families was to strengthen their socialist consciousnesses. For those of us who were from other class backgrounds, the task was to turn ourselves into Workers with socialist consciousnesses. The teacher never explained exactly how we were supposed to "turn" into Workers. Instead, we were given samples of the ritualistic annual plans we had to write at the beginning of each term. In these plans, we performed "self-criticism" on our consciousnesses and made vows to turn ourselves into Workers with socialist consciousnesses. The teacher's division between those who did and those who didn't have a socialist consciousness led me to reify the notion of "consciousness" into a thing one possesses. I equated this intangible "thing" with a concrete way of dressing, speaking, and writing. For instance, I never doubted that my political philosophy teacher had a socialist consciousness because she was from a steel-worker's family (she announced this the first day of class) and was a Party member who wore grey cadre suits and talked like a philosophy textbook. I noticed other things about her. She had beautiful eyes and spoke Standard Chinese with such a pure accent that I thought she should be a film star. But I was embarrassed that I had noticed things that ought not to have been associated with her. I blamed my observation on my Bourgeois consciousness.

At the same time, the way reading and writing were taught through memorization and imitation also encouraged me to reduce concepts and ideas to simple definitions. In literature and political philosophy classes, we were taught a large number of quotations from Marx, Lenin, and Mao Tse-tung. Each concept that appeared in these quotations came with a definition. We were required to memorize the definitions of the words along with the quotations. Every time I memorized a definition, I felt I had learned a word: "The national red flag symbolizes the blood shed by Revolutionary ancestors for our socialist cause"; "New China rises like a red sun over the eastern horizon." As I memorized these sentences, I reduced their metaphors to dictionary meanings: "red" meant "Revolution" and "red sun" meant "New China" in the "language" of the Working class. I learned mechanically but eagerly. I soon became quite fluent in this new language.

As school began to define me as a political subject, my parents tried to buildup my resistance to the "communist poisoning" by exposing me to the "great books"—novels by Charles Dickens, Nathaniel Hawthorne, Emily Bronte, Jane Austen, and writers from around the turn of the century. My parents implied that these writers represented how I, their child, should read and write. My parents replaced the word "Bourgeois" with the word "cultured." They reminded me that I was in school only to learn math and science. I needed to pass the other courses to stay in school, but I was not to let the "Red doctrines" corrupt my mind. Gone were the days when I could innocently write, "I saw the red, red rose among the green leaves," collapsing, as I did, English and Chinese cultural traditions. "Red" came to mean Revolution at school, "the Commies" at home, and adultery in *The Scarlet Letter*. Since I took these symbols and metaphors as meanings natural to people of the same class, I abandoned my earlier definitions of English and Standard Chinese as the language of home and the language of school. I now defined English as the language of the Bourgeois and Standard Chinese as the language of the Working class. I thought of the language of the Working class as someone else's language and the language of the Bourgeois as my language. But I also believed that, although the language of the Bourgeois was my real language, I could and would adopt the language of the Working class when I was at school. I began to put on and take off my Working class language in the same way I put on and took off my school clothes to avoid being criticized for wearing Bourgeois clothes.

In my literature classes, I learned the Working-class formula for read- 15 ing. Each work in the textbook had a short "Author's Biography": "XXX, born in 19-- in the province of XX, is from a Worker's family. He joined the Revolution in 19--. He is a Revolutionary realist with a passionate love for the Party and Chinese Revolution. His work expresses the thoughts and emotions of the masses and sings praise to the prosperous socialist construction on all fronts of China." The teacher used the "Author's Biography" as a yardstick to measure the texts. We were taught to locate details in the texts that illustrated these summaries, such as words that expressed Workers' thoughts and emotions or events that illustrated the Workers' lives.

I learned a formula for Working-class writing in the composition classes. We were given sample essays and told to imitate them. The theme was always about how the collective taught the individual a lesson. I would write papers about labor-learning experiences or school-cleaning days, depending on the occasion of the collective activity closest to the assignment. To make each paper look different, I dressed it up with details about the date, the weather, the environment, or the appearance of the Master-worker who had taught me "the lesson." But as I became more and more fluent in the generic voice of the Working-class Student, I also became more and more self-conscious about the language we used at home.

For instance, in senior high we began to have English classes ("to study English for the Revolution," as the slogan on the cover of the textbook said), and I was given my first Chinese-English dictionary. There I discovered the English version of the term "class-struggle." (The Chinese characters for a school "class" and for a social "class" are different.) I had often used the English word "class" at home in sentences such as, "So and so has class," but I had not connected this sense of "class" with "class-struggle." Once the connection was made, I heard a second layer of meaning every time someone at home said a person had "class." The expression began to mean the person had the style and sophistication characteristic of the Bourgeoisie. The word lost its innocence. I was uneasy about hearing that second layer of meaning because I was sure my parents did not hear the word that way. I felt that therefore I should not be hearing it that way either. Hearing the second layer of meaning made me wonder if I was losing my English.

My suspicion deepened when I noticed myself unconsciously merging and switching between the "reading" of home and the "reading" of school. Once I had to write a report on *The Revolutionary Family*, a book about an illiterate woman's awakening and growth as a Revolutionary through the deaths of her husband and all her children for the cause of the Revolution. In one scene the woman deliberated over whether or not she should encourage her youngest son to join the Revolution. Her memory of her husband's death made her afraid to encourage her son. Yet she also remembered her earlier married life and the first time her husband tried to explain the meaning of the Revolution to her. These memories made her feel she should encourage her son to continue the cause his father had begun.

I was moved by this scene. "Moved" was a word my mother and sisters used a lot when we discussed books. Our favorite moments in novels were moments of what I would now call internal conflict, moments which we said "moved" us. I remember that we were "moved" by Jane Eyre when she was torn between her sense of ethics, which compelled her to leave the man she loved, and her impulse to stay with the only man who had ever loved her. We were also moved by Agnes in *David Copperfield* because of the way she restrained her love for David so that he could live happily with the woman he loved. My standard method of doing a book report was to model it on the review by the Publishing Bureau and to dress it up with detailed quotations from the book. The review of *The Revolutionary Family* emphasized the woman's Revolutionary spirit. I decided to use the scene that had moved me to illustrate this point. I wrote the report the night before it was due. When I had finished, I realized I couldn't possibly hand it in. Instead of illustrating her Revolutionary spirit, I had dwelled on her internal conflict, which could be seen as a moment of weak sentimentality that I should never have emphasized in a Revolutionary heroine. I wrote another report, taking care to illustrate the grandeur of her Revolutionary spirit by expanding on a quotation in which she decided that if the life of her son could change the lives of millions of sons, she should not begrudge his life for the cause of Revolution. I handed in my second version but kept the first in my desk.

I never showed it to anyone. I could never show it to people outside 20 my family, because it had deviated so much from the reading enacted by the jacket review. Neither could I show it to my mother or sisters, because I was ashamed to have been so moved by such a "Revolutionary" book. My parents would have been shocked to learn that I could like such a book in the same way they liked Dickens. Writing this book report increased my fear that I was losing the command over both the "language of home" and the "language of school" that I had worked so hard to gain. I tried to remind myself that, if I could still tell when my reading or writing sounded incorrect, then I had retained my command over both languages. Yet I could no longer be confident of my command over either language because I had discovered that when I was not careful— or even when I was—my reading and writing often surprised me with its impurity. To prevent such impurity, I became very suspicious of my thoughts when I read or wrote. I was always asking myself why I was using this word, how I was using it, always afraid that I wasn't reading or writing correctly. What confused and frustrated me most was that I could not figure out why I was no longer able to read or write correctly without such painful deliberation.

I continued to read only because reading allowed me to keep my thoughts and confusion private. I hoped that somehow, if I watched myself carefully, I would figure out from the way I read whether I had really mastered the "languages." But writing became a dreadful chore. When I tried to keep a diary, I was so afraid that the voice of school might slip in that I could only list my daily activities. When I wrote for school, I worried that my Bourgeois sensibilities would betray me.

The more suspicious I became about the way I read and wrote, the more guilty I felt for losing the spontaneity with which I had learned to "use" these "languages." Writing the book report made me feel that my reading and writing in the "language" of either home or school could not be free of the interference of the other. But I was unable to acknowledge, grasp, or grapple with what I was experiencing, for both my parents and my teachers had suggested that, if I were a good student, such interference would and should not take place. I assumed that once I had "acquired" a discourse, I could simply switch it on and off every time I read and wrote as I would some electronic tool. Furthermore, I expected my readings and writings to come out in their correct forms whenever I switched the proper discourse on. I still regarded the discourse of home as natural and the discourse of school alien, but I never had doubted before that I could acquire both and switch them on and off according to the occasion.

When my experience in writing conflicted with what I thought should happen when I used each discourse, I rejected my experience because it contradicted what my parents and teachers had taught me. I shied away from writing to avoid what I assumed I should not experience. But trying to avoid what should not happen did not keep it from recurring whenever I had to write. Eventually my confusion and frustration over these recurring experiences compelled me to search for an explanation: how and why had I failed to learn what my parents and teachers had worked so hard to teach me?

I now think of the internal scene for my reading and writing about *The Revolutionary Family* as a heated discussion between myself, the voices of home, and those of school. The review on the back of the book, the sample student papers I came across in my composition classes, my philosophy teacher—these I heard as voices of one group. My parents and my home readings were the voices of an opposing group. But the conversation between these opposing voices in the internal scene of my writing was not as polite and respectful as the parlor scene Kenneth Burke has portrayed (see epigraph). Rather, these voices struggled to dominate the discussion, constantly incorporating, dismissing, or suppressing the arguments of each other, like the battles between the hegemonic and counterhegemonic forces described in Raymond Williams' *Marxism and Literature* (108–14).

When I read *The Revolutionary Family* and wrote the first version of my report, I began with a quotation from the review. The voices of both home and school answered, clamoring to be heard. I tried to listen to one group and turn a deaf ear to the other. Both persisted. I negotiated my way through these conflicting voices, now agreeing with one, now agreeing with the other. I formed a reading out of my interaction with both. Yet I was afraid to have done so because both home and school had implied that I should speak in unison with only one of these groups and stand away from the discussion rather than participate in it.

My teachers and parents had persistently called my attention to the intensity of the discussion taking place on the external social scene. The story of my grandfather's failure and my father's success had from my early childhood made me aware of the conflict between Western and traditional Chinese cultures. My political education at school added another dimension to the conflict: the war of Marxist-Maoism against them both. Yet when my parents and teachers called my attention to the conflict, they stressed the anxiety of having to live through China's transformation from a semi-feudal, semi-capitalist, and semi-colonial society to a socialist one. Acquiring the discourse of the dominant group was, to them, a means of seeking alliance with that group and thus of surviving the whirlpool of cultural currents around them. As a result, they modeled their pedagogical practices on this utilitarian view of language. Being the eager student, I adopted this view of language as a tool for survival. It came to dominate my understanding of the discussion on the social and historical scene and to restrict my ability to participate in that discussion.

To begin with, the metaphor of language as a tool for survival led me to be passive in my use of discourse, to be a bystander in the discussion. In Burke's "parlor," everyone is involved in the discussion. As it goes on through history, what we call "communal discourses"—arguments specific to particular political, social, economic, ethnic, sexual, and family groups—form, re-form and transform. To use a discourse in such a scene is to participate in the argument and to contribute to the formation of the discourse. But when I was growing up, I could not take on the burden of such an active role in the discussion. For both home and school presented the existent conventions of the discourse each taught me as absolute laws for my action. They turned verbal action into a tool, a set of conventions produced and shaped prior to and outside of my own verbal acts. Because I saw language as a tool, I separated the process of producing the tool from the process of using it. The tool was made by someone else and was then acquired and used by me. How the others made it before I acquired it determined and guaranteed what it produced when I used it. I imagined that the more experienced and powerful members of the community were the ones responsible for making the tool. They were the ones who participated in the discussion and fought with opponents. When I used what they made, their labor and accomplishments would ensure the quality of my reading and writing. By using it, I could survive the heated discussion. When my immediate experience in writing the book report suggested that knowing the conventions of school did not guarantee the form and content of my report, when it suggested that I had to write the report with the work and responsibility I had assigned to those who wrote book reviews in the Publishing Bureau, I thought I had lost the tool I had earlier acquired.

Another reason I could not take up an active role in the argument was that my parents and teachers contrived to provide a scene free of conflict for practicing my various languages. It was as if their experience had made them aware of the conflict between their discourse and other discourses and of the struggle involved in reproducing the conventions of any discourse on a scene where more than one discourse exists. They seemed convinced that such conflict and struggle would overwhelm someone still learning the discourse. Home and school each contrived a purified space where only one discourse was spoken and heard. In their choice of textbooks, in the way they spoke, and in the way they required me to speak, each jealously silenced any voice that threatened to break the unison of the scene. The homogeneity of home and of school implied that only one discourse could and should be relevant in each place. It led me to believe I should leave behind, turn a deaf ear to, or forget the discourse of the other when I crossed the boundary dividing them. I expected myself to set down one discourse whenever I took up another just as I would take off or put on a particular set of clothes for school or home.

Despite my parents' and teachers' attempts to keep home and school discrete, the internal conflict between the two discourses continued whenever I read or wrote. Although I tried to suppress the voice of one discourse in the name of the other, having to speak aloud in the voice I had just silenced each time I crossed the boundary kept both voices active in my mind. Every "I think . . ." from the voice of home or school brought forth a "However . . ." or a "But . . ." from the voice of the opponents. To identify with the voice of home or school, I had to negotiate through the conflicting voices of both by restating, taking back, qualifying my thoughts. I was unconsciously doing so when I did my book report. But I could not use the interaction comfortably and constructively. Both my parents and my teachers had implied that my job was to prevent that interaction from happening. My sense of having failed to accomplish what they had taught silenced me.

To use the interaction between the discourses of home and school con- 30 structively, I would have to have seen reading or writing as a process in which I worked my way towards a stance through a dialectical process of identification and division. To identify with an ally, I would have to have grasped the distance between where he or she stood and where I was positioning myself. In taking a stance against an opponent, I would have to have grasped where my stance identified with the stance of my allies. Teetering along the "wavering line of pressure and counterpressure" from both allies and opponents, I might have worked my way towards a stance of my own (Burke, *A Rhetoric of Motives* 23). Moreover, I would have to have understood that the voices in my mind, like the participants in the parlor scene, were in constant flux. As I came into contact with new and different groups of people or read different books, voices entered and left. Each time I read or wrote, the stance I negotiated out of these voices would always be at some distance from the stances I worked out in my previous and my later readings or writings.

I could not conceive such a form of action for myself because I saw reading and writing as an expression of an established stance. In delineating the conventions of a discourse, my parents and teachers had synthesized the stance they saw as typical for a representative member of the community. Burke calls this the stance of a "god" or the "prototype"; Williams calls it the "official" or "possible" stance of the community. Through the metaphor of the survival tool, my parents and teachers had led me to assume I could automatically reproduce the official stance of the discourse I used. Therefore, when I did my book report on *The Revolutionary Family*, I expected my knowledge of the official stance set by the book review to ensure the actual stance of my report. As it happened, I began by trying to take the official stance of the review. Other voices interrupted. I answered back. In the process, I worked out a stance approximate but not identical to the official stance I began with. Yet the experience of having to labor to realize my knowledge of the official stance or to prevent myself from wandering away from it frustrated and confused me. For even though I had been actually reading and writing in a Burkean scene, I was afraid to participate actively in the discussion. I assumed it was my role to survive by staying out of it.

Not long ago, my daughter told me that it bothered her to hear her friend "talk wrong." Having come to the United States from China with little English, my daughter has become sensitive to the way English, as spoken by her teachers, operates. As a result, she has amazed her teachers with her success in picking up the language and in adapting to life at school. Her concern to speak the English taught in the classroom "correctly" makes her uncomfortable when she hears people using "ain't" or double negatives, which her teacher considers "improper." I see in her the me that had eagerly learned and used the discourse of the Working class at school. Yet while I was torn between the two conflicting worlds of school and home, she moves with seeming ease from the conversations she hears over the dinner table to her teacher's words in the classroom. My husband and I are proud of the good work she does at school. We are glad she is spared the kinds of conflict between home and school I experienced at her age. Yet as we watch her becoming more and more fluent in the language of the classroom, we wonder if, by enabling her to "survive" school, her very fluency will silence her when the scene of her reading and writing expands beyond that of the composition classroom.

For when I listen to my daughter, to students, and to some composition teachers talking about the teaching and learning of writing, I am often alarmed by the degree to which the metaphor of a survival tool dominates their understanding of language as it once dominated my own. I am especially concerned with the way some composition classes focus on turning the classroom into a monological scene for the students' reading and writing. Most of our students live in a world similar to my daughter's, somewhere between the purified world of the classroom and the complex world of my adolescence. When composition classes encourage these students to ignore those voices that seem irrelevant to the purified world of the classroom, most students are often able to do so without much struggle. Some of them are so adept at doing it that the whole process has for them become automatic.

However, beyond the classroom and beyond the limited range of these students' immediate lives lies a much more complex and dynamic social and historical scene. To help these students become actors in such a scene, perhaps we need to call their attention to voices that may seem irrelevant to the discourse we teach rather than encourage them to shut them out. For example, we might intentionally complicate the classroom scene by bringing into it discourses that stand at varying distances from the one we teach. We might encourage students to explore ways of practicing the conventions of the discourse they are learning by negotiating through these conflicting voices. We could also encourage them to see themselves as responsible for forming or transforming as well as preserving the discourse they are learning.

As I think about what we might do to complicate the external and 35 internal scenes of our students' writing, I hear my parents and teachers saying: "Not now. Keep them from the wrangle of the marketplace until they have acquired the discourse and are skilled at using it." And I answer: "Don't teach them to 'survive' the whirlpool of crosscurrents by avoiding it. Use the classroom to moderate the currents. Moderate the currents, but teach them from the beginning to struggle." When I think of the ways in which the teaching of reading and writing as classroom activities can frustrate the development of students, I am almost grateful for the overwhelming complexity of the circumstances in which I grew up. For it was this complexity that kept me from losing sight of the effort and choice involved in reading or writing with and through a discourse.

[1987]

Works Cited

Burke, Kenneth. *The Philosophy of Literary Form: Studies in Symbolic Action.* 2nd ed. Baton Rouge: Louisiana State UP, 1967.

———. *A Rhetoric of Motives.* Berkeley: U of California P, 1969.

Freire, Paulo. *Pedagogy of the Oppressed.* Trans. M. B. Ramos. New York: Continuum, 1970.

Williams, Raymond. *Marxism and Literature.* New York: Oxford UP, 1977.

SCOTT McCLOUD [b. 1960]

Understanding Comics

Born in Boston, Massachusetts, and raised in Lexington, **Scott McCloud** is a cartoonist and comics theorist. After graduating from Syracuse University with a fine arts degree in illustration, McCloud worked in the production department of DC Comics before creating *Zot!*—a lighthearted, thirty-six-issue alternative series published by Eclipse Comics between 1984 and 1991—in response to the darker, violent comics that dominated the scene during the 1980s. McCloud followed *Zot!* with *Destroy!!* (1986), a single, oversized volume parodying the archetypal, violent superhero; *The New Adventures of Abraham Lincoln* (1998), his first attempt with computer-generated artwork; and *Superman: Adventures of the Man of Steel* (1998), a compilation of the first six of twelve superman stories scripted for DC Comics. Cited as the "Aristotle of comics," McCloud is best known as the author of *Understanding Comics: The Invisible Art* (1993), in which his self-caricature guides the reader through a study of sequential art, by tracing the relationship between words and images. Following the belated success of *Understanding Comics*, he published *Reinventing Comics* (2000) and *Making Comics* (2006), in which his self-caricature reemerged.

In the following excerpts from *Understanding Comics*, McCloud suggests that the influence of new media on the written word is often misunderstood, and that comics are more than simple juxtapositions of words and images. Drawing first on the idea of "show and tell," McCloud proposes "unlimited" benefits to the interdependent use of words and images in comics, comparing the two to dance partners: "[E]ach one takes turns leading."

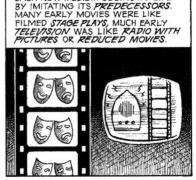

WORDS AND PICTURES IN COMBINATION MAY NOT BE MY *DEFINITION* OF COMICS, BUT THE COMBINATION HAS HAD *TREMENDOUS INFLUENCE* ON ITS *GROWTH*.

com.ics (kom'iks) n. p____ form, used with a singula___ Juxtaposed pictori___ ___er images in deliber___ ___nce, intended to conve___ ___ and/or to prod___ ___ response in t___ **2.**___roes ___costumes, ___ villains ___ ___ words ___

A HUGE RANGE OF HUMAN EXPERIENCES CAN BE *PORTRAYED* IN COMICS THROUGH EITHER WORDS OR PICTURES.

AS A RESULT--AND DESPITE ITS MANY *OTHER* POTENTIAL USES-- COMICS HAVE BECOME *FIRMLY IDENTIFIED* WITH THE ART OF *STORYTELLING*.

AND *INDEED*, WORDS AND PICTURES HAVE *GREAT* POWERS TO TELL STORIES WHEN CREATORS FULLY EXPLOIT THEM *BOTH*.

DADA

BIOGRAPHY HORROR

ROMANCE SURREALISM

BLANK VERSE HISTORICAL FICTION

EPIC POETRY FOLK TALES

SOCIAL ALLEGORY | SEQUENTIAL ART | EROTICA

MYSTERY

ADAPTATIONS RELIGIOUS TOPICS

STREAM OF CONSCIOUSNESS

SATIRE

AND SO FAR, WE'VE ONLY SEEN THE *TIP OF THE ICEBERG!*

AS CHILDREN, WE "SHOW AND TELL" *INTERCHANGEABLY*, WORDS AND IMAGES COMBINING TO TRANSMIT A *CONNECTED SERIES OF IDEAS*.

IT'S GOT ONE OF *THESE* THINGS.

THE DIFFERENT WAYS IN WHICH WORDS AND PICTURES CAN *COMBINE* IN COMICS IS VIRTUALLY *UNLIMITED*.

BUT LET'S TRY TO BREAK IT DOWN INTO SOME DISTINCT *CATEGORIES*.

FIRST, WE HAVE THE *WORD SPECIFIC* COMBINATIONS, WHERE PICTURES *ILLUSTRATE,* BUT DON'T SIGNIFICANTLY *ADD* TO A LARGELY *COMPLETE* TEXT.

WE STUMBLED BACK TO THE APARTMENT SHORTLY BEFORE DAWN, *VOMITING* EVERY 20 YARDS.

JUDY GAVE ME HER KEYS AND SMILED.

THE *UNITED STATES CONSTITUTION* WAS ADOPTED BY THE *SECOND CONTINENTAL CONGRESS* IN 1787 AND PUT INTO EFFECT IN 1789.

THEN THERE ARE *PICTURE SPECIFIC* COMBINATIONS WHERE WORDS DO LITTLE MORE THAN ADD A *SOUNDTRACK* TO A VISUALLY TOLD SEQUENCE.

HE DID IT!

MMM... MMM...

AND, OF COURSE, *DUO-SPECIFIC* PANELS IN WHICH BOTH WORDS AND PICTURES SEND ESSENTIALLY THE *SAME* MESSAGE.

GRIM-FACED, GEORGE LIFTED HIS LOLLYPOP.

BUT THE CAPTAIN'S MIGHTY BLOW *MISSES* ITS INTENDED TARGET!

BLAST! HE *DODGED* MY PUNCH AND I STRUCK THIS *BRICK WALL!*

HA! I *DODGED* YO

I FEEL SO *SAD!*

...THOUGHT AMY.

PERHAPS THE MOST *COMMON* TYPE OF WORD/PICTURE COMBINATION IS THE *INTER-DEPENDENT,* WHERE WORDS AND PICTURES GO *HAND IN HAND* TO CONVEY AN IDEA THAT NEITHER COULD CONVEY *ALONE.*

MEANWHILE...

DID ANYONE *SEE* YOU?

THIS IS ALL I NEED TO *STOP* HIM!

I ASK YOU, DOES THIS GUY LOOK LIKE A *C.E.O.* TO YOU ??

"AND JUST *GUESS* WHO DROVE UP IN BOB'S TRUCK AN HOUR LATER!"

HEY, MARGE!

OH, MY GOD!

"AFTER COLLEGE, I PURSUED A CAREER IN *HIGH FINANCE.*"

HURRY UP, WILLYA ?!

HE'S LYING.

UH-HUH.

INTERDEPENDENT COMBINATIONS AREN'T ALWAYS AN *EQUAL BALANCE* THOUGH AND MAY FALL *ANYWHERE* ON A SCALE BETWEEN TYPES ONE AND TWO.

GENERALLY SPEAKING, THE MORE IS SAID WITH *WORDS,* THE MORE THE PICTURES CAN BE FREED TO GO EXPLORING AND *VICE VERSA.*

$$\frac{P}{W}$$

$$\frac{W}{P}$$

148

IN COMICS AT ITS *BEST,* WORDS AND PICTURES ARE LIKE *PARTNERS* IN A *DANCE* AND EACH ONE TAKES TURNS *LEADING.*

WHEN *BOTH* PARTNERS TRY TO LEAD, THE COMPETITION CAN *SUBVERT* THE OVERALL GOALS...

YOW!

...THOUGH A LITTLE *PLAYFUL* COMPETITION CAN SOMETIMES PRODUCE *ENJOYABLE RESULTS.*

BUT WHEN THESE PARTNERS EACH *KNOW* THEIR ROLES--

--AND *SUPPORT* EACH OTHER'S *STRENGTHS*--

--COMICS CAN MATCH *ANY* OF THE ART FORMS IT DRAWS SO MUCH OF ITS STRENGTH FROM.

[1993]

149

DONALD MURRAY   [1924–2007]

The Maker's Eye: Revising Your Own Manuscripts

Donald Murray, an acclaimed novelist, poet, and journalist, was born in Boston, Massachusetts. He graduated from the University of New Hampshire, where he later worked as an English professor. Murray is considered an expert on the writing process, and he has written several composition textbooks and sourcebooks. These works include *A Writer Teaches Writing: A Complete Revision* (1985), *Learning by Teaching* (1982), and *Write to Learn* (Seventh Edition, 2004). Murray's editorials in *The Boston Globe* won him the Pulitzer Prize in 1954. He died from heart failure on December 30, 2007.

In his essay "The Maker's Eye: Revising Your Own Manuscripts," Murray emphasizes that writers can only rely on themselves to bring their work to success. While stressing the importance of revising and rewriting, Murray challenges writers to be their own critics, to review their work as if they were seeing it for the first time, and to rework their writing through multiple drafts. In the essay, he outlines the steps necessary to "edit oneself" in order to yield the most polished work possible.

When students complete a first draft, they consider the job of writing done—and their teachers too often agree. When professional writers complete a first draft, they usually feel that they are at the start of the writing process. When a draft is completed, the job of writing can begin.

That difference in attitude is the difference between amateur and professional, inexperience and experience, journeyman and craftsman. Peter F. Drucker, the prolific business writer, calls his first draft "the zero draft"—after that he can start counting. Most writers share the feeling that the first draft, and all of those which follow, are opportunities to discover what they have to say and how best they can say it.

To produce a progression of drafts, each of which says more and says it more clearly, the writer has to develop a special kind of reading skill.

In school we are taught to decode what appears on the page as finished writing. Writers, however, face a different category of possibility and responsibility when they read their own drafts. To them the words on the page are never finished. Each can be changed and rearranged, can set off a chain reaction of confusion or clarified meaning. This is a different kind of reading which is possibly more difficult and certainly more exciting.

Writers must learn to be their own best enemy. They must accept the criticism of others and be suspicious of it; they must accept the praise of others and be even more suspicious of it. Writers cannot depend on others. They must detach themselves from their own pages so that they can apply both their caring and their craft to their own work.

Such detachment is not easy. Science-fiction writer Ray Bradbury sup- 5 posedly puts each manuscript away for a year to the day and then rereads it as a stranger. Not many writers have the discipline or the time to do this. We must read when our judgment may be at its worst, when we are close to the euphoric moment of creation.

Then the writer, counsels novelist Nancy Hale, "should be critical of everything that seems to him most delightful in his style. He should excise what he most admires, because he wouldn't thus admire it if he weren't . . . in a sense protecting it from criticism." John Ciardi, the poet, adds, "The last act of the writing must be to become one's own reader. It is, I suppose, a schizophrenic process, to begin passionately and to end critically, to begin hot and to end cold; and, more important, to be passion-hot and critic-cold at the same time."

Most people think that the principal problem is that writers are too proud of what they have written. Actually, a greater problem for most professional writers is one shared by the majority of students. They are overly critical, think everything is dreadful, tear up page after page, never complete a draft, see the task as hopeless.

The writer must learn to read critically but constructively, to cut what is bad, to reveal what is good. Eleanor Estes, the children's book author, explains: "The writer must survey his work critically, coolly, as though he were a stranger to it. He must be willing to prune, expertly and hard-heartedly. At the end of each revision, a manuscript may look . . . worked over, torn apart, pinned together, added to, deleted from, words changed and words changed back. Yet the book must maintain its original freshness and spontaneity."

Most readers underestimate the amount of rewriting it usually takes to produce spontaneous reading. This is a great disadvantage to the student writer, who sees only a finished product and never watches the craftsman who takes the necessary step back, studies the work carefully, returns to the task, steps back, returns, steps back, again and again. Anthony Burgess, one of the most prolific writers in the English-speaking world, admits, "I might revise a page twenty times." Roald Dahl, the popular children's writer, states, "By the time I'm nearing the end of a story, the first part will have been reread and altered and corrected at least 150 times. . . . Good writing is essentially rewriting. I am positive of this."

Rewriting isn't virtuous. It isn't something that ought to be done. It is 10 simply something that most writers find they have to do to discover what they have to say and how to say it. It is a condition of the writer's life.

There are, however, a few writers who do little formal rewriting, primarily because they have the capacity and experience to create and review a large number of invisible drafts in their minds before they approach the page. And some writers slowly produce finished pages, performing all the tasks of revision simultaneously, page by page, rather than draft by draft. But it is still possible to see the sequence followed by most writers most of the time in rereading their own work.

Most writers scan their drafts first, reading as quickly as possible to catch the larger problems of subject and form, and then move in closer and closer as they read and write, reread and rewrite.

The first thing writers look for in their drafts is *information*. They know that a good piece of writing is built from specific, accurate, and interesting information. The writer must have an abundance of information from which to construct a readable piece of writing.

Next writers look for *meaning* in the information. The specifics must build to a pattern of significance. Each piece of specific information must carry the reader toward meaning.

Writers reading their own drafts are aware of *audience*. They put 15 themselves in the reader's situation and make sure that they deliver information which a reader wants to know or needs to know in a manner which is easily digested. Writers try to be sure that they anticipate and answer the questions a critical reader will ask when reading the piece of writing.

Writers make sure that the *form* is appropriate to the subject and the audience. Form, or genre, is the vehicle which carries meaning to the reader, but form cannot be selected until the writer has adequate information to discover its significance and an audience which needs or wants that meaning.

Once writers are sure the form is appropriate, they must then look at the *structure*, the order of what they have written. Good writing is built on a solid framework of logic, argument, narrative, or motivation which runs through the entire piece of writing and holds it together. This is the time when many writers find it most effective to outline as a way of visualizing the hidden spine by which the piece of writing is supported.

The element on which writers may spend a majority of their time is *development*. Each section of a piece of writing must be adequately developed. It must give readers enough information so that they are satisfied. How much information is enough? That's as difficult as asking how much garlic belongs in a salad. It must be done to taste, but most beginning writers underdevelop, underestimating the reader's hunger for information.

As writers solve development problems, they often have to consider questions of *dimension*. There must be a pleasing and effective proportion among all the parts of the piece of writing. There is a continual process of subtracting and adding to keep the piece of writing in balance.

Finally, writers have to listen to their own voices. *Voice* is the force 20 which drives a piece of writing forward. It is an expression of the writer's authority and concern. It is what is between the words on the page, what glues the piece of writing together. A good piece of writing is always marked by a consistent, individual voice.

As writers read and reread, write and rewrite, they move closer and closer to the page until they are doing line-by-line editing. Writers read their own pages with infinite care. Each sentence, each line, each clause, each phrase, each word, each mark of punctuation, each section of white space between the type has to contribute to the clarification of meaning.

Slowly the writer moves from word to word, looking through language to see the subject. As a word is changed, cut, or added, as a construction is rearranged, all the words used before that moment and all those that follow that moment must be considered and reconsidered.

Writers often read aloud at this stage of the editing process, muttering or whispering to themselves, calling on the ear's experience with language. Does this sound right—or that? Writers edit, shifting back and forth from eye to page to ear to page. I find I must do this careful editing in short runs, no more than fifteen or twenty minutes at a stretch, or I become too kind with myself. I begin to see what I hope is on the page, not what actually is on the page.

This sounds tedious if you haven't done it, but actually it is fun. Making something right is immensely satisfying, for writers begin to learn what they are writing about by writing. Language leads them to meaning, and there is the joy of discovery, of understanding, of making meaning clear as the writer employs the technical skills of language.

Words have double meanings, even triple and quadruple meanings. 25 Each word has its own potential of connotation and denotation. And when writers rub one word against the other, they are often rewarded with a sudden insight, an unexpected clarification.

The maker's eye moves back and forth from word to phrase to sentence to paragraph to sentence to phrase to word. The maker's eye sees the need for variety and balance, for a firmer structure, for a more appropriate form. It peers into the interior of the paragraph, looking for coherence, unity, and emphasis, which make meaning clear.

I learned something about this process when my first bifocals were prescribed. I had ordered a larger section of the reading portion of the glass because of my work, but even so, I could not contain my eyes within this new limit of vision. And I still find myself taking off my glasses and bending my nose toward the page, for my eyes unconsciously flick back and forth across the page, back to another page, forward to still another, as I try to see each evolving line in relation to every other line.

When does this process end? Most writers agree with the great Russian writer Tolstoy, who said, "I scarcely ever reread my published writings, if by chance I come across a page, it always strikes me: all this must be rewritten; this is how I should have written it."

The maker's eye is never satisfied, for each word has the potential to ignite new meaning. This article has been twice written all the way through the writing process. . . . Now it is to be republished in a book. The editors made a few small suggestions, and then I read it with my maker's eye. Now it has been re-edited, re-revised, re-read, and re-re-edited, for each piece of writing to the writer is full of potential and alternatives.

A piece of writing is never finished. It is delivered to a deadline, torn 30 out of the typewriter on demand, sent off with a sense of accomplishment and shame and pride and frustration. If only there were a couple more days, time for just another run at it, perhaps then. . . .

[1973]

154

PAUL ROBERTS   [1917–1967]

How to Say Nothing in Five Hundred Words

California-born **Paul Roberts** received his B.A. from San Jose State College and his M.A. and Ph.D. from the University of California at Berkeley, where he taught for fourteen years after serving in the mer-chant marine during World War II. Writing in a down-to-earth, often humorous style, Roberts published several books on English composi-tion, including *Understanding Grammar* (1954), *English Sentences* (1962), and *Modern Grammar* (1954). He died in Rome in 1967.

"How to Say Nothing in Five Hundred Words" is from Roberts's best-known book, *Understanding English* (1958), and is representative of his clarity and wit. Roberts recommends that composition students check their tendency to state the obvious and instead strive for inter-esting content backed by concrete examples.

NOTHING ABOUT SOMETHING

It's Friday afternoon, and you have almost survived another week of classes. You are just looking forward dreamily to the week end when the English instructor says: "For Monday you will turn in a five-hundred word composition on college football."

Well, that puts a good big hole in the week end. You don't have any strong views on college football one way or the other. You get rather excited during the season and go to all the home games and find it rather more fun than not. On the other hand, the class has been reading Robert Hutchins in the anthology and perhaps Shaw's "Eighty-Yard Run," and from the class discussion you have got the idea that the instructor thinks college football is for the birds. You are no fool, you. You can figure out what side to take.

After dinner you get out the portable typewriter that you got for high school graduation. You might as well get it over with and enjoy Saturday and Sunday. Five hundred words is about two double-spaced pages with normal margins. You put in a sheet of paper, think up a title, and you're off:

WHY COLLEGE FOOTBALL SHOULD BE ABOLISHED

College football should be abolished because it's bad for the school and also bad for the players. The players are so busy practicing that they don't have any time for their studies.

This, you feel, is a mighty good start. The only trouble is that it's only thirty-two words. You still have four hundred and sixty-eight to go, and you've pretty well exhausted the subject. It comes to you that you do your best thinking in the morning, so you put away the typewriter and go to the movies. But the next morning you have to do your washing and some math problems, and in the afternoon you go to the game. The English instructor turns up too, and you wonder if you've taken the right side after all. Saturday night you have a date, and Sunday morning you have to go to church. (You shouldn't let English assignments interfere with your religion.) What with one thing and another, it's ten o'clock Sunday night before you get out the typewriter again. You make a pot of coffee and start to fill out your views on college football. Put a little meat on the bones.

WHY COLLEGE FOOTBALL SHOULD BE ABOLISHED

In my opinion, it seems to me that college football should be abolished. The reason why I think this to be true is because I feel that football is bad for the colleges in nearly every respect. As Robert Hutchins says in his article in our anthology in which he discusses college football, it would be better if the colleges had race horses and had races with one another, because then the horses would not have to attend classes. I firmly agree with Mr. Hutchins on this point, and I am sure that many other students would agree too.

One reason why it seems to me that college football is bad is that it has become too commercial. In the olden times when people played football just for the fun of it, maybe college football was all right, but they do not play football just for the fun of it now as they used to in the old days. Nowadays college football is what you might call a big business. Maybe this is not true at all schools, and I don't think it is especially true here at State, but certainly this is the case at most colleges and universities in America nowadays, as Mr. Hutchins points out in his very interesting article. Actually the coaches and alumni go around to the high schools and offer the high school stars large salaries to come to their colleges and play football for them. There was one case where a high school star was offered a convertible if he would play football for a certain college.

Another reason for abolishing college football is that it is bad for the players. They do not have time to get a college education, because they are so busy playing football. A football player has to practice every afternoon from three to six, and then he is so tired that he can't concentrate on his studies. He just feels like dropping off to sleep after dinner, and then the next day he goes to his classes without having studied and maybe he fails the test.

(Good ripe stuff so far, but you're still a hundred and fifty-one words from home. One more push.)

Also I think college football is bad for the colleges and the universities because not very many students get to participate in it. Out of a college of ten thousand students only seventy-five or a hundred play football, if that many. Football is what you might call a spectator sport. That means that most people go to watch it but do not play it themselves.

(Four hundred and fifteen. Well, you still have the conclusion, and when you retype it, you can make the margins a little wider.)

These are the reasons why I agree with Mr. Hutchins that college football should be abolished in American colleges and universities.

On Monday you turn it in, moderately hopeful, and on Friday it comes 5 back marked "weak in content" and sporting a big "D."

This essay is exaggerated a little, not much. The English instructor will recognize it as reasonably typical of what an assignment on college football will bring in. He knows that nearly half of the class will contrive in five hundred words to say that college football is too commercial and bad for the players. Most of the other half will inform him that college football builds character and prepares one for life and brings prestige to the school. As he reads paper after paper all saying the same thing in almost the same words, all bloodless, five hundred words dripping out of nothing, he wonders how he allowed himself to get trapped into teaching English when he might have had a happy and interesting life as an electrician or a confidence man.

Well, you may ask, what can you do about it? The subject is one on which you have few convictions and little information. Can you be expected to make a dull subject interesting? As a matter of fact, this is precisely what you are expected to do. This is the writer's essential task.

All subjects, except sex, are dull until somebody makes them interesting. The writer's job is to find the argument, the approach, the angle, the wording that will take the reader with him. This is seldom easy, and it is particularly hard in subjects that have been much discussed: College Football, Fraternities, Popular Music, Is Chivalry Dead?, and the like. You will feel that there is nothing you can do with such subjects except repeat the old bromides. But there are some things you can do which will make your papers, if not throbbingly alive, at least less insufferably tedious than they might otherwise be.

AVOID THE OBVIOUS CONTENT

Say the assignment is college football. Say that you've decided to be against it. Begin by putting down the arguments that come to your mind: it is too commercial, it takes the students' minds off their studies, it is hard on the players, it makes the university a kind of circus instead of an intellectual center, for most schools it is financially ruinous. Can you think of any more arguments just off hand? All right. Now when you write your paper, *make sure that you don't use any of the material on this list.* If these are the points that leap to your mind, they will leap to everyone else's too, and whether you get a "C" or a "D" may depend on whether the instructor reads your paper early when he is fresh and tolerant or late, when the sentence "In my opinion, college football has become too commercial," inexorably repeated, has brought him to the brink of lunacy.

Be against college football for some reason or reasons of your own. If they are keen and perceptive ones, that's splendid. But even if they are trivial or foolish or indefensible, you are still ahead so long as they are not everybody else's reasons too. Be against it because the colleges don't spend enough money on it to make it worth while, because it is bad for the characters of the spectators, because the players are forced to attend classes, because the football stars hog all the beautiful women, because it competes with baseball and is therefore un-American and possibly Communist inspired. There are lots of more or less unused reasons for being against college football.

Sometimes it is a good idea to sum up and dispose of the trite and conventional points before going on to your own. This has the advantage of indicating to the reader that you are going to be neither trite nor conventional. Something like this: 10

> We are often told that college football should be abolished because it
> has become too commercial or because it is bad for the players. These

158

arguments are no doubt very cogent, but they don't really go to the heart of the matter.

Then you go to the heart of the matter.

TAKE THE LESS USUAL SIDE

One rather simple way of getting interest into your paper is to take the side of the argument that most of the citizens will want to avoid. If the assignment is an essay on dogs, you can, if you choose, explain that dogs are faithful and lovable companions, intelligent, useful as guardians of the house and protectors of children, indispensable in police work—in short, when all is said and done, man's best friends. Or you can suggest that those big brown eyes conceal more often than not, a vacuity of mind and an inconstancy of purpose; that the dogs you have known most intimately have been mangy, ill-tempered brutes, incapable of instruction; and that only your nobility of mind and fear of arrest prevent you from kicking the flea-ridden animals when you pass them on the street.

Naturally, personal convictions will sometimes dictate your approach. If the assigned subject is "Is Methodism Rewarding to the Individual?" and you are a pious Methodist, you have really no choice. But few assigned subjects, if any, will fall in this category. Most of them will lie in broad areas of discussion with much to be said on both sides. They are intellectual exercises, and it is legitimate to argue now one way and now another, as debaters do in similar circumstances. Always take the side that looks to you hardest, least defensible. It will almost always turn out to be easier to write interestingly on that side.

This general advice applies where you have a choice of subjects. If you are to choose among "The Value of Fraternities" and "My Favorite High School Teacher" and "What I Think About Beetles," by all means plump for the beetles. By the time the instructor gets to your paper, he will be up to his ears in tedious tales about the French teacher at Bloombury High and assertions about how fraternities build character and prepare one for life. Your views on beetles, whatever they are, are bound to be a refreshing change.

Don't worry too much about figuring out what the instructor thinks about the subject so that you can cuddle up with him. Chances are his views are no stronger than yours. If he does have convictions and you oppose them, his problem is to keep from grading you higher than you deserve in order to show he is not biased. This doesn't mean that you should always cantankerously dissent from what the instructor says;

that gets tiresome too. And if the subject assigned is "My Pet Peeve," do not begin, "My pet peeve is the English instructor who assigns papers on 'my pet peeve.'" This was still funny during the War of 1812, but it has sort of lost its edge since then. It is in general good manners to avoid personalities.

SLIP OUT OF ABSTRACTION

If you will study the essay on college football in [the "Nothing about 15 Something" section], you will perceive that one reason for its appalling dullness is that it never gets down to particulars. It is just a series of not very glittering generalities: "football is bad for the colleges," "it has become too commercial," "football is a big business," "it is bad for the players," and so on. Such round phrases thudding against the reader's brain are unlikely to convince him, though they may well render him unconscious.

If you want the reader to believe that college football is bad for the players, you have to do more than say so. You have to display the evil. Take your roommate, Alfred Simkins, the second-string center. Picture poor old Alfy coming home from football practice every evening, bruised and aching, agonizingly tired, scarcely able to shovel the mashed potatoes into his mouth. Let us see him staggering up to the room, getting out his econ textbook, peering desperately at it with his good eye, falling asleep and failing the test in the morning. Let us share his unbearable tension as Saturday draws near. Will he fail, be demoted, lose his monthly allowance, be forced to return to the coal mines? And if he succeeds, what will be his reward? Perhaps a slight ripple of applause when the third-string center replaces him, a moment of elation in the locker room if the team wins, of despair if it loses. What will he look back on when he graduates from college? Toil and torn ligaments. And what will be his future? He is not good enough for pro football, and he is too obscure and weak in econ to succeed in stocks and bonds. College football is tearing the heart from Alfy Simkins and, when it finishes with him, will callously toss aside the shattered hulk.

This is no doubt a weak enough argument for the abolition of college football, but it is a sight better than saying, in three or four variations, that college football (in your opinion) is bad for the players.

Look at the work of any professional writer and notice how constantly he is moving from the generality, the abstract statement, to the concrete example, the facts and figures, the illustration. If he is writing on juvenile delinquency, he does not just tell you that juveniles are (it seems to him) delinquent and that (in his opinion) something should be done about it. He shows you juveniles being delinquent, tearing up movie theatres in Buffalo, stabbing high school principals in Dallas, smoking marijuana in Palo Alto. And more than likely he is moving toward some specific remedy, not just a general wringing of the hands.

It is no doubt possible to be *too* concrete, too illustrative or anecdotal, but few inexperienced writers err this way. For most the soundest advice is to be seeking always for the picture, to be always turning general remarks into seeable examples. Don't say, "Sororities teach girls the social graces." Say, "Sorority life teaches a girl how to carry on a conversation while pouring tea, without sloshing the tea into the saucer." Don't say, "I like certain kinds of popular music very much." Say, "Whenever I hear Gerber Spinklittle play 'Mississippi Man' on the trombone, my socks creep up my ankles."

GET RID OF OBVIOUS PADDING

The student toiling away at his weekly English theme is too often tormented by a figure: five hundred words. How, he asks himself, is he to achieve this staggering total? Obviously by never using one word when he can somehow work in ten. 20

He is therefore seldom content with a plain statement like "Fast driving is dangerous." This has only four words in it. He takes thought, and the sentence becomes:

In my opinion, fast driving is dangerous.

Better, but he can do better still:

In my opinion, fast driving would seem to be rather dangerous.

If he is really adept, it may come out:

In my humble opinion, though I do not claim to be an expert on this complicated subject, fast driving, in most circumstances, would seem to be rather dangerous in many respects, or at least so it would seem to me.

Thus four words have been turned into forty, and not an iota of content has been added.

Now this is a way to go about reaching five hundred words, and if you are content with a "D" grade, it is as good a way as any. But if you aim higher, you must work differently. Instead of stuffing your sentences with straw, you must try steadily to get rid of the padding, to make your sentences lean and tough. If you are really working at it, your first draft will greatly exceed the required total, and then you will work it down, thus:

> It is thought in some quarters that fraternities do not contribute as much as might be expected to campus life.
> Some people think that fraternities contribute little to campus life.

> The average doctor who practices in small towns or in the country must toil night and day to heal the sick.
> Most country doctors work long hours.

> When I was a little girl, I suffered from shyness and embarrassment in the presence of others.
> I was a shy little girl.

> It is absolutely necessary for the person employed as a marine fireman to give the matter of steam pressure his undivided attention at all times.
> The fireman has to keep his eye on the steam gauge.

You may ask how you can arrive at five hundred words at this rate. Simply. You dig up more real content. Instead of taking a couple of obvious points off the surface of the topic and then circling warily around them for six paragraphs, you work in and explore, figure out the details. You illustrate. You say that fast driving is dangerous, and then you prove it. How long does it take to stop a car at forty and at eighty? How far can you see at night? What happens when a tire blows? What happens in a head-on collision at fifty miles an hour? Pretty soon your paper will be full of broken glass and blood and headless torsos, and reaching five hundred words will not really be a problem.

CALL A FOOL A FOOL

Some of the padding in freshman themes is to be blamed not on anxiety about the word minimum but on excessive timidity. The student writes, "In my opinion, the principal of my high school acted in ways that I believe every unbiased person would have to call foolish." This isn't exactly what he means. What he means is, "My high school principal

162

was a fool." If he was a fool, call him a fool. Hedging the thing about with "in-my-opinion's" and "it-seems-to-me's" and "as-I-see-it's" and "at-least-from-my-point-of-view's" gains you nothing. Delete these phrases whenever they creep into your paper.

The student's tendency to hedge stems from a modesty that in other 25 circumstances would be commendable. He is, he realizes, young and inexperienced, and he half suspects that he is dopey and fuzzy-minded beyond the average. Probably only too true. But it doesn't help to announce your incompetence six times in every paragraph. Decide what you want to say and say it as vigorously as possible, without apology and in plain words.

Linguistic diffidence can take various forms. One is what we call *euphemism*. This is the tendency to call a spade "a certain garden implement" or women's underwear "unmentionables." It is stronger in some eras than others and in some people than others but it always operates more or less in subjects that are touchy or taboo: death, sex, madness, and so on. Thus we shrink from saying "He died last night" but say instead "passed away," "left us," "joined his Maker," "went to his reward." Or we try to take off the tension with a lighter cliché: "kicked the bucket," "cashed in his chips," "handed in his dinner pail." We have found all sorts of ways to avoid saying *mad:* "mentally ill," "touched," "not quite right upstairs," "feeble-minded," "innocent," "simple," "off his trolley," "not in his right mind." Even such a now plain word as *insane* began as a euphemism with the meaning "not healthy."

Modern science, particularly psychology, contributes many polysyllables in which we can wrap our thoughts and blunt their force. To many writers there is no such thing as a bad schoolboy. Schoolboys are maladjusted or unoriented or misunderstood or in need of guidance or lacking in continued success toward satisfactory integration of the personality as a social unit, but they are never bad. Psychology no doubt makes us better men or women, more sympathetic and tolerant, but it doesn't make writing any easier. Had Shakespeare been confronted with psychology, "To be or not to be" might have come out, "To continue as a social unit or not to do so. That is the personality problem. Whether 'tis a better sign of integration at the conscious level to display a psychic tolerance toward the maladjustments and repressions induced by one's lack of orientation in one's environment or—" But Hamlet would never have finished the soliloquy.

Writing in the modern world, you cannot altogether avoid modern jargon. Nor, in an effort to get away from euphemism, should you salt your paper with four-letter words. But you can do much if you will mount guard against those roundabout phrases, those echoing polysyllables that tend to slip into your writing to rob it of its crispness and force.

BEWARE OF THE PAT EXPRESSION

Other things being equal, avoid phrases like "other things being equal." Those sentences that come to you whole, or in two or three doughy lumps, are sure to be bad sentences. They are no creation of yours but pieces of common thought floating in the community soup.

Pat expressions are hard, often impossible, to avoid, because they 30 come too easily to be noticed and seem too necessary to be dispensed with. No writer avoids them altogether, but good writers avoid them more often than poor writers.

By "pat expressions" we mean such tags as "to all practical intents and purposes," "the pure and simple truth," "from where I sit," "the time of his life," "to the ends of the earth," "in the twinkling of an eye," "as sure as you're born," "over my dead body," "under cover of darkness," "took the easy way out," "when all is said and done," "told him time and time again," "parted the best of friends," "stand up and be counted," "gave him the best years of her life," "worked her fingers to the bone." Like other clichés, these expressions were once forceful. Now we should use them only when we can't possibly think of anything else.

Some pat expressions stand like a wall between the writer and thought. Such a one is "the American way of life." Many student writers feel that when they have said that something accords with the American way of life or does not they have exhausted the subject. Actually, they have stopped at the highest level of abstraction. The American way of life is the complicated set of bonds between a hundred and eighty million ways. All of us know this when we think about it, but the tag phrase too often keeps us from thinking about it.

So with many another phrase dear to the politician: "this great land of ours," "the man in the street," "our national heritage." These may prove our patriotism or give a clue to our political beliefs, but otherwise they add nothing to the paper except words.

COLORFUL WORDS

The writer builds with words, and no builder uses a raw material more slippery and elusive and treacherous. A writer's work is a constant struggle to get the right word in the right place, to find that particular word that will convey his meaning exactly, that will persuade the reader or soothe him or startle or amuse him. He never succeeds altogether—sometimes he feels that he scarcely succeeds at all—but such successes as he has are what make die thing worth doing.

164

There is no book of rules for this game. One progresses through 35
ever-lasting experiment on the basis of ever-widening experience. There
are few useful generalizations that one can make about words as words,
but there are perhaps a few.

Some words are what we call "colorful." By this we mean that they are
calculated to produce a picture or induce an emotion. They are dressy
instead of plain, specific instead of general, loud instead of soft. Thus, in
place of "Her heart beat," we may write "Her heart *pounded, throbbed,
fluttered, danced.*" Instead of "He sat in his chair," we may say, "He
lounged, sprawled, coiled." Instead of "It was hot," we may say, "It was
blistering, sultry, muggy, suffocating, steamy, wilting."

However, it should not be supposed that the fancy word is always better. Often it is as well to write "Her heart beat" or "It was hot" if that is all
it did or all it was. Ages differ in how they like their prose. The nineteenth century liked it rich and smoky. The twentieth has usually pre-
ferred it lean and cool. The twentieth century writer, like all writers, is
forever seeking the exact word, but he is wary of sounding feverish. He
tends to pitch it low, to understate it, to throw it away. He knows that if
he gets too colorful, the audience is likely to giggle.

See how this strikes you: "As the rich, golden glow of the sunset died
away along the eternal western hills, Angela's limpid blue eyes looked
softly and trustingly into Montague's flashing brown ones, and her heart
pounded like a drum in time with the joyous song surging in her soul."
Some people like that sort of thing, but most modern readers would say,
"Good grief," and turn on the television.

COLORED WORDS

Some words we would call not so much colorful as colored—that is,
loaded with associations, good or bad. All words—except perhaps structure words—have associations of some sort. We have said that the
meaning of a word is the sum of the contexts in which it occurs. When
we hear a word, we hear with it an echo of all the situations in which we
have heard it before.

In some words, these echoes are obvious and discussable. The word 40
mother, for example, has, for most people, agreeable associations. When
you hear *mother* you probably think of home, safety, love, food, and various other pleasant things. If one writes, "She was like a mother to me,"
he gets an effect which he would not get in "She was like an aunt to me."
The advertiser makes use of the associations of *mother* by working it in
when he talks about his product. The politician works it in when he talks
about himself.

So also with such words as *home, liberty, fireside, contentment, patriot, tenderness, sacrifice, childlike, manly, bluff, limpid.* All of these words are loaded with favorable associations that would be rather hard to indicate in a straightforward definition. There is more than a literal difference between "They sat around the fireside" and "They sat around the stove." They might have been equally warm and happy around the stove, but *fireside* suggests leisure, grace, quiet tradition, congenial company, and *stove* does not.

Conversely, some words have bad associations. *Mother* suggests pleasant things, but *mother-in-law* does not. Many mothers-in-law are heroically lovable and some mothers drink gin all day and beat their children insensible, but these facts of life are beside the point. The thing is that *mother* sounds good and *mother-in-law* does not.

Or consider the word *intellectual.* This would seem to be a complimentary term, but in point of fact it is not, for it has picked up associations of impracticality and ineffectuality and general dopiness. So also with such words as *liberal, reactionary, Communist, socialist, capitalist, radical, schoolteacher, truck driver, undertaker, operator, salesman, huckster, speculator.* These convey meanings on the literal level, but beyond that— sometimes, in some places—they convey contempt on the part of the speaker.

The question of whether to use loaded words or not depends on what is being written. The scientist, the scholar, try to avoid them; for the poet, the advertising writer, the public speaker, they are standard equipment. But every writer should take care that they do not substitute for thought. If you write, "Anyone who thinks that is nothing but a Socialist (or Communist or capitalist)" you have said nothing except that you don't like people who think that, and such remarks are effective only with the most naïve readers. It is always a bad mistake to think your readers more naïve than they really are.

COLORLESS WORDS

But probably most student writers come to grief not with words that are   45 colorful or those that are colored but with those that have no color at all. A pet example is *nice*, a word we would find it hard to dispense with in casual conversation but which is no longer capable of adding much to a description. Colorless words are those of such general meaning that in a particular sentence they mean nothing. Slang adjectives, like *cool* ("That's real cool") tend to explode all over the language. They are applied to everything, lose their original force, and quickly die.

Beware also of nouns of very general meaning, like *circumstances, cases, instances, aspects, factors, relationships, attitudes, eventualities,* etc. In most circumstances you will find that those cases of writing which contain too many instances of words like these will in this and other aspects have factors leading to unsatisfactory relationships with the reader resulting in unfavorable attitudes on his part and perhaps other eventualities, like a grade of "D." Notice also what "etc." means. It means "I'd like to make this list longer, but I can't think of any more examples."

WILLIAM ZINSSER

Clutter

William Zinsser was born in New York City, graduated from Princeton University in 1944, and subsequently began a long association with the *New York Herald Tribune* as a writer, editor, and critic. Since, Zinsser has contributed to *Life* and the *New Yorker*, among other magazines. His experience teaching writing at Yale (1970–1979) led to the publication of *On Writing Well* in 1976, now a classic guide for nonfiction writers in its seventh edition. In *On Writing Well*, Zinsser recounts his own struggles to both master and impart on his students the writer's "craft." His other books include *Writing to Learn* (1988) and *Writing about Your Life: A Journey into the Past* (2004), a guide to memoir encouraging writers to focus on small, authentic moments and to be themselves in their writing. Zinsser's most recent work includes *Writing Places: The Life and Journey of a Writer and Teacher* (2010).

In "Clutter," excerpted from *On Writing Well*, Zinsser identifies how linguistic flourishes can often interfere with a writer's clarity. Language, according to Zinsser, must serve a purpose: A writer cannot hold onto words simply because he or she thinks they are "beautiful."

Fighting clutter is like fighting weeds — the writer is always slightly behind. New varieties sprout overnight, and by noon they are part of American speech. Consider what President Nixon's aide John Dean accomplished in just one day of testimony on television during the Watergate hearings. The next day everyone in America was saying "at this point in time" instead of "now."

Consider all the prepositions that are draped onto verbs that don't need any help. We no longer head committees. We head them up. We don't face problems anymore. We face up to them when we can free up a few minutes. A small detail, you may say — not worth bothering about. It *is* worth bothering about. Writing improves in direct ratio to the number of things we can keep out of it that shouldn't be there. "Up" in "free up" shouldn't be there. Examine every word you put on paper. You'll find a surprising number that don't serve any purpose.

Take the adjective "personal," as in "a personal friend of mine," "his personal feeling" or "her personal physician." It's typical of hundreds of words that can be eliminated. The personal friend has come into the language to distinguish him or her from the business friend, thereby debasing both language and friendship. Someone's feeling *is* that person's personal feeling—that's what "his" means. As for the personal physician, that's the man or woman summoned to the dressing room of a stricken actress so she won't have to be treated by the impersonal physician assigned to the theater. Someday I'd like to see that person identified as "her doctor." Physicians are physicians, friends are friends. The rest is clutter.

Clutter is the laborious phrase that has pushed out the short word that means the same thing. Even before John Dean, people had stopped saying "now." They were saying "currently" ("all our operators are currently assisting other customers"), or "at the present time," or "presently" (which means "soon"). Yet the idea can always be expressed by "now" to mean the immediate moment ("Now I can see him"), or by "today" to mean the historical present ("Today prices are high"), or simply by a form of the verb "to be" ("It is raining"). There's no need to say, "At the present time we are experiencing precipitation."

"Experiencing" is one of the worst clutterers. Even your dentist will 5 ask if you are experiencing any pain. If he had his own kid in the chair he would say, "Does it hurt?" He would, in short, be himself. By using a more pompous phrase in his professional role, he not only sounds more important; he blunts the painful edge of truth. It's the language of the flight attendant demonstrating the oxygen mask that will drop down if the plane should run out of air. "In the unlikely possibility that the aircraft should experience such an eventuality," she begins—a phrase so oxygen-depriving in itself that we are prepared for any disaster.

Clutter is the ponderous euphemism that turns a slum into a depressed socioeconomic area, garbage collectors into waste-disposal personnel and the town dump into the volume reduction unit. I think of Bill Mauldin's cartoon of two hoboes riding a freight car. One of them says, "I started as a simple bum, but now I'm hard-core unemployed." Clutter is political correctness gone amok. I saw an ad for a boys' camp designed to provide "individual attention for the minimally exceptional."

Clutter is the official language used by corporations to hide their mistakes. When the Digital Equipment Corporation eliminated 3,000 jobs its statement didn't mention layoffs; those were "involuntary methodologies." When an Air Force missile crashed, it "impacted with the ground prematurely." When General Motors had a plant shutdown, that was a "volume-related production-schedule adjustment." Companies that go belly-up have "a negative cash-flow position."

Clutter is the language of the Pentagon calling an invasion a "reinforced protective reaction strike" and justifying its vast budgets on the need for "counterforce deterrence." As George Orwell pointed out in "Politics and the English Language," an essay written in 1946 but often cited during the wars in Cambodia, Vietnam and Iraq, "political speech and writing are largely the defense of the indefensible. . . . Thus political language has to consist largely of euphemism, question-begging and sheer cloudy vagueness." Orwell's warning that clutter is not just a nuisance but a deadly tool has come true in the recent decades of American military adventurism. It was during George W. Bush's presidency that "civilian casualties" in Iraq became "collateral damage."

Verbal camouflage reached new heights during General Alexander Haig's tenure as President Reagan's secretary of state. Before Haig, nobody had thought of saying "at this juncture of maturization" to mean "now." He told the American people that terrorism could be fought with "meaningful sanctionary teeth" and that intermediate nuclear missiles were "at the vortex of cruciality." As for any worries that the public might harbor, his message was "leave it to Al," though what he actually said was, "We must push this to a lower decibel of public fixation. I don't think there's much of a learning curve to be achieved in this area of content."

I could go on quoting examples from various fields—every profession 10 has its growing arsenal of jargon to throw dust in the eyes of the populace. But the list would be tedious. The point of raising it now is to serve notice that clutter is the enemy. Beware, then, of the long word that's no better than the short word: "assistance" (help), "numerous" (many), "facilitate" (ease), "individual" (man or woman), "remainder" (rest), "initial" (first), "implement" (do), "sufficient" (enough), "attempt" (try), "referred to as" (called) and hundreds more. Beware of all the slippery new fad words: paradigm and parameter, prioritize and potentialize. They are all weeds that will smother what you write. Don't dialogue with someone you can talk to. Don't interface with anybody.

Just as insidious are the word clusters with which we explain how we propose to go about our explaining: "I might add," "It should be pointed out," "It is interesting to note." If you might add, add it. If it should be pointed out, point it out. If it is interesting to note, *make* it interesting; are we not all stupefied by what follows when someone says, "This will interest you"? Don't inflate what needs no inflating: "with the possible exception of" (except), "due to the fact that" (because), "he totally lacked the ability to" (he couldn't), "until such time as" (until), "for the purpose of" (for).

Is there any way to recognize clutter at a glance? Here's a device my students at Yale found helpful. I would put brackets around every component in a piece of writing that wasn't doing useful work. Often just one word got bracketed: the unnecessary preposition appended to a verb ("order up"), or the adverb that carries the same meaning as the verb ("smile happily"), or the adjective that states a known fact ("tall skyscraper"). Often my brackets surrounded the little qualifiers that weaken any sentence they inhabit ("a bit," "sort of"), or phrases like "in a sense," which don't mean anything. Sometimes my brackets surrounded an entire sentence—the one that essentially repeats what the previous sentence said, or that says something readers don't need to know or can figure out for themselves. Most first drafts can be cut by 50 percent without losing any information or losing the author's voice.

My reason for bracketing the students' superfluous words, instead of crossing them out, was to avoid violating the students' sacred prose. I wanted to leave the sentence intact for them to analyze. I was saying, "I may be wrong, but I think this can be deleted and the meaning won't be affected. But *you* decide. Read the sentence without the bracketed material and see if it works." In the early weeks of the term I handed back papers that were festooned with brackets. Entire paragraphs were bracketed. But soon the students learned to put mental brackets around their own clutter, and by the end of the term their papers were almost clean. Today many of those students are professional writers, and they tell me, "I still see your brackets—they're following me through life."

You can develop the same eye. Look for the clutter in your writing and prune it ruthlessly. Be grateful for everything you can throw away. Reexamine each sentence you put on paper. Is every word doing new work? Can any thought be expressed with more economy? Is anything pompous or pretentious or faddish? Are you hanging on to something useless just because you think it's beautiful?

Simplify, simplify. 15

[1976]

Introduction to English 100 Award-Winning Essays

Each year the English 100 Program sponsors a Student Writing Award contest. Students are invited to submit work completed in their English 100 class in several categories (see the guidelines at the back of this book). The essays included here were selected from writing completed in the spring 2013 and fall 2013 semesters. This year's selections include an award winner and "honorable mention" for each category. Each essay is accompanied by a "Writer's Memo," which describes his or her approach to the assignment and the process of writing the piece. You'll also find an "Instructor's Memo," which describes the strengths and qualities that made the essay stand out.

We include these essays to recognize and illustrate the excellent writing that occurs in our classes. We also want you to view these essays by your peers alongside those produced by professional writers. You will see that the strengths and qualities of effective writing exist across a spectrum of writers, from novice to expert. As you read these essays, notice how the topics and approaches vary. This reflects the diversity in teaching and learning styles across sections of English 100, which share common goals for students' development as writers within a flexible structure of assignments. Although these essays are exemplary, they should not be viewed as singular models of the "right way" to complete an assignment. Each author has made a personal connection to his or her topic and taken an individual approach to communicating ideas effectively. Emulating this kind of behavior in your writing will support your success, even though imitating specific model essays will not.

For more information about the English 100 Student Writing Awards, please see the announcement on page 230.

KELLY URBANEK

Eternity in Ten Seconds

It's a beautiful day in the Costa Rican jungle. Rays of sunlight pass though the canopy above us and dance across the pool of wading water below. From under the waterfall, my sister emerges completely serene and tranquil despite what has suddenly happened. In fact, it is a miracle that she even emerged from the water at all. Just moments before, our hearts stopped beating and breaths became still as we witnessed what could have been a deathly tragedy. Despite the gentle and peaceful hums that resonate from a waterfall, these sounds transport me back to the longest ten seconds of my life.

Ten seconds pass six times every minute, 720 times every hour, and 17,280 times every day. In the course of one's life, the passing of ten seconds can seem uneventful. It is next to impossible to accomplish any significant task during this short amount of time, and it is safe to assume that the average individual does not always acknowledge how much can happen in such a short span of time. For example, an average person blinks twice and takes an average of six breaths in ten seconds. If the individual were walking, he/she would be able to cover a total of three yards in distance. Although the scale of this may seem small and one may ask—"What could possibly happen in a ten-second window?"—a lot can happen. We just need to pay attention to it.

Ten seconds can have a tremendous impact on a life. Around the world, someone dies every ten seconds from starvation (Alexander, 2013). Every ten seconds a child abuse case is reported (Child Abuse Statistics, 2013). But ten seconds can also hold personal impact. It wasn't until the day my sister emerged from underneath the waterfall that I fully understood how powerful a seemingly short ten seconds could be. It is my hope that after becoming familiar with what the passing of ten seconds potentially can hold, you will understand the power harbored in this seemingly insignificant amount of time.

A series of unique circumstances brought me to a Costa Rican jungle that spring. First and foremost, my sister had been traveling throughout Costa Rica as a photographer for the previous five months. My generous aunt and uncle had invited me to come along when they decided to partake in some international travel. I was fortunate because if the trip had been planned at any other time, I would have not been able to go due to academic conflicts. However, after some pleading, my instructors allowed me to turn in homework ahead of time and take moderated exams prior to leaving for our Central American adventure. Even my soon-to-be soccer coach supported this trip and allowed me to miss the first week of tryouts to travel abroad with my aunt and uncle.

Before I knew it, I was sitting on a plane and on my way to Costa Rica. The plane ride lasted for about six hours but "flew by" in comparison to the ten-second event that would occur soon after my arrival. In the initial days of my vacation, I woke up beside my sister in the small Costa Rican village of Arenal. The highly admired volcano of Arenal sits an inactive 50 yards away from our sleeping quarters. Our proximity to the volcano was only possible because we stayed away from commercialized resorts. Instead, we stayed in locally run Cabiñas, which offered us a new perspective on the country and its people. Every morning we woke up to a freshly prepared meal that consisted of an array of colorful and exotic fruits. We also ate plentiful amounts of the typical plate of the Costa Rican breakfast, Pinto de Gallo. Pinto de Gallo, or rice and beans, although simple, gave us all the energy we needed for that day's adventures.

Among the many adventures that were experienced on this trip, one stands out more than the rest. On this particular day, most of our experiences occurred from heights 350 feet above ground and consisted of the four of us gliding across the jungle from platform to platform like Tarzan swinging among the trees. After our amazing zip lining adventure across the lush rain forest of the Costa Rican jungle, we had the luxury of our guide taking us to a secluded, majestic waterfall. This waterfall was hidden deep within the rainforest and measured up to be at least 30 feet tall. At the bottom of the waterfall was a deep reservoir surrounded by pointed rocks. The rocks on the side of the waterfall served as an organic staircase that led to the top of the falls, and our guide easily climbed it. As the rest of our tour group caught up to us, my sister and I had already begun swimming across the pool with the intentions of following our guide up the waterfall.

The rock path to the top of the waterfall seemed safe enough. We had watched the tour guide negotiate it with ease, and figured that we were capable of the same feat. The first time we attempted the steep climb, we were too afraid to make it to the top and decided to jump off the first ledge instead. However, at a height of 15 feet, this was easier said than done. Making matters even worse, a slippery, green residue covered each rock we tried to climb with a small stream of water trickling between each one of them. Standing from ground level, these obstacles were not anything that we could have anticipated. Even so, we proudly embraced these challenges and after our first jump off the first ledge and into the refreshing pool of water below, we were determined to make it to the top of the waterfall.

Our guide was still at the top of the waterfall as we began climbing for the second time. My sister made me go in front of her on the climb, having a better understanding of the conditions of the rocks. Being the older sister, she felt that this would allow her to protect me if I were to slip while climbing. However, if I were to fall, there was not much she nor anyone else would have been able to do to help me. Despite my recent declaration about my determination to reach it to the top of the waterfall, I did not make it to the top. Instead, I stopped again at the first ledge and jumped off. However, my sister, filled with bravery, continued her treacherous climb to the top. After my second jump, I looked back to the waterfall and scanned it for my sister. By the time I found her, she was nearly to the top.

A second passes and her foot fails to find a firm spot on the rock, and then slides. Another second passes, and her hands fail to grasp the rock in front of her. Her body falls backward and goes limp as she begins to cascade down the endless waterfall. Four seconds pass. Her body continues to follow the path of least resistance and bypasses a huge boulder sticking out from the far left side. She is still falling. By this time, seven seconds have passed and she is still on her descent down. Her hands and body flop in the way that the waterfall decides. There is nothing anyone can do for her. All we are able to do is watch and pray.

In just these few seconds so many thoughts raced through my mind. I didn't believe that there was a way a person would be able to survive such conditions and live to tell the tale. I thought that she was going to be dead by the time she hit the water. Even if she did make it to the bottom alive, the pointy rocks were sure to finish the job. I thought that I was never going to see my beloved sister again. Before she hit the water, I already had blamed myself for her falling. Finally she hit the water with a big splash. The air became still, voices were silent and even the critters of the jungle held their breath. Two more seconds have passed. There was still no movement. Everyone prayed even harder. Then, we see her body begin to move. She is alive and even more impressively, smiling and laughing without even a scratch. Everyone takes a second to catch their breath. The birds begin to chirp again and the critters of the jungle go about their normal business. We rush over to my sister and ask her if she is hurt anywhere. We check her head for concusses. We scan her body for gashes, scratches or cuts. Thankfully, there is no physical evidence of the horrifying event I just witnessed. I embrace her and hold her in my arms for what seems like an eternity. Of course, it was likely only ten seconds. The following ten seconds after our long hug, I blinked to look at her and took a few breaths to listen to her *begin* to explain what happened. Time resumed its normal speed and seemed to pass with ease again. The impact of a mere ten seconds, although seemingly insignificant, has the capability to determine life or death.

Works Cited

Alexander, R. (2013). Does a child die of hunger every 10 seconds? *BBC News Magazine*, 1. Retrieved from http://www.bbc.com/ news/magazine-22935692

Child Abuse Statistics. (2013). *ARK of Hope*. Retrieved from http://arkofhopeforchildren.org/child-abuse/child-abuse-statistics-info

Instructor's Memo

Early in the semester, Kelly came to my office to discuss my expectations for the course and her writing. During that conversation, I encouraged her to use the class to experiment and to think about assignments in terms of what she wanted to say, rather than regurgitating what she thought I wanted to hear. My sense then was that Kelly left my office with some trepidation—that my request made her uncomfortable—but when I saw the first draft of this assignment, I was blown away. Kelly took a creative risk by using narrative in an innovative way, and the result was a compelling essay that felt truly literary.

Kelly had the benefit of producing a strong first draft, but she also spent a lot of time revising this piece. In early drafts, the writing was a bit uneven: the narrative was compelling and interesting, but the analysis seemed vague and tangential. It took Kelly and me a few drafts (plus some discussion) to figure out the larger point she was trying to make and to integrate it into the narrative, but we eventually did. Kelly took revision very seriously: she came to our conferences engaged and also made use of campus resources and her peers—visiting the English 100 Tutorial Program and asking friends to proofread her work.

Ultimately, I felt that Kelly's final piece lived up to the promise shown in her first draft. Because it was so creative, it stands out in my mind to the point that I can remember it now, months later. I hope English 100 students who read her essay are inspired to take risks and try things that make them uncomfortable: often, that's when you're doing your best work.

—Emma Needleman

Writer's Memo

During the first few weeks of English 100, we focused a lot on narrative. My classmates and I soon discovered that descriptive detail plays an essential role in that style of writing. I chose the subject of my narrative piece accordingly. I knew that I would be able to acutely depict the story of my sister falling down the waterfall in Costa Rica. However, this was not my only reason for choosing this topic. This essay was also written about a truly genuine experience that impacted my life and altered my mindset. Through this assignment I learned that if I write about a topic that I have a strong feeling towards, the words flow more easily and I produce a higher quality essay. The motif of "ten seconds" that I use in this narrative was established as a result of starting my paper in the climax of the story. Inspired by another published student in CCC, I thought that this strategy would allow me to create a dramatic and suspenseful effect. I wanted to give my readers clues about the tragedy that almost took place during that beautiful day in the Costa Rican jungle without revealing too much. Keeping the scenario vague at first allowed me to gain the reader's attention in order to fully develop the scene leading up to the moments of falling. It was my hope that through this, I could intensify each moment and fully illustrate my changed mindset in regards to the significance that the passing of ten seconds can hold.

Despite all the strategies I used in writing this paper, the most important strategy I utilized was the process of revision. What helped me produce the quality of paper that I did was my ability to take criticisms from others, which helped me change and mold my paper accordingly. Although I did not take all suggestions that were given to me, I considered every one and chose those that I thought would help make my paper stronger. Not only did I get recommendations from my peers and my English 100 teacher but I also sought out help from the English 100 Tutorial Program as well as from family members. At the beginning of the revision process I got a lot of feedback stating that there was confusion about the chronological order of events within my paper. As I worked though these mistakes I began to receive more and more nitpicky feedback relating to diction, indicating to me that my paper was improving. After each person read my paper, I would make corrections before handing it off to another individual to read. Often times, this process would take longer than expected because while making recommended changes, I would come up with my own ideas of how to improve my paper. Although it was a tedious process, in the end my paper showed major improvement from the initial draft. Personally, I believe that a paper is never really done because it can always be improved. The best advice I have for future English 100 students is to take the revision process seriously and to not be afraid to utilize resources. The progress you see comparing your first draft to your final draft can make all the hard work worth it!

INDIA PUNGARCHER

An Injured Runner with Strength

I am an eighteen-year-old girl. I lace up my shoes, step outside, and start to walk towards the sidewalk. The cement foundation is so much more than a convenient walkway to me though. The sidewalk is the starting point of my escape. It is the cure to my obsession. It is the road to my own personal nirvana and the road to a clear, healthy mind. The sidewalk is where it all begins. I have my own secret trap door, waiting to escort me into a whole new, perfect world at virtually any moment that I choose. The sidewalk is where I start each and every run.

So here I am, making my way to this common slab of concrete. I lift my right index finger and begin to press its plush, yet calloused surface onto the purple, overused start button on my Timex watch. I have stretched out my muscles, paying special attention to each and every push and pull, to each and every fiber and ligament, to each and every want and need demanded by my body. I am ready. I take a step, and I fall.

I am eighteen years old and I am lying on the ground. I am lying on the cold, hard, unforgiving ground, the ground that once provided me with more comfort, joy, satisfaction, and pleasure than I knew what to do with. I am eighteen years old and I cannot even take one step without my leg giving out. The ground that normally responds to my footstep with a generous thrust of energy surging back in my direction is now sucking me towards it, selfishly deciding not to return the favor. I cannot take one step, let alone run one mile. I am stuck in the quicksand. To some people, this might sound like a godsend: an excuse to never have to run again. To me, it was like a death sentence. My body screaming at me, "India, you cannot run," basically translated, in my mind, to, "You cannot do the thing that you love most. You cannot do the thing that gives you life itself".

Let me take a step back for a moment. This whole comparison probably seems a bit drastic, a bit overdramatic. So, some girl cannot run anymore. Big deal. She is young and able; she can just find a different sport or pick up a new hobby. To this conclusion, I laugh. I cry too. Running is so much more than just a sport or some hobby I do when I am bored. Running has slowly become my life, my world, my everything. It is more than just a sport; it is a lifestyle. Changing one's lifestyle is no simple task. Lying there on the ground, I felt as though my whole world had been plucked out from underneath me, both literally and figuratively, and there was nothing I could do about it.

So how did I get here? "Here," as in on the ground? Well, it has been a journey of about three years or so that has finally brought me to this point. As an avid cross country runner in high school, I dealt with mysterious, reoccurring calf pains. Undiagnosed by multiple doctors, the pain would eventually go away after a short break from running. Relentlessly, my deep, throbbing, sharp pains would always return near the end of each season though, leaving me unsatisfied with my final performances, frustrated, and always longing for more. More what? More miles, more personal records, more blood, sweat, and tears, more pain, more triumph. More life.

I am eighteen years old and I am on the ground. I have reached my breaking point, and clearly so has my body. This marked the start of my two month break from running, as well as my downward cycle into depression. This broke me, this changed me, and this healed me. I am still healing.

Fast forward. I am now an eighteen-year-old girl going off to college. I have no way to relieve my stress. I have a thousand different things going on back at home that constantly cause me to worry. I am worried about my family, about my uncle who has cancer, about my mom who does not have a job, and about my dad who is also depressed. I am gaining weight. Now I am self-conscious about my body. I hate my body; it is depriving me of the thing I love. Now, to top it all off, I do not like how it looks. I am trapped inside this shell. I am a being inside this edifice, stuck. I do not recognize myself. I am lost. I need to get back on track. I need to run. I have no life.

Fast forward. I am at a new physical therapist, who tells me it is how I am running that is causing me to be in such pain. In other words, I am doing this to myself. My form is putting an abnormal amount of pressure on my calf, and it just could not handle the force anymore. Now what? This marked the beginning of a new journey that also would start on the sidewalk. It would be a very arduous journey. I would have to teach myself how to run again, and I would have to do this very slowly.

So my journey began. Yes, it was nice to get back into running, but it was also almost torturous at the same time. Running for a few minutes is nothing compared to the eight mile minimum I was running daily last summer. I was still physically and mentally deprived from that euphoric feeling. It was like a sick joke. I was being teased. All I wanted to do was to go on a long distance run and zone out. I had forgotten what it felt like. I forgot what it felt like to put on my favorite pair of tennis shoes, shut the door behind me, and run away from all my problems. I just wanted more than anything to go for a run and come back with a clear, fresh mind, ready to conquer any obstacle thrown my way. I wanted to be happy. I quickly realized I could no longer run away from my problems. I had to face them, head on. I had to learn to accept things and make myself happy.

Fast forward. Now, I can run five miles three times a week. This is still nothing compared to the level of fitness I used to be in. I used to have a goal: to walk onto the Badger's cross country team. Now, this has been postponed and turned into a dream. It is a dream that seems so unachievable and so far away, but running has impacted my life so profoundly that I still do everything in my power each and every day in order to get just a little bit closer to making my dream a reality.

I am at the starting line, my stomach is churning, I feel a little dizzy, and I wipe a bead of sweat across my forehead. My muscles are warm and loose, begging me to unleash their limitless power. My breathing is heavy and the only sound I can hear is my own heartbeat. Everything else, the entire world, is still. Then suddenly the gun goes off and there is a rush, a whirlwind of emotions, people, scents, and noises all racing forward and brushing against me. A few minutes go by and this excitement in the atmosphere is replaced with a calm, cool, and collective disposition. I feel infinite, limitless, and powerful beyond measure. Slowly, the burn starts creeping into my veins. My muscles start to whisper intentions of giving in. The voice inside my head begins its usual plea. I make my choice. I continue. I can see it now; the finish line is near. It is in the distance, a blurry object losing its turbidity with each stride. Each movement feels more and more strenuous now. My lungs are gasping for air, my throat is covered in cotton, and my tongue is searching for any remaining saliva to moisten itself with. I cannot really control my legs anymore; they are just going. They are burning. The fire is intense. The pain is explicit. The pain is beautiful. It is beautiful because I can choose to overcome it, to push past it, and to achieve my wildest dreams.

It is moments like these that keep me going now. My persistence today relies on my memories of years past. When I feel like quitting, I think of my very first cross country race. I think of how I felt when I finished a race, and I take myself back to that moment. I remember being completely conscious of each and every individual function happening in my body. I am fully aware of every aspect of pain. I feel each muscle strain. I feel the sandpaper that has replaced my tongue and the peanut-butter-like effect occurring on the roof of my mouth. The world is still, but I am incessant. The world is bustling, yet it is silent, much like those scenes in the movies. Everything is rushing past me, screaming at me, but I am so focused on one single object that everything else is irrelevant. Everything else becomes nonexistent. Suddenly, the stillness breaks. The instant I cross the white line, the world resumes at warp speed, as if to catch up for its momentary lapse. Slowly, the agony that filled my veins begins to exit my body. I can feel it gradually leak out and replace itself with a sense of accomplishment and success.

This memory evokes enough feeling in me to keep fueling the fire of my passion. Throughout the journey that this injury has taken me on, I have developed a greater appreciation for not only running, but for life in general. I have realized that yes, it is kind of scary that one thing has the power to ultimately control my happiness or send my world tumultuously crashing down. At the same time, it is also astonishing and breathtaking that we, as humans, have the capacity to create such a strong connection with our actions. They say actions define us; I would certainly agree. Running has molded me into the eighteen-year-old girl I am today. I am still a girl who has an overzealous affinity for running, but I also have a newfound affection for living a fruitful, gratifying life. Being deprived of the one thing I thought I could not live without made me a stronger person. It made me redefine my goals, and look to myself to find a sense of inner peace and fulfillment, not to an outer source or action, such as running. Granted, I still want running to continue to play an essential role in my lifestyle. I take comfort in knowing that I will always have a back-up plan when things do get difficult and present a challenge. I will always have my secret trap door, waiting for me to succumb to the sanctuary inside my own mind, with the entrance at the nearest sidewalk. However, now I have the tools to find this happiness through my own thoughts, and most importantly, now I have the strength to do so.

Instructor's Memo

India Pungarcher's essay, "An Injured Runner With Strength," was created in response to an assignment that asked students to write a narrative about an emotional and/or physical scar that illustrated how their lives had been shaped and informed by their process of healing. Many of the smaller assignments leading up to this essay focused on learning how to write with specificity. Some assignments involved pulling powerful details out of texts we read and discussed as a class and other assignments emphasized writing with detail rather than abstraction. I believe this foundation helped prepare India for the writing of this essay. India's enthusiasm for writing and running was obvious in the outpouring that came in the first draft. I pushed her to create even more vivid imagery and also to be as honest as possible about her experience. This poetic essay is what evolved.

—Heather Swan

Writer's Memo

One of my favorite professors I have had thus far, Heather Swan, assigned my class the task of writing a scar narrative. We were instructed to write a piece that detailed a difficult event in our life and explain how it impacted and then changed us. I am a running addict, so naturally I defaulted to writing about my tumultuous relationship with the sport. I didn't really know where my writing was going to take me and, as I often do when writing essays, I just sat down and started typing anything and everything that began to flow out of my mind. In its primitive state, it was just overflow, spillage. I knew I would definitely need to connect it all somehow and make it a more cohesive piece, but how?

We were instructed to use as much imagery as possible, so that is what I tried to do. I tried to paint a picture of running that even those who have never partaken could grasp onto. I knew my use of imagery was also essential in order to accurately portray the defeat and helplessness I felt when I was robbed of my favorite hobby. I decided to use these descriptive blurbs as intermissions between my transitions back to reality. Here, I would explain my journey with running in somewhat of a chronological order. I also like using repetition when I write in order to create a more unified piece, so I employed that technique as well in these transitions. After I constructed the foundation of my piece and achieved something that, to me, was pleasing to follow, the end of this paper sort of wrote itself. I really came to the conclusion of how my scar had affected me through the actual act of writing. It really was a pleasant way to reflect upon what I had been through, try to make sense of it all, and receive some closure.

As I write this memo, it has been almost a year now since I wrote this piece, and I must say I am almost embarrassed about my overly ambitious goals that it contains. I guess that is what I have found that running does to you; it makes you a dreamer. I suppose I would rather be a dreamer though and move through life with passion than just idly let it pass me by. Revisiting this piece reminded of something one of favorite professional runners, Lauren Fleshman, once said: "When you're a dreamer, heart break and failure come with the territory, but I can tell you it's worth it because it's a way of living that is both moving and memorable." I hope when others read this piece they too are reminded of something that moves them and makes them never stop dreaming those big, crazy dreams.

JACOB GRABOSKI

Walleye War

The police force continuously increased as they attempted to subdue the growing tensions between the protesters and the Indians on the banks of Trout Lake. Thousands of protesters had gathered on the Trout Lake boat landing to form a barricade against the Ojibwe Indians. A rally, held by an anti-treaty group "Stop Treaty Abuse, Wisconsin" (STA/W), had brought in many protesters from all over Wisconsin in a unified effort to take over the boat landing and essentially stop the Ojibwe Indians from harvesting walleye. Tom Maulson, an avid Ojibwe hunter and fisherman living on the Lac du Flambeau reservation, recalls that this night at Trout Lake was the most dangerous night in all of the years of spearing (Nesper, *Walleye* 138). Maulson explains, "They could have killed us all, and they was [sic] saying that that is what they wanted to do" (139). Rocks were thrown as racial epithets flew from the mouths of the angry crowds who were barely held back by mere snow fences and the brute force of police officers. The Ojibwe fisherman, fearing for their lives, armed themselves with anything they could find and waited for the anger to subside. That Friday night, 109 protesters were arrested as the police forced the mobs back. Fourteen Flambeau spearers took 175 walleyes and 27 muskies, but the war was just beginning (Nesper, *Walleye* 139).

The night at Trout Lake was a product of years of tensions and political debates between the Ojibwe tribe of Lac du Flambeau, Wisconsin, and non-Indians of Wisconsin. Patty Loew, professor in the Department of Life Sciences Communication at the University of Wisconsin-Madison, and co-author James Thannum explain the origins of the political debate: "The contemporary struggles had their roots in four treaties signed in 1836, 1837, 1842, and 1854 in which the Ojibwe ceded millions of acres in the Great Lakes region" (162). They locate the tensions between non-Indian and Ojibwe tribe members in treaties signed nearly 200 years ago. An article published by the Wisconsin Historical Society on its website provides background:

> In 1837 and 1842, the Ojibwe had signed treaties forfeiting their land titles while retaining their right to hunt and fish on that ceded territory — a guarantee known as "reserved rights." Another treaty, signed in 1854, created reservations for the Ojibwe but did not cancel the rights guaranteed in earlier treaties. Despite this protection, the state consistently denied the Ojibwe these lawfully protected reserved rights ("Ojibwe Treaty Rights: 15 Years Later").

Simply stated, the Ojibwe bands of Wisconsin were hunting and spearing in the lands they ceded to the United States of America and some non-Indians believed they had no rights to those lands. Many elements contributed to the controversy of whether or not Ojibwe bands had different rights for hunting and fishing over non-Indians, and these elements were explored greatly in the late 1980s and early 1990s.

Wisconsin Indian reservations are most commonly perceived as low-income areas. Larry Nesper, an ethnographer who studied the Ojibwe Tribe, found that "over fourteen hundred [Ojibwe] band members live on the reservation, 41 percent of them below the poverty line" (*Walleye* 14). This finding supports the Ojibwe claim that they rely on spearfishing to survive on the low-income reservations. Although the non-Indians who oppose treaty rights in Wisconsin might recognize the poverty of the Ojibwe, many feel that the fish more than make up for their lack of income. For example, on April 24, 1986, 54 spearers took 1,192 walleye (Nesper, *Walleye* 83). The ability to sell those fish for money created an unequal economic advantage for Ojibwe tribe members over non-Indian sports fishermen because the Ojibwe could take whatever they needed for sustenance and sell the rest for surplus. Also, the Ojibwe bands had unlimited rights to walleye when compared to sports fishermen who had bag limits. Dennis Anderson, in *The Minnesota Star Tribune*, clarified the bag limit dilemma asserting that "[i]n recent years, the six Wisconsin Ojibwe bands have set harvest quotas between 41,000 and 45,000 walleye on 200 to 230 lakes. Bag limits for sport anglers are then adjusted down from the state limit of five walleye to three or two." In essence, the Ojibwe control the amount of fish that sports fishermen are able to catch each season.

Some non-Indians even considered the Ojibwe spear fishing actions a form of "rape." Even the Lac Du Flambeau Department of Natural Resources (DNR) used the word "rape" to describe the Ojibwes' taking of vulnerable spawning females. However, Nesper critiques the DNR statement by showing that in 1990, 84.6 percent of the walleye speared during spawning were males (*Walleye* 104). Regardless of the gender of the fish, most non-Indian protesters felt that the spawning fish should be respected simply because mating is a biological instinct. Tom Hook, a non-Indian who took part in a boat landing protest on Big Arbor Vitae Lake in 1990 states, "If the fish are spawning and should be left alone, they should be left alone by everyone" (qtd. in Loew 170). The Ojibwe, however, had legal rights to these fish and they would spear as many as they desired.

The northern third of Wisconsin had an economic boom in the tourist industry in the 1990s. The north woods were the perfect getaway to a land of trees and lakes filled with bountiful trophy fish. These fish bring many jobs to people in the Lac du Flambeau area through fish hatcheries, taverns, resorts, and much more. Residents prided themselves on tourism, and many believed that spearfishing and tourism simply could not coexist. Technically, the Ojibwe tribe is allotted 100 percent of "safe harvest." The term "safe harvest" represents the amount of fish that can be taken before the population of fish is in danger. In 1996, *The Minnesota Star Tribune* announced, "The Wisconsin Ojibwe bands...intend to spear all of the safe allowable walleye harvest" (Anderson). More likely than not, the Ojibwe bands were attempting to threaten the state of Wisconsin in order to reduce protester violence and to demonstrate their rights to fishing and hunting to the non-Indians. DNR Secretary George Meyer boldly responded to this threat: "This [threat] is absolutely unacceptable. Under both the spirit and the letter of the federal court decision, the resource was to be shared." Meyer is referring to the Voight decision in the Wisconsin Supreme Court which demanded that the Ojibwe treaties be followed by state officials and that the tribes should work to negotiate a proper harvesting of resources. Meyer was calling for collaboration and sharing between the groups, whereas, according to him, the Ojibwe were intentionally attempting to preclude non-Indian fishers from catching walleye.

Spearfishing is also culturally embedded in the Ojibwe bands of Wisconsin. Even now in 2013, when Native Americans have access to the dominating society in which they live, many hold close the traditions and values of their people. The ancient Anishinaabe (Ojibwe) language provides insight into why the Ojibwe tribe values spearfishing. The name for the lands of Lac du Flambeau in Anishinaabe language is Waswaaganing; "Waswa," means spearing with torch, "ganing," means the locator, the place where it happens. Waswaaganing literally means the place where they fish with a torch (Nesper, *Walleye* 159). Spearing during the nighttime with a torch is a tradition of the Ojibwe who follow similar methods today only they use halogen lights on their boats. Ojibwe spearfish*ing* is also a spiritual process. A 2007 article in *Current Anthropology* discusses the relationship between the Ojibwe natives and the spirits of the animals they kill:

> Before these subsistence activities became symbols of local Indian ethnic identity theywere the basis of what is referred to as "traditional law" in some of the trials that would take place in the 1980s and 90s. At the root of this law were cosmological ideas about the reciprocal moral obligations entailed in the relationships between communities of human beings and animals and the reproductive consequences thereof, as well as the idea that the source of an individual's power, identity, and morality lay in a personal relationship with a spiritual source (Nesper, "Negotiating Jurisprudence").

Many tribes, not only the Ojibwe, share this animistic belief. They believe that all life contains a spirit and those spirits shape their ways of living. Spearing a fish, to the Ojibwe, not only feeds their families and friends, but the spirit of the fish that has died will feed their ancestors' spirits. Nesper confirms, "Ignoring resources...was tantamount to refusing to exchange with spirits, who would then offer no beneficence of any kind" (*Walleye* 38). The non-Indians' attempts to disrupt this process of hunting and fishing would anger the Ojibwe ancestors and the fish would not reproduce. Non-Indians countered this argument, claiming most Ojibwe tribe members had converted to Christianity and could therefore not believe in a world of spirits and hungry ancestors. Many non-Indians also observed that the treaty was signed a few hundred years ago when the Ojibwe tribe had been pure. Now the Ojibwe bands were not full-blooded natives of the land and therefore they did not deserve the same rights as those who were true Ojibwe members in the 1800s (Nesper, "Negotiating").

During the late 1980s, many Ojibwe members were arrested for spearing outside of the reservation even though those rights were given to them in the treaties of the 1800s. The Wisconsin Department of Natural Resources (DNR) proposed to negotiate with bands to compensate for the lost spearing time but non-Indians did not want to pay for the negotiation process. In their article on treaty rights, Loew and Thannum mention the perspective of a protester: "I'm paying taxes to support them every week—to support this [spearfishing], to send them welfare checks, to give them all different kinds of aid....If we're supporting them in those ways, why can't they learn to live like the white man does?" (172). Such beliefs held by non-Indians held that the state of Wisconsin should not compensate the Ojibwe tribe through the taxpayer's money. Although the Supreme Court of Wisconsin decided that Ojibwe bands had the right to hunt and fish on ceded lands, the debate continues today. The tensions climaxed in the 1980s and 90s, but they are not resolved.. The hostile walleye war has assisted in the rebirth of the Ojibwe traditions and ethnic identity. Today the Ojibwe proudly exercise the rights that were given to them when they gave up their land to the United States of America. Meanwhile, the State of Wisconsin and non-Indian protesters continue to search for ways to negotiate and strategically control the natural resources that profit capitalist society.

Works Cited

Anderson, Dennis. "Wisconsin Ojibwe Lay Claim to All Walleye in 79 Lakes." *Star Tribune* 20 March 1996. Web. 30 March 2013.

Loew, Patty and Thannum, James. "After the Storm: Ojibwe Treaty Rights Twenty-Five Years After the Voight Decision." *American Indian Quarterly* 35.2 (2011): 161-191. Print.

Nesper, Larry. "Negotiating Jurisprudence in Tribal Court and Emergence of a Tribal State." *Current Anthropology* 48.5 (2007): 675-699. Print.

---. *The Walleye War: The Struggle for Ojibwe Treaty and Spearfishing Rights*. Lincoln: Univ. of Nebraska Press, 2002. Print.

"Ojibwe Treaty Rights: 15 Years Later." *Wisconsin Historical Society*. N.p., 19 May 2006. Web. 1 March 2013.

Instructor's Memo

Writing Project 2 in my English 100 class asked students to write a literature review in which they would summarize, synthesize, and evaluate an ongoing conversation. Coming up with a conversation to research can be one of the most challenging aspects of such an assignment. Choose too broad a topic, and you could wind up with generalizations and large gaps in the conversation. Choose too narrow, and your claims might become one-sided and circuitous. Many writing prompts you'll receive in college will be too open-ended to offer much help on picking a topic. My main advice for finding a topic, then, is to think about what interests you as a person and as a student (what are you thinking of majoring in and why? What interests you about a particular career? What concerns are pressing for you as an individual?). The English 100 literature review provides an opportunity to think deeply about something that matters to you, your future profession, or your home state (to offer a few general directions you might look for a topic).

Jake's literature review is an excellent example of how choosing a topic you're invested in can lead to a compelling, well-researched account of an issue. He narrowed his broader interest in history and politics by focusing on the fishing rights of the Ojibwe in Wisconsin. He had been learning about the Ojibwe in an anthropology course that semester, and he found himself interested in the conversation surrounding their rights. This interest shows. In his literature review, Jake presents and evaluates the specific grounds on which the Ojibwe's rights have been staged (legal, economic, and spiritual), effectively integrating historical and current perspectives in his review. Another strength of Jake's paper is that he uses concrete examples to support his claims, with clear topic sentences that foreground the shape of the conversation he's researching. Throughout the review, Jake demonstrates a deep understanding about the stakes of his topic for readers – he persuasively illustrates why it matters that we think about the Ojibwe's rights in Wisconsin specifically and the motivations behind our treatment of people more generally.

—Catherine DeRose

Writer's Memo

Choosing a topic for sequence two in my English 100 class was the most difficult part in the writing process. Initially, I wanted to compose an essay on a highly debated issue in the medical community since that is where my interest lies. However, I decided to avoid writing about a medical debate since this would only appeal to readers with a passion for medicine and would be uninteresting for all other readers. Choosing a topic that interested all readers was vital to writing a good paper and I made sure to take a lot of time to find a topic worth pursuing. It wasn't until about three days before our first draft was due that I found the topic I was looking for. I chose to write on the Ojibwe tribes of Wisconsin and their treaty rights to hunting and fishing since I believed most people would be interested in learning about a vital part of Wisconsin history that is often overlooked.

I used many sources, both scholarly and popular, to start piecing together my essay and creating a conversation between the authors. I was especially intrigued by the ethnography *The Walleye War* by Larry Nesper, in which he interacts with the Ojibwe tribes of Wisconsin for many years and researches their culture. His personal insight and research proved to be very useful in finding factual information about both the perspectives of the Ojibwe tribes, the non-Indians, and the Wisconsin state government. Other sources came from the 1996 *Minnesota Star Tribune*, the Wisconsin Historical Society, and other online articles using the UW-Madison library database. I received feedback from two fellow students and my English 100 instructor before I was able to produce the final product.

The goal of this paper was to accurately present the arguments of the Ojibwe tribes of Wisconsin, the non-Indian protesters, and the Wisconsin government. I felt myself side overwhelmingly with the Ojibwe tribes but I hope I have created a paper in which readers can form their own opinions on this topic. I also tried to present a historical view of this conversation while showing the overall arguments that are still prevalent in modern society.

Student Writing Award Honorable Mention:
Informative/Synthesis Essay

LUKE VOEGELL

Trouble in Syria

On August 21st, 2013, President Assad of Syria shocked the world by using chemical weapons against his own people. A short time after the initial attack, videos of civilian victims, visibly sick and frothing at the mouth, were uploaded to the internet. At least 355 people were killed by the gas attack ("Syria Chemical Attack"). United Nations chemical weapons inspectors have since confirmed the chemical in the footage as the nerve agent, sarin. Sarin is a lethal chemical weapon banned by the Chemical Weapons Convention of 1993 (CWC). President Obama had previously drawn a line in the sand saying that if President Assad were to use chemical weapons against civilians, it would call for U.S. intervention. The use of chemical weapons by Assad's forces is one of the factors that underlines the complexities of the scope and wisdom of United States' involvement in the Syrian civil war. This paper will examine the pros and cons of the United States' involvement in the Syrian civil war. The issues are complex because both action and inaction have effects on myriad groups, coalitions and power structures. The Syrian civil war presents the United States with few good options and a great risk of not only strengthening our enemies, but of endangering the stability of the Middle East.

The use of chemical weapons by Syria in 2013 calls attention to the long-debate concerning the use of chemical and nuclear weapons by Middle Eastern countries. In a 1993 article, political scientist Frances Harbour articulates the moral difference between taking life with traditional arms versus chemical weapons in the Muslim world. She points out that Muslim scholars have long debated the use of both nuclear and chemical weapons. (Harbour). Although there seem to be clear moral objections to the use of such weapons, there are also arguments that justify their use as a means of defense and reciprocity. Assad's use of these weapons sets an ugly and disturbing precedent that could well be emulated by other Islamic countries if nothing is done. Wary of involvement in yet another conflict in the Middle East, the Obama administration is faced with a difficult decision: what is the role of the United States in the Syrian civil war? Washington and the Obama administration seem to have very mixed feelings about involvement in Syria. The options are varied, and some have already come and gone. Retired Army General James "Spider" Marks says that "there is an array of bad options and you have to take the least bad option that is out there" (Foreman). Before even considering the options, it is necessary to articulate why it is important to intervene in Syria at all. Michael Doran argues that by bringing down Assad, Iran's influence in the Middle East will be diminished. He argues that a "muscular American policy would keep the conflict from spreading." Frida Ghitis argues that other dictators are watching and if there is no price to pay, the use of chemical weapons may well be used again. Ezra Klein suggests that limited strikes may well deter the Iranians from developing and obtaining nuclear weapons. By intervening and arming the more secular rebels, the rise and influence of radical al Qaeda elements could be limited. Klein also argues that Syria is a humanitarian tragedy that requires American intervention to stop the horrendous bloodshed.

Although each of these pro-intervention opinions have supporters, there are counterarguments that question whether an aggressive American response is a good idea. John Tate, an author for the Campaign for Liberty organization, points out that it is foolish to get involved in a conflict when only 9 percent of the American public favors military action. He argues that we have no goal and no national security interest, and if we do pursue a military option and Assad survives, it may well empower him. Striking Syria might actually embolden Iran, and could lead to a conflict that draws in the entire Middle East (Tate). It is also not clear that intervention would reduce violence, and it could actually make the killing worse. Getting involved in Syria may well risk the loss of American lives. This is exactly what many Americans do not want. America is in the process of extracting itself from two protracted and costly wars in the Middle East that have stretched the American military to a dangerous level. The last thing that America needs is to involve itself in another Middle East war.

Involvement in the Syrian civil war is more complicated than a gas attack, American lives, and taxpayer dollars. In order to understand these complications, we must understand some of the background of the uprising and the important groups involved. The Syrian revolution has been going on for the last two years, and is still running strong today. The UN estimates 100,000 dead and millions of displaced persons. One third of the entire population of Syria has been driven from their homes during the war (Arkin). Political unrest began in 2011 during the Arab spring. Protesters demonstrated against Bashar Assad in hopes of overthrowing his regime. A lot of the unrest comes as a result of an 80% Sunni majority being subject to the 19% Alawite minority (Slattery). In response to the non-violent protests, the Syrian military opened fire on the demonstrators and killed thousands. As a result of Assad's harsh crackdown, the protests escalated into a full-fledged civil war, and now, more and more players are getting involved in the murky power struggle that is unfolding in Syria.

As the conflict grew and changed, it morphed into a many faceted, violent, and often confusing conflict. Gram Slattery, a writer for the *Harvard Political Review*, wrote that "Contrary to neoconservative innuendos, the story of Syria is not that of a unified rebel army acting on a popular mandate against an unsupported tyrant. Rather, it is the story of a multi-layered, kaleidoscopic civil war." This un-united front against President Bashar Assad makes it very difficult for the U.S to get involved for fear of what a post-Assad Syrian state will look like. Complicating matters further, Russia is an important ally and the arms supplier of the Syrian regime. Russia continues to maintain its last naval installation outside the former Soviet Union in Syria, and has a decades-old Cold War connection with Assad (Fisher).

Though Sunnis make up most of the rebels, there are several other groups fighting in the opposition. The Free Syrian Army is not one force, but rather a cohort of groups that share the common goal of ousting Assad. Major General Noam Tibon, commander of the IDF Northern Corps, was quoted in the *Jerusalem Post* explaining that a lot of the Syrian civil war is fueled by groups that are not Syrian: "We must understand that this is not a war in Syria where Syrians are fighting against Syrians anymore" (Reuters). This disconnected opposition includes foreign jihadist fighters from Chechnya, Pakistan, Iraq and other surrounding regions that have come to join in the fight against Assad. Several groups such as Islamic State in Iraq and Syria (ISIS) and al-Nusra have strong links to al-Qaeda. Many of these groups are strongly opposed to American ideals and staunch foes of Israel. In an article in *The Australian*, Shahran Akabarzadeh states that "ISIS is essentially a legion of foreign fighters who have come to Syria to wage jihad" (Akabarzadeh). This makes directing funds to rebels extremely difficult for U.S. foreign policy. If we aid the rebels in any way, including striking chemical weapons depots, we could be directly supporting al-Qaeda. The important question facing the Obama administration and lawmakers is what will be more advantageous for U.S. foreign policy: a state controlled by al-Qaeda, or an oppressive pro-Soviet minority government that regularly brutalizes and kills its own citizens. Many would argue that having Assad remain in control would better benefit the U.S. However, Assad has blatantly violated humanitarian laws, put in place by the UN, and is allied with Iran and the fiercely anti-Israeli Hezbollah. Elite Hezbollah forces (who are Shi'ite Muslims) have joined the fight against the Sunni rebels, mainly based on the age-old feud between Shi'ite and Sunni Muslims (Reuters). Hezbollah is classified by the EU, Israel, and the U.S. as a terrorist organization. Hezbollah is also funded and armed by Iran. If the U.S were to engage in military action within Syria, it would be in opposition to Assad's regime and lead to the complicated question of who the funds and arms would benefit. Would the arms we supply ultimately end up in the hands of our most dangerous enemies and further the aims of Iran and Hezbollah? Gram Slattery argues that, "The basic unit of anti-Assad resistance could best be described as a gang." Because there are so many different groups involved, it is extremely difficult to direct funds. Most likely U.S military action would end up helping one of the many groups within the Syrian opposition that has ties to al-Qaeda.

The violence in Syria has displaced millions. Refugees fleeing the fighting in Syria have created severe strains on both Turkey and Jordan. Jordan has taken on 790,000 refugees, raising its population by 20 percent. Even Bulgaria is seeing the effects of the war in Syria. Bulgaria has received 4,760 refugees from Syria (Brown). Not only is this mass exodus of people inhumane, but it creates problems for our allies. Who will pay to feed, clothe, and educate these refugees? If the war continues, what will happen to these growing populations? Will the growing camps destabilize the accepting countries?

If no action is taken, murder and violence will continue in Syria for an indefinite period of time. Humanitarian violations take place on both sides. This instability and violence might well play into the hands of the radical al-Qaeda militias. Although Assad's forces have used chemical weapons against civilians, they are not the only culprits of unjustifiable violence. In several instances, Sunni rebels have murdered Alawite civilians for the sole reason of ethnicity. In one incident in the town of Rabia, Sunni rebels murdered 39 Alawite civilians, including women and children (Slattery). The struggle in Syria has grown from a political to an ethnic struggle. It is also alarming that caught in the middle of this conflict are Syria's 2.1

million Christians. The Syrian Orthodox Church has reported ethnic cleansing from Sunni rebels. In the city of Homs where a great deal of fighting has been taking place, the al-Farouq brigade, an Islamic brigade composed of Syrian Army deserters, has expelled 90 percent of the Syrian Christians (Slattery). Pro-government factions believe that if Sunni rebels are able to take power, there would be a massacre and massive displacement of Alawite civilians. On the other side, the Free Syrian army is driven by fear of the abuse and oppression that defeat by Assad's forces would bring. If the U.S involves itself, it would be supporting a massacre, but if the U.S abstains from entering the conflict, it is allowing a massacre to continue. If violence continues at the present rate, the entire moral fiber of Syria is likely to unravel. The chance of Syria ending up as a broken, dysfunctional state like Libya and Iraq seems ever more likely. In these countries the central government is so weak that armed Islamic militias control ever larger areas of the country.

One of the main fears of the U.S is that power will fall into the hands of a radical Islamist group. Whenever religion gets involved, U.S foreign policy seems to operate in an area of poorly defined objectives. In Syria there are Islamist groups on both sides of the conflict; Iranian-backed Shiite Hezbollah and Iraqi Shiites on the side of the Alawites and radical Sunni militias often affiliated with al-Qaeda on the side of the Sunni rebels. Almost 50% of the Free Syrian Army is made up by the Syrian Liberation Front (Slattery). Because there is no united power in the resistance, it is hard to tell who will be left in charge of Syria if the U.S did involve itself.

The location of Syria in the very center of the Middle East raises the stakes both for the Middle East and the United States. Syria borders on three important United States allies: Jordan, Israel and Turkey. Instability in Syria increases the risk to each of these important American allies. The chance of this conflict spreading or involving neighboring countries cannot be overlooked. Hezbollah fighters are already actively involved in the fighting, as well as both Sunni and Shia fighters from Iraq. There is an increase of fighting in Lebanon which borders Syria to the west. Turkey has strengthened its borders and has served as a conduit of arms to the Syrian rebels (Brown). On the east Iran has funneled in arms and equipment to the Assad forces. The Middle East has, for generations, been considered a powder keg waiting to explode. The proxy fighting in Syria has the potential to involve the entire area.

For the last ten years the U.S has been involved in conflicts in the Middle East, spending massive amounts of money and also American lives. Involvement in Syria is not popular in the eyes of many Americans. If we do choose to involve ourselves and overthrow Assad's regime, we are faced with the problem of who will lead Syria. Because of dislocation in the ranks of the opposition, it is very difficult to support a group. Fifty percent of the Free Syrian Army is the Syrian Liberation Front which has strong Islamic ties, and is strongly anti-American. We also risk upsetting international relations with Russia. Involvement could spread into a regional war, threatening and destabilizing many of our most important allies. If the United States chooses to stay uninvolved, even after President Obama's chemical weapons ultimatum, we are sitting on the sidelines of humanitarian violations, murder of civilians, and ethnic cleansing. Currently, Hezbollah and al-Qaeda who are both sworn enemies of the U.S, are viciously fighting within Syria. This could be good for U.S. foreign policy, but there are millions of civilians caught in the middle. Where does the U.S as leader of the free world draw the line? There is no clear answer as to what is the right decision in Syria, but there are valid pros and cons on both sides. Syria presents a confusing set of options that directly challenges both our morals and the stability of an area that has long had geopolitical importance to the United States.

Works Cited

Akbarzadeh, Shahram. "The Danger When Faith, Conflict Collide." *The Australian.* 7 Oct. 2013. Web. 28 Oct. 2013.

Arkin, Daniel. "Syrian Refugees Flood Neighboring States Amid Carnage - but Few Settling in US." NBC News. 28 Oct. 2013. Web. 02 Nov. 2013.

Brown, Hayes. "As Neighbors Strain, Other States Grant Syria's Refugees Cold Reception." ThinkProgress RSS. 17 Oct. 2013. Web. 30 Oct. 2013.

Doran, Michael and Max Boot. "5 Reasons to Intervene in Syria Now." *New York Times* Opinion Pages. 26 September. 2013. Web. 29 Oct. 2013.

Fisher, Max. "Understanding the Roots of the Syrian Conflict." *The Miami Herald.* 31 Aug. 2013. Web. 02 Nov. 2013.

Foreman, Tom. "So, What Exactly Are Obama's Options on Syria?" CNN. Cable News Network, 01 Jan. 1970. Web. 02 Nov. 2013.

Ghitis, Frida. "5 Reasons the U.S. Must Intervene in Syria." CNN. Cable News Network, 01 Jan.1970. Web. 31 Oct. 2013.

Harbour, Frances V. "Islamic Principles and the Chemical Weapons Convention of 1993." *Wiley Journal of Religious Ethics* 23.1 (1995): 69-92. Online.

Klein, Ezra. "The Five Best Arguments for Striking Syria — and the Best Rebuttals." *The Washington Post.* 10 Sept. 2013. Web. 30 Oct. 2013.

Reuters. "Hezbollah's Role in the Syrian Civil War." *The Jerusalem Post.* 26 Sept. 2013 Web. 30 Oct. 2013.

Slattery, Gram. "The Gangs of Syria." *Harvard Political Review.* Web. 27 Oct. 2013.

"Syria Chemical Attack: What We Know." BBC News Middle East. 24 September 2013. Web. 30 Oct. 2013.

Tate, John. "11 Reasons Not to Intervene in Syria." Campaign for Liberty. 30 Aug. 2013. Web. 31 Oct. 2013.

"The Chemical Weapons Convention (CWC) at a Glance." Arms Control Association. September 2013. Web. 30 Oct. 2013.

Instructor's Memo

For my class's Sequence Two project, I asked them to focus most on drawing together different sources so that the whole became more than the sum of its parts. To illustrate what I meant by this, we did an exercise looking at groups of statistics; viewed together, these statistics made an overall point about some aspect of American culture that wasn't visible when the statistics were viewed individually. I encouraged my students to do similar work in their papers - to bring together multiple sources of information to tell the reader something more about a topic of their choice than they could get reading each source on its own. I told them I would be looking for strong integration and synthesis of sources, as well as a clear and focused research question around which this synthesis would be based.

Luke came to me shortly after I gave out the assignment, asking about using the recent Syrian conflict as a topic. The original assignment had required multiple peer-reviewed sources, and Luke was concerned about finding them because his topic was so new. I encouraged him to pursue it anyhow and to view the challenge of finding relevant scholarly work as a kickstart to the task of integrating different types of information. Luke rose to the challenge and then some. Over the course of at least three separate drafts and multiple visits to my office hours (in addition to his peer review sessions), Luke constructed a paper that turned a long list of articles – on many different aspects of the Syrian conflict and its associated issues – into a clear, focused discussion of the elements involved in considering an American intervention. Luke uses his considerable research to really convey the complexity of the issues involved; in reading the paper, I genuinely felt as if I had been given a new perspective on the difficulty our government was having in choosing a path. In addition, Luke's deep reading on the topic allowed him to write a paper that presents a fairly even-handed view of the issue. Had it not been for our in-person meetings, I would not have been able to tell from just the paper what his own feelings were about intervention in Syria. This objective presentation of the research emphasized the assignment's focus on synthesis and clarity, and it encourages readers to do some work themselves – to think for themselves about what this information adds up to altogether.

—Becca Tarsa

Writer's Memo

I decided to write about the civil war in Syria because it is a constantly evolving topic that is frequently in the international spotlight. Since the early days of the civil war, I have been intrigued by the conflict, but did not study it in depth until writing this paper. When I began this project, the question I was seeking to answer was: What, if any, options did the United States have in this conflict? Should the United States abstain from involvement or take military action? Through my research, I learned how complex and difficult this question really is. One of the most important things I learned about the civil war is how difficult it is to weigh and balance the pros and cons of the conflict. On both sides of the issue are innumerable costs and benefits that defy easy answers. In the Syrian civil war there is no one correct answer.

In my research process I relied heavily on newspaper articles. Since my topic was so recent, there were no scholarly articles directly on it. Every day brought a constantly changing milieu that only the international news media could keep up with. My one scholarly article was very relevant, in spite of the fact that it was written prior to the beginnings of the civil war. This source was about Islamic Principles regarding the Chemical Weapons Convention of 1993. Considering that chemical weapons have recently been a controversial issue in the Syrian civil war, the use of this article in my paper helped explain the conflict.

The writing process in research papers is constantly subject to change. As one thing leads to another, the topic itself changes and grows. Research papers are like solving a mystery in which you are the detective. What you expect to find is not always what you end up with.

GIOVANNA STERN

Ditch the Jury, Do Justice

We live in a society where we put value on justice, but what exactly does it mean to be *just*? Many people consider that our system is *just* because it assumes our innocence, provides counsel to those who cannot afford a lawyer, and prohibits cruel and unusual punishments. But can we say it is just to put innocent people in jail? Or is it just to discriminate against certain groups of people? Of course not—but these things happen in our current legal system. As concerned members of society, we need to evaluate the 6th Amendment's right to an impartial jury in order to address these flaws in the system (Constitution). Our jury system needs to be eliminated because it inhibits our criminal justice system from achieving greater justice due to jurors' lack of expertise; inherent discrimination that undermines the democratic value of a jury; lack of awareness or control over psychological factors; and some ineffective trial procedures.

Take a moment to consider the case of John White. White served more than 22 years in a cell, living a harsh, restricted lifestyle for a crime that he did not commit. He wasn't released until an organization, The Innocence Project, investigated his case and proved his innocence. The crime he was accused of occurred when a man broke into an elderly woman's home and beat, raped, and robbed her before fleeing the scene. At the scene, police collected skin and hair samples from the couch, but they were never tested for DNA for the trial. Some time later, the victim was presented with a lineup where she was "almost positive" that the offender was White. Because memory is constructive and not nearly as reliable as we'd like to believe, it is not the victim's fault that she chose the wrong person in the lineup (Lichstein). Nevertheless, a jury found White guilty based on this unreliable but influential evidence. In the end, White was sentenced to life in prison for a crime that he had nothing to do with. It sounds like a distant, twisted nightmare, but to John White and many others this is their reality. In total, there have been more than 300 innocent people released from prison in the US simply due to properly examining DNA evidence (The Innocence Project).

201

Although there are multiple causes for wrongful convictions, many can be traced back to the inexperience of the jury. Currently it is estimated that "between 2.3% and 5% of all prisoners in the U.S. are innocent." That may appear to be a small number but that translates to between 46,000 and 100,000 innocent people in prison (Innocence Project). To a jury, the most influential piece of evidence is eyewitness identification (Lichstein). This is when the victim or another witness attempts to identify the offender in a lineup. Eyewitness identification also happens to be the "single greatest cause of wrongful convictions nationwide" (The Innocence Project). This is mainly because memory is "not like a tape recorder," but it is more malleable (Lichstein). When victims are presented with a lineup, they are pressured to pick an offender. Studies have shown that someone is more likely to choose the person that looks most like the offender rather than choosing no one at all (Lichstein). Byron Lichstein, from the Wisconsin Innocence Project, explains how the witness who identifies the "offender" is asked in front of the jury how confident they feel that the person who they identified is the real offender. More likely than not, their answer is 100% confident. The Innocence Project explains that this may be due to how actors in the system often encourage the witness on their identification by saying things like "good job, we thought that was the guy" or even by clapping (Lichstein). In short, a witness's confidence can turn from partially confident when they first identify an offender to completely sure by the time they face the jury at the time of the trial.

False confessions are another cause of wrongful convictions (The Innocence Project). Many may question why anyone would ever plead guilty to a crime that they did not commit, but it happens more often than we think mainly due to interrogations. These interrogations "prey on psychological vulnerabilities" with hours of continual questioning and accusations until the suspect either truly begins to believe that they committed the crime or until they confess in order to be released from the stressful interrogation (Leo). Inexperienced jurors may fail to question the validity of eyewitness identifications or consider the possibility of false confessions, which can lead to punishing the innocent. Overall, punishing innocent people is too frequent a phenomenon for a society that puts an emphasis on justice.

In addition, psychological factors can have a negative effect on the reliability of a jury. It is known that people tend to favor the group to which they belong and often discriminate based on group membership. These groups include race, age, gender, religion and many more. A juror's personal biases may affect the outcome of the trial. Psychology research at Harvard University emphasizes that jurors may not even be aware of their prejudices (Cromie). Social psychology also plays a role in influencing juries. The Asch Experiment concluded that people easily conform to the group, either because the group truly convinces them that their opinions are wrong, or because the individual fears the criticism that comes when they deviate from the group (McLeod). The experiment consisted of a group where everyone except for one person was aware of the experiment. The group was then presented with a simple visual matching task, and the people involved in the experiment were, at times, directed to pick answers that were clearly wrong. The researchers discovered that the actual participant would go against his or her own judgment and agree with the people who had already given clearly incorrect answers. This behavior is important to note because in a jury it is very unlikely for one person to challenge the opinions of others, even when that one person may be right. Both inherent prejudice and this tendency to conform may cloud a juror's ability to make an impartial decision.

Many would agree with the American Bar Association when they say that "trial by jury is a vital part of our democracy," but the discrimination in our current jury system seems to undermine this democratic value. This discrimination extends to both the juror selection process and the decisions jurors make once they are on a jury. An article in the *Boston College Journal of Law and Justice* explains a 2012 study done by the Equal Justice Initiative. The researchers found that prosecutors in Houston County, Alabama have removed "eighty percent of qualified African Americans" (Weddell 458). In theory, I agree that the jury system epitomizes democratic values, but many fail to acknowledge that it overlooks the idea that jury selection is inherently biased. Although the "Supreme Court mandated [...] that jurors represent a 'fair cross section of the community,' in reality it only draws from a pool of registered voters" (Weddell 459). By doing this, it potentially leaves out many people from lower socioeconomic backgrounds or others who have not registered to vote. Keller, a writer for *The New York Times*, focuses on the idea that the jury system is beneficial because it gives citizens an opportunity to be educated on the criminal justice system. However, he fails to understand that the cost of juries may be too great just so someone can "feel like a more dutiful member of society" (Keller).

There are many safeguards in place for keeping a jury as impartial as possible, but these often fail. One attempt to safeguard justice is to have twelve people make the decision as opposed to one judge. I have to disagree with Weddell that many people are more "capable of achieving a wisdom together that no one person is capable of achieving alone" (Weddell 486). She is resting that statement on the questionable assumption that quantity automatically equals quality. Even the process of the trial tends to limit the potential of the jury. As the fact finders of the court, one would think that juries could be allowed to take notes or ask questions to try to understand the case to the best of their ability, but these things are not allowed. Also, the judge is required to "instruct" the jury right before they leave to make their decision. This instruction is essentially extra information about the case or legal procedures. This practice should be helpful, but the instructions commonly consist of full-on legal jargon that ends up confusing the jury and thus the outcome of the trial. One criminal justice professor used the analogy that if you needed surgery, you wouldn't just hand over instructions on how to perform the surgery to someone who is not a trained doctor.

For our legal system to function effectively without juries, we would need to instill more power into the judge's role, because in our system, judges, and not juries, symbolize impartiality. Many people assume that a "jury can soften the rough edges of the law," but studies have shown that "federal judges are more likely to acquit than juries" (Keller, Krause). Keller, in his article in *The New York Times,* admits that there are even cases where a jury can be "razzle-dazzled by a skillful attorney or lost in the complications of evidence" (Keller). The law is complicated; that is why people dedicate years of their life to study it. Putting not just the law, but also someone's life, in a jury's hands is not a logical solution. I also agree with Keller that "judges are human too," and they are not immune to these influences. Since a judge can make mistakes as well, I am proposing that there be a panel of judges to make an even greater step towards justice. I am not saying that judges are perfect, but we cannot overlook the fact that they have more experience than the typical juror. For example, they may be more familiar with organizations like The Innocence Project, and thus more likely to be aware of the potential for witnesses to identify an innocent person and or for innocent people to make false confessions. In the end, the judge should take over the role of the jury in our criminal justice system in order to create true justice.

Works Cited

American Bar Association. *americanbar.org.* N/A. Web. 16 Nov 2013.

Cromie, William. "Brain Shows Unconscious Prejudices." *Harvard Gazette,* 17 July 2003. Web. 21 December 2013.

Keller, Ben. "A Jury of Whose Peers?" *The New York Times,* 22 Sept. 2013. Web. 16 Nov. 2013.

Krause, Jason. "Judge v. Jury." *abajournal.com.* American Bar Association, 5 June 2007. Web. 17 Nov. 2013

Leo, Richard A. "Miranda's Revenge: Police Interrogation as a Confidence Game." *Law and Society Review.* 30.2 (1996): 58-75. Print.

Lichstien, Byron. Lecture. 11 November 2013.

McLeod, Sam. "Asch Experiment." *Simply Psychology.* 2008. Web. 17 Nov. 2013.

The Innocence Project. *innocenceproject.org.* 2013. Web. 16 Nov 2013.

United States. "The Constitution of the United State." *archives.gov.* N.D. Web. 17 Nov. 2013.

Weddell, Hilary. "A Jury of Whose Peers?: Eliminating Racial Discrimination in Jury Selection

Procedures." *Boston College Journal of Law and Social Justice* 33:453 (Year): 453-486. *Academic Search Premier.* Web. 16 Nov. 2013.

Instructor's Memo

In our section of English 100, the Sequence 3 project was an extension of the student's research in Sequence 2. Students wrote informative essays about an issue in Sequence 2 and then narrowed in on their own argument related to that issue in Sequence 3. The benefit of this structure is that each student becomes an expert on his or her chosen topic; the challenge is that students often have several sources from Sequence 2 that do not end up fitting into the Sequence 3 project. This was certainly the case for Giovanna, who researched the relationship between students and Madison police in her Sequence 2 project, and then found a related but different issue that she felt strongly about arguing in her Sequence 3 project. The evidence that Giovanna uses in this essay impresses me, but I am almost as impressed by how much research I know she left out. I think that one of the biggest challenges for writers can be cutting those sentences, paragraphs, or pieces of evidence that we have spent time and effort finding and writing when they turn out to be tangential or unnecessary for our final project. Giovanna accomplished this by including only those pieces of evidence that directly supported her argument about abolishing the jury system, resisting the urge to show her readers all the additional information she had about the justice system more broadly. This resulted in a focused and persuasive essay.

One of the challenges for Giovanna in this project was making her argument accessible to her intended audience. Because she had spent a lot of time researching the topic and was taking a criminal justice class, she was comfortable with terminology and background knowledge that her classmates were not. The first draft of the essay was much more technical and might have been accessible to her criminal justice classmates but was difficult for an audience without that background to follow. When her peers brought this up, she had to think deeply about which audience she was trying to reach. Ultimately, she decided that she wanted to introduce this issue to an audience that was not already familiar with criminal justice scholarship, and so she changed the style and explained her evidence to make it more accessible. For me as an instructor, it was interesting to read the same argument written for two different audiences and to see how Giovanna changed her writing choices depending on how much prior knowledge her audience shared with her.

There are many things I admire about this essay, but what impresses me most is how challenging it is to me as a reader. Giovanna doesn't make a safe or familiar argument that many people would already agree with. Instead, she argues against something that most of her readers (including me) take for granted and assume is good—the jury system. She challenges us to think differently about it, and presents strong evidence for why we should do so. This essay tries to persuade an audience, but it also represents Giovanna's process of trying to figure one whether common sense is right or not. I enjoy reading this essay because it makes me think differently about familiar ideas.

—Jennifer Maclure

Writer's Memo

This writing project was assigned around the time that my criminal justice class had three guest speakers. One of the speakers was in prison for more than ten years until The Innocence Project proved his innocence. In class, we had been learning about wrongful convictions and the role of the jury for quite some time, but it was an entirely different experience to hear the story come to life from someone sitting in front of you. After listening to the speaker, the topic for my paper became very clear to me. I was also enrolled in an introductory psychology class where I learned about memory and perception, which also influenced my thinking for this paper. It was from these two classes that I drew the majority of my ideas. The writing process, however, was not as easy as deciding on a topic.

It is one thing to be passionate about what you're presenting as a writer, but it is another thing to effectively argue for what you believe. One main struggle I had was keeping my audience in mind. The peer-review process was especially helpful in this area. My instructor and peers pointed out that I used a lot of the legal jargon that was fresh in my mind from my criminal justice class, without realizing the majority of my audience wouldn't have had that legal background. For my final draft of this paper, I simplified my arguments and evidence for an audience that may not be familiar with the criminal justice system. Because my peers helped me to see that listing fact after fact can get pretty dry, I also included the specific case of John White to add more of an emotional appeal. During the revision process, to stay focused on my major points, I even narrowed down how much evidence I put into my paper. One main challenge that I came across was trying to figure out what exactly to simplify or remove completely to make the clearest argument without bringing in too many different ideas. Receiving feedback from my classmates allowed me to figure out which ideas were the most persuasive: for example, the John White case example, the surgery analogy from my professor, and some psychology principles. In the end, these revisions helped to express the overall two-fold purpose of my paper. First of all, I am trying to establish that there is something wrong with our current system. Second of all, and most importantly, I want to persuade my audience that eliminating the jury would lead to greater justice in our system.

Student Writing Award Honorable Mention:
Critical/Analytical Essay

GABRIELLA NEGRETE

The Great Pacific Garbage Patch: A Case Study in Public Awareness

The Great Pacific Garbage Patch, located in the middle of the Pacific Ocean, is the largest landfill in the world. This immense mass of garbage, consisting mostly of small plastic particles, is not very well known, yet its presence in the global environment affects all of us. I believe this oceanic landfill needs to be addressed so it can gain international attention. Without public awareness, there is no way to make a change in consumption patterns or develop new environmental regulations. Knowledge of the invisible elements of our environment and acknowledgment of changes in environmental conditions are the door to reality.

Large amounts of marine litter collect in the Great Pacific Gyre. The environmental activist group Greenpeace explains that, "the North Pacific central gyre is an area of convergence where clockwise ocean currents prevent plastic debris from moving towards mainland coasts" (Allsopp 28). Marine litter gets trapped in the oceanic currents and continues accumulating without hope of disintegration. Regardless of the garbage's origin on land, the convergence currents trap litter in the Pacific Ocean and separate the floating plastic into two primary sub-patches. The Eastern patch is located between Hawaii and California and the Western garbage patch is between Hawaii and Japan.

While public awareness of this garbage patch is low, the size and shape of the Great Pacific Garbage Patch has been a prominent topic of discussion and uncertainty among Oceanographers. While some might imagine it as an island composed of garbage, a more accurate description would be a mass of plastic stretching across hundreds of miles of the Pacific Ocean. Russell McLendon, from the Mother Nature Network, describes the patch as "a galaxy of garbage, populated by billions of smaller trash islands that may be hidden underwater or spread out over many miles" (McLendon). There is also much speculation about the geographic extent of the garbage patch. Many science writers say that it is the size of Texas, France or even a continent. However, they have little evidence to prove the extent of the garbage patch because of the difficulty of measuring floating material. The massive amount of litter is composed of some "hot spots," zones of highly concentrated floating debris spread around the Pacific Ocean Gyre. Although the precise size of the garbage patch is uncertain, it has been generally estimated to be twice the size of the state of Texas.

The majority of this muck is composed of plastic and synthetic material coming from everyday human activity and ordinary production. Tsunamis and hurricanes in Japan have carried garbage away from the land. However, large storms are not the only reason debris has accumulated in the oceans. Rivers and storm drains carry debris from inland urban areas and deposit in the ocean. Tourism-related litter along the coasts, fishing debris, and waste from ships are other critical factors. All of us who do not dispose of our garbage properly contribute to the Great Pacific garbage patch. Most of the plastic and synthetic materials come from more developed countries like the United States and China. Therefore, as Michelle Allsopp writes, "in the future, as less developed countries become more industrialized, it is likely that they will also produce more plastic and synthetic wastes and this will increase further the threat of pollution of the marine environment" (6). People need to be informed about the debris floating in the ocean because if this accumulation is not stopped, the ocean will be at risk.

A substantial complication in reducing the Great Pacific Garbage Patch is the fact that it is mostly composed of plastic. Anthony L. Andrady, an experienced Senior Research Scientist from the Research Triangle Park in North Carolina notes, "Plastic in the ocean undergoes both chemical and photochemical weathering, as plasticizers and other chemicals leach out of the polymer matrix and photodegrade, and mechanical weathering, as wind and wave action break the plastic into pieces. The most important process controlling the rate of degradation is heat" (Andrady). This explains how the plastic is incapable of fully disintegrating; the plastic in the ocean is currently breaking down into extremely small fragments through weathering, sunlight and other processes. These pieces, no matter how small, remain plastic and therefore will never decompose. Instead, we have accumulating organic pollutants in the ocean.

Life becomes dangerous for species in the ocean trying to drink the contaminated water or confusing the plastic of the Great Pacific Garbage Patch for food. Miriam Chanita Goldstein, an oceanographer, mentions that 17 out of 24 marine species in a study conducted by researchers were found to have ingested plastic. Furthermore, more than 80% of the birds studied contained ingested plastic. There are striking similarities between plastic ingestion rates in the Pacific and plastic ingestion rates in the North Atlantic: 21 of 38 Atlantic seabird species contained plastic particles (9). Goldstein notes that although plastic ingestion is not fatal for seabirds, it results in a high body pollutant load. The enormous accumulation of debris in the middle of the ocean is a substantial contributor to harm of marine animals in the Pacific. The Great Pacific Garbage Patch has affected at least 267 species worldwide. Some of these species include sea turtles, sea birds, seals, sea lions, whales and fish. Most of the autopsy results have concluded that the primary cause of death was the swallowing of plastic and consequent suffocation in the oceans. Confusing garbage with food has been correlated with these results. The accumulation of plastic in the oceans is the most common and atrocious factor harming marine animals.

In addition to harming marine animals, debris on the ocean floor also affects coral reefs Most of the litter that affects these reefs is fish lining and nets. In a study done by the National Oceanic and Atmospheric Association it was found that, "Nets and lines become snagged on coral and subsequent wave action causes coral heads to break off at points where the debris was attached. Once freed, debris can again snag on more coral and the whole process is repeated. This cycle continues until the debris is removed or becomes weighted down with enough broken coral to sink" (NOAA). All of the suspended debris doesn't just affect a single species. Instead, it creates a positive feedback loop that keeps affecting the oceans.

When tourists notice pollution in oceans, they tend to move away from the region instead of educating themselves about the causes of the pollution. It's important to realize that the earth is composed of about 71% water coming from the oceans. This is most of the earth, and if nothing is done, our resources and lifespans will decrease exponentially. As mentioned previously, most of this garbage is composed of plastic, which will not disintegrate. There have been research studies and programs trying to clean the oceans and "make the world right again", but that is an optimist's dream We cannot make the world pure or go back in time to how it used to be hundreds of years ago. However, if we keep producing large amounts of plastic, the situation will only get worse. Even though oceanic garbage patches are an ongoing problem, there are ways to minimize the amount of debris leaving the continents as well as to decrease the volume of the plastics already in the oceans.

One of the most promising projects is the idea of greener plastics. Paul Anastas, the director of the Yale University Center for Green Chemistry and Green Engineering, has been working on creating plastics that don't pollute or poison the environment. He emphasizes the ability of green plastics to disintegrate:

> Plastics created using the principles of "green chemistry" are designed to reduce or eliminate the use and generation of hazardous substances throughout their life cycle. This means nontoxic, renewable feed stocks, a manufacturing process that yields little or no waste, and a final plastic that, when discarded, degrades into harmless products on a human rather than a geologic time scale (Anastas).

Green plastics have the potential to eliminate waste material and production.

Additionally, activist and community projects such as "Zero Waste" help the environment through simple tasks such as recycling and reducing resource use. Other beneficial measures could include manual cleanup operations focused on shorelines and the sea floor with the help of school and public educational programs. Likewise, according to Greenpeace, "Attempts to address the problem of marine debris range from international legislation to prevent shipping from dumping plastic at sea and campaigns to prevent losses due to poor industrial practice to beach and seabed clean-up operations and public awareness campaigns" (Allsopp 5). There are many ways to alleviate the accumulation of plastic in our oceans, and increasing awareness in communities will improve the possibility of positive change.

The Great Pacific Garbage Patch remains a critical issue, and education is therefore an essential tool in environmental change. The majority of society remains oblivious to this floating debris, which prevents people from adjusting their lifestyles. These oceans are a significant source of life and improving our treatment of the environment will positively benefit us all. There should be international laws developed to regulate the production and consumption of plastic in addition to economic measures instated to promote green plastic use. There should also be more public presentations made in order for people to understand how the Great Pacific Garbage Patch is created. Attention and communication the keys to solving this problem. Our population is not naturally destructive we just do not yet understand what is threatening the well being of the ocean.

Works Cited

Allsopp, Michelle, Adam Walters, David Santillo, and Paul Johnston. "Plastic Debris In The World's Oceans." Greenpeace. Web. 21 Nov. 2013.

Andrady, Anthony L., Microplastics in the marine environment, *Marine Pollution Bulletin*, Volume 62, Issue 8, August 2011, Pages 1596-1605, ISSN 0025-326X

Anastas, Paul. "Greener Plastics." *Technology review* Jul 2013: 12.

Duenas, Ashlee. "Ocean is Choking on Trash: Research Vessel Returns from 7-Week Study in the Great Pacific Garbage Patch." *McClatchy - Tribune Business News*. Aug 04 2009. *ProQuest.* Web. 29 Nov. 2013

Gillis, Charlie. "ENVIRONMENT: Trashing the Island: Why the 'Garbage Patch' in the Mid-Pacific is Not nearly the Disaster it's been made Out to be." *Maclean's* Jan 31 2011: 53.

Goldstein, Miriam Chanita. "Abundance and Ecological Implications of Microplastic Debris in the North Pacific Subtropical Gyre." University of California, San Diego, 2012. Ann Arbor: ProQuest. Web. 20 Nov. 2013.

McLendon Russel. "What is the Great Pacific Garbage Patch?" Mother Nature Network. Feb 24 2010. Web. 29 Nov. 2013.

NOAA (2005), National Oceanic and Atmospheric Association, US Department of Commerce. Coral reef restoration through marine debris mitigation. Background. Web. 2 December. 2013.

Rios, L. M., et al. "Quantitation of Persistent Organic Pollutants Adsorbed on Plastic Debris from the Northern Pacific Gyre's 'Eastern Garbage Patch'." *Journal of Environmental Monitoring* 12.12 (2010): 2226-36. *ProQuest.* Web. 29 Nov. 2013.

Robards, Martin D., Patrick J. Gould, and John F. Piatt. "The Highest Global Concentrations and Increased Abundance of Oceanic Plastic Debris in the North Pacific." 1997 Springer-Verlag New York, Inc. Web. 2 December. 2013.

Thompson R.C., Olsen Y., Mitchell R.P., Davis A., Rowland S.J., John A.W.G., McGonigle D and Russell A.E. (2004). Lost at sea: where is all the plastic? *Science* 304: 838.

Thompson R.C., Moore C., Andrady A., Gregory M., Takada H. and Weisburg S. (2005) New directions in Plastic Debris. *Science* 310: 1117.

Weiss, Kenneth R. "Plague of Plastic Choke's the Seas." *Los Angeles Times* 2013. Web. 30 Nov. 2013.

Instructor's Memo

The writer Wallace Stegner claims, "No place is a place until things that have happened in it are remembered in history, ballads, yarns, legends or monuments." With this relationship between place and story in mind, our course explored how writing can grant meaning to places, rendering them not simply as abstract locations on a map but as sites of emotion, context, and significance. Gaby's essay on the Great Pacific Garbage Patch emerged from our discussions of politically or culturally contested places. Gaby decided to write about the incongruities of environmental awareness, noting that while the Great Pacific Garbage Patch is "coming from our own palms," few of us spend much time thinking about this place.

In the process of writing this essay, Gaby confronted the challenges of interdisciplinary work. She explored everything from cutting-edge chemical engineering to Greenpeace press releases. Once we specialize in a field—declaring a major or choosing a career—we often forget that the best writers are ones who move easily across disciplinary boundaries. I think English 100 gives students an opportunity to write more holistically, and Gaby's essay demonstrates how an expansive, interdisciplinary paper can feel like a conversation between a wide variety of experts. From the technology of green plastics to philosophical questions about what it takes to translate knowledge into action, this paper is interested in making connections and bridges between fields of knowledge.

I love this essay because it proves how research can translate into hope. When Gaby announced that she wanted to write about the Great Pacific Garbage Patch, I anticipated a cynical, despairing argument about the irrevocability of environmental damage. Given the scale of this gyre of plastic, I think a pessimistic argument would have been the easiest one to make. Gaby's essay acknowledges that we cannot "make the world right again," but she chooses not to stop there. She guides her readers forward, delving into articles about green plastics and highlighting community and activist clean-up projects. In the face of a dire crisis, Gaby employs research to maintain a sense of possibility about the future.

—Sarah Dimick

Writer's Memo

This project started as the last paper for my English 100 class. We were supposed to find a topic of our interest that was controversial and then research it. I wasn't very sure what to pick, but when one of my classmates informed me about the Great Pacific Garbage Patch, I was instantly hooked. My dream is to become an oceanographer some day. Anything talking about the ocean instantly grabs my attention, but this topic was completely different. The first thing I heard about it was that it was an island made of plastic in the middle of the Pacific Ocean. I could not understand how this was going on and I had no idea about it. I was very interested, and I knew that it was the perfect topic for me.

Doing the research was probably one of the best parts of the writing process because I got to learn about so many different opinions in the subject. Every article I read had a very distinct view and different information. For the first time, I got to use the resources that the library offers and, thanks to that I borrowed a couple of books that opened my understanding of the argument. I became very passionate about the subject, which assured me that dealing with these problems and researching about them really is what I want to do when I graduate. That fascination helped me pick the voice that I wanted to portray in the paper, the voice that my English instructor encouraged us to find.

One of my biggest difficulties was organizing my thoughts in a way that would make the paper flow and resemble my actual views. That's very challenging because it's easy to have an idea of what you want to say, but actually writing it in a way that makes since to you and to the readers is very difficult. I learned that there are a lot of rough drafts to go through before the paper is actually presentable, and the first one is one of the most important ones because even if it's very bad, it helps you write all of your ideas and opinions on paper. The actual motive of rewriting and reshaping is to bring your further thoughts to light.

After many drafts and changes I went to the English 100 Tutorial for additional help. It was very beneficial because I got to read my essay in front of the instructor while she gave me her opinion on what needed reshaping, but overall she was very entertained and my draft left her wanting to know more.

My last step was making my final revisions, which my English instructor helped me think about. By the end, I understood why she encouraged us to show off our voices in our writing. That is the most fundamental way to share your passion about a topic, and I like to think that this is what I accomplished.

MANDY THOR

Color Blind: An Exploration of Hmong American Experiences and the Controversy of White Privilege

You can find Mandy Thor's Project through the English 100 website.

Instructor's Memo

Our English 100 class studied composition in the context of graphic narratives and new media. While reading graphic novels alongside journalistic and scholarly prose, students explored how visual and other non-textual modes of composition might transform their approaches to traditional forms of academic writing. For their final projects, I asked students to create a graphic or multimedia research essay on a topic of their choice. One of the goals of this assignment was to provoke students to translate what they had learned about graphic rhetoric into an argumentative writing project. Another of the assignment's goals was to encourage students to engage with the writing process in a new way: to understand it not simply as the penning of words on a page, but rather as the rhetorical negotiation of a shifting visual, aural and linguistic landscape.

Mandy Thor's video essay, "Color Blind: An Exploration of Hmong American Experiences and the Controversy of White Privilege," realizes these goals to stunning effect. I admire this essay not only for its formal and conceptual innovation, but also and perhaps most importantly for the extraordinary strength, courage and originality of Mandy's voice. When Mandy first started work on the project she was unsure about whether to include her own personal narratives, as well as those of other Hmong, wondering whether these narratives would detract from the essay's credibility. In our conferences, I encouraged Mandy to view this assignment as an opportunity to do precisely what might otherwise be deemed too informal or experimental for a piece of academic writing. Mandy took this advice and ran with it, creating an essay that is remarkable for its intertwinement of analytical and intensely personal modes of expression. And though I was initially skeptical of Mandy's decision to leave the electronic voiceover unexplained until the essay's conclusion, I later realized how right Mandy was about this aspect of her project. By deferring this revelation, Mandy demonstrated the extent to which white privilege comes to bear on voice, and the acts of reading and listening. Thus, the essay is a marvelous testament not only to the power of Mandy's voice, but also to her self-knowledge as a writer.

—Devin Garofalo

Writer's Memo

When I embarked on this project I was already pretty certain about what the topic would be because it was something that I was passionate about. My head was swimming with ideas and concepts that I thought would be important for people to know about so it wasn't very difficult for me to find content about my subject. The biggest problem for me was how to present my information and organize it in a way that made sense to the reader. I had so much to say that I felt writing a paper wouldn't do it justice. In creating a video for the essay project, I was able to show what I meant visually which would eliminate the need to explain little details, such as where Laos was located, as well as use a narrative to help organize the information.

I was very torn in the beginning between whether or not to use an electronic voiceover versus just narrating the whole thing myself. In the end I decided that if I had narrated it myself, that the point of the project would have gotten lost in my personal story and biased opinions. Although it was a personal project for me, I wanted my experience to be just a little part of the bigger picture. Using the voiceover disconnected me from the project and made me a subject that I could use as an example. After coming to this conclusion and playing around with the voice over program, I found the option of changing the accent of the computed voice and I knew right away what I wanted to do with it. I wanted to use it in a way that would show exactly how privilege works. Although in the beginning it may have been strange to hear the computed voice, people would eventually ignore it and focus on the content of the video. At the end then, it would be revealed that even this little attribute—an accent—was a huge privilege. I tried to make this a profound point and didn't feel the need to include images in the last couple seconds. It would be up to the audience then, to think over what they just saw and heard.

Getting to the finished product took lots of time and effort. While creating the video, I kept in mind what I knew about documentaries as a general guide and attempted to create something that was interesting to watch while still clearly presenting my information. Because I had audio, pictures and distinct examples, I had to constantly edit the entire video. Even as I was putting it together I was editing and revising and changing the way I said certain things. It had been my first time trying something like this so it was a learning process but the general feedback was positive and I was ultimately satisfied with what I produced.

BARBARA FISTER

Working with Sources: Using MLA, Seventh Edition Style

A. A Checklist for Working with Sources

B. For MLA-Style In-Text Citations

C. For an MLA-Style Works Cited List

Sources not only provide information and ideas but can help establish your credibility and strengthen your argument when used as "expert witnesses." You should cite your sources to allow readers to track down your sources easily and to avoid plagiarizing words and ideas, a serious academic offense. Consult the *MLA Handbook for Writers of Research Papers*, Seventh Edition, for additional examples and advice.

A. A CHECKLIST FOR WORKING WITH SOURCES

Did I Use the Best Possible Evidence for My Assertions?

- **Are all of my claims supported by evidence?** If a section of your paper needs stronger support or if you need to verify a fact, consult with a reference librarian for suggestions.

- **Do my sources present balanced perspectives?** If a source you rely on promotes an agenda and ignores alternative viewpoints, you may want to substitute one that is more balanced and less likely to be dismissed by your readers as unreliable. Make sure to address alternate perspectives.

- **Will my readers consider my sources persuasive evidence for my assertions?** A medical research report on a treatment for cancer is more impressive as a source than a magazine article that describes the treatment. If you need scholarly sources, look for ones written by researchers that include documented references to other sources.

- **If writing about literature, have I chosen effective illustrations to support my thesis?** Choose quotations from the text or summarize passages that illustrate your main points. Be sure to explain how each quotation or summary relates to your thesis.

Are My Sources Integrated into My Writing Smoothly and Correctly?

- **Have I used more sources than necessary?** Use sources to support your ideas, not replace them. If two sources provide similar information, use the one that carries the most clout.

- **Do my sources back up what I say—or do they speak for me?** When possible, convey information in your own words. Don't quote a source when paraphrase or summary will do.

- **Have I used my sources ethically?** Provide a reference for anything from a source that isn't common knowledge, even if you have put it in your own words. Facts available in multiple sources—such as dates and well-known historical events—are considered common knowledge and do not need to be cited.

- **Are quotations presented correctly?** If quoting four lines or more from a source, set it off as a block quote by indenting the entire passage an inch from the left margin; do not put quotation marks around a block quote. If quoting two lines from a poem, separate the lines with a slash. If quoting three or more lines, set them off as a block quote.

- **Have I introduced each source effectively?** Never drop in a quote without introducing it. Use signal phrases such as "according to..." or "...Smith argues." If possible, include the author's credentials: "Poet Seamus Heaney has noted...."

Are My Sources Cited Clearly and Completely?

- **Did I provide a reference for every idea that came from a source?** Indicate the original source by naming the author and page.

- **Do all of my in-text references have a complete citation in my bibliography or works cited list?** Double-check to make sure every source referred to in the text can be found easily in your bibliography or works cited list.

- **Did I provide all the information necessary for my readers to locate my sources?** Make sure you include all required information, specified on the following pages, including information about electronic versions of print sources.

B. FOR MLA-STYLE IN-TEXT CITATIONS

In-text citations point your readers toward the full citations for sources that you provide in the works cited list at the end of your paper. Provide author and page numbers for in-text citations. Readers can look up the author's name in the alphabetized list of works cited at the end of the paper. The page number will lead them directly to the portion of the work that you are citing.

- Use the author's name to introduce the quote in your text and put page numbers in parentheses after the material you are citing. Or you can include the author's name with the page number in parentheses: Jones asserts... (15) or (Jones 15).
- If there is no author, use a shortened version of the title: ("Mind" 69).
- If there are multiple works by one author, include a short title: (Markoff, "Attack" A1); if there are multiple authors with the same last name, include the first initial (J. Markoff A1).
- Leave out page numbers if the source doesn't have them. Use a PDF version of an online source if it is an option; it will usually include original page numbers.
- When quoting from a Shakespeare play, use act, scene, and line numbers instead of page numbers. For quotations from the Bible, use chapter and verse.
- When quoting from a source found in another source, indicate the original author and the page of the source you found it in: According to philosopher Michael Oakeshott... (qtd. in Smith 22).

C. FOR AN MLA-STYLE WORKS CITED LIST

At the end of your paper, provide all the details readers need to find the sources you used in your text. Arrange the entries alphabetically by authors' last names (or, if a source has no author, by the title). Some of the information may be hard to find, especially in online sources. The sponsor of a Web site, for instance, may appear at the bottom of an internal page, on the home page, or on an information page ("Contact Us," "About Us"). Don't give up too easily; do your best to uncover all the information about the sources you are citing.

If a source has no author, begin with the title. For sources without other required information, use the following abbreviations: "n.d." (no date), "n. pag." (no page numbers), and "n.p." (no publisher; no sponsor for an online source). Include the medium of publication or delivery for all sources (for example, "Print," "Web," "Television," "Film," "DVD," "Photograph"). Do not include a URL for online sources (except for a source that would be difficult for readers to find in a search).

An alternative to a works cited list is a bibliography that includes sources consulted but not necessarily cited. The examples that follow are based on the *MLA Handbook for Writers of Research Papers*, Seventh Edition. For more examples and for explanations, see the *MLA Handbook*.

Articles

Journal Article

Last name, First name. "Title of Article." *Title of Journal* volume.issue (year): page number(s). Medium.

Moore, Peter. "The Nature of *King Lear*." *English Studies* 87.2 (2006): 169-90. Print.

O'Connor, Stephen. "Words and the World at a New York Public School: Can Writing Really Matter to Inner City Children?" *Teachers and Writers* 32.2 (Nov.-Dec. 2000): 1-8. Print.

Journal Article from an Electronic Database

Last name, First name. "Title of Article." *Title of Journal* volume.issue (year): page number(s) [n. pag. if no page numbers in database]. *Name of Database*. Medium. Date accessed.

Dougherty, James. "Presence, Silence, and the Holy in Denise Levertov's Poems." *Renascence* 58.4 (2006): 305-26. *Academic Search Premier*. Web. 12 May 2007.

Magazine Article

Last name, First name. "Title of Article." *Title of Magazine* date: page number(s). Medium.

Gladwell, Malcolm. "Open Secrets." *New Yorker*. 8 Jan. 2007: 44-53. Print.

Magazine Article from an Electronic Database

Last name, First name. "Title of Article." *Title of Magazine* date: page number(s) [n. pag. if no page numbers in database]. *Name of Database.* Medium. Date accessed.

Graeber, David. "Army of Altruists: On the Alienated Right to Do Good." *Harper's* Jan. 2007: 31-38. *Expanded Academic.* Web. 15 Feb. 2007.

Online Magazine Article

Last name, First name. "Title of Article." *Title of Online Magazine.* Sponsor of Web Site, date. Medium. Date accessed.

Burton, Robert. "The Certainty Epidemic." *Salon.com.* Salon Media Group, 29 Feb. 2008. Web. 18 Jan. 2009.

Newspaper Article

Last name, First name. "Title of Article." *Title of Newspaper* date, edition [if any], section title, number, or letter [if not part of page number(s)]: page number(s). Medium.

Markoff, John. "Attack of the Zombie Computers Is a Growing Threat, Experts Say." *New York Times* 7 Jan. 2007: A1+. Print.

Newspaper Article from an Electronic Database

Last name, First name. "Title of Article." *Title of Newspaper* date, edition [if any], section title, number, or letter [if not part of page number(s)]: page number(s) [n. pag. if no page numbers in database]. Medium. Date accessed.

Eberstadt, Nicholas. "Why Poverty Doesn't Rate." *Washington Post* 3 Sept. 2006: B1. *Newspaper Source.* Web. 12 Feb. 2007.

Online Newspaper Article

Last name, First name. "Title of Article." *Title of Online Newspaper.* Sponsor of Web Site, date. Medium. Date accessed.

Choi, Candice. "Modest Earners to Get Relief for Student Loans." *Boston Globe*. NY Times, 29 June 2009. Web. 6 Jul. 2009.

Books

Book by One Author

Last name, First name. *Title of Book*. City: Publisher, year. Medium.

Updike, John. *Terrorist*. New York: Knopf, 2006. Print.

Book by Multiple Authors

Last name, First name, First name Last name, and First name Last name. *Title of Book*. City: Publisher, year. Medium.

Singer, Peter, and Jim Mason. *The Way We Eat: Why Our Food Choices Matter*. Emmaus, PA: Rodale, 2006. Print.

Book with an Editor

Last name of editor, First name, ed. *Title of Book*. City: Publisher, year. Medium.

Lerer, Seth, ed. *The Yale Companion to Chaucer*. New Haven: Yale UP, 2006. Print.

Book with an Author and an Editor

Last name of author, First name. *Title of Book*. Ed. Editor's First name Last name. City: Publisher, year. Medium.

Plath, Sylvia. *The Unabridged Journals of Sylvia Plath*. Ed. Karen V. Kukil. New York: Anchor-Doubleday, 2000. Print.

Book in an Edition Other than First

Last name, First name. *Title of Book*. Number of edition. City: Publisher, year. Medium.

Smith, Steven S., Jason M. Roberts, and Ryan J. Vander Weilen. *The American Congress*. 4th ed. Cambridge: Cambridge UP, 2006. Print.

Work in an Anthology or Collection of Essays

Last name, First name. "Title of Essay." *Title of Anthology*. Ed. Editor's First name Last name [if different from essay author]. City: Publisher, year. Page number(s) of essay. Medium.

Dvorak, Marta. "Margaret Atwood's Humor." *The Cambridge Companion to Margaret Atwood*. Ed. Coral Ann Howells. Cambridge: Cambridge UP, 2006. 114-29. Print.

Short Story in a Collection

Last name, First name. "Title of Short Story." *Title of Collection*. Ed. Editor's First name Last name [if different from short story author]. City: Publisher, year. Page number(s) of short story. Medium.

Braverman, Kate. "Cocktail Hour." *Pushcart Prize XXXI: Best of the Small Presses*. Ed. Bill Henderson. Wainscott: Pushcart Press, 2007. 52-68. Print.

Poem in a Collection

Last name, First name. "Title of Poem." *Title of Collection*. Ed. Editor's First name Last name [if different from author of poem]. City: Publisher, year. Page number(s) of poem. Medium.

Reed, Ishmael. "Poison Light." *New and Collected Poems, 1964-2006*. New York: Carroll & Graf, 2006. 123-24. Print.

Play

Last name, First name. *Title of Play*. City: Publisher, year. Medium.

Wilson, August. *Seven Guitars*. New York: Dutton, 1996. Print.

Encyclopedia or Dictionary Entry

Last name, First name [if given]. "Title of Entry." *Title of Encyclopedia or Dictionary*. Number of edition. City: Publisher, year. Medium.

Frakes, Jerold C. "Literature, Jewish." *Encyclopaedia Judaica*. 2nd ed. Detroit: Macmillan Reference, 2007. Print.

Online Book

Last name, First name. *Title of Book [or Book-Length Work]*. City: Publisher, year. *Title of Web Site or Scholarly Project*. Medium. Date accessed.

Tienda, Marta, and Faith Mitchell, eds. *Hispanics and the Future of America*. Washington, DC: National Academies Press, 2006. *National Academies Press*. Web. 10 Feb. 2007.

Web Pages

Entire Web Site

Last name, First name [if given]. *Title of Web Site*. Sponsor of Web Site, update date. Medium. Date accessed.

Nobelprize.org. Nobel Foundation Rights Association, 2009. Web. 12 Feb. 2009.

Short Work from a Web Site

Last name, First name [if given]. "Title of Short Work." *Title of Web Site*. Sponsor of Web Site, date. Medium. Date accessed.

Pamuk, Orhan. "My Father's Suitcase." *Nobelprize.org*. Nobel Foundation Rights Association, 7 Dec. 2006. Web. 15 Jan. 2007.

Entry in a Weblog (Blog)

Last name, First name. "Title of Blog Entry." *Title of Blog*. Sponsor of Blog, date of entry. Medium. Date accessed.

Mayer, Caroline. "Some Surprising Findings about Identity Theft." *The Checkout*. Washington Post, 28 Feb. 2006. Web. 19 Jan. 2009.

Entry in a Wiki

"Title of Wiki Entry." *Title of Wiki.* Sponsor of Wiki, date of entry. Medium. Date accessed.

"Negation in Languages." *UniLang Wiki.* UniLang, 25 Oct. 2004. Web. 9 Dec. 2008.

Other Sources (Print and Online Versions)

Work of Art

Last name of artist, First name. *Title of Work.* Date of composition. Medium of composition. Institution, City.

Cézanne, Paul. *Postman Joseph Roulin.* 1888. Oil on canvas. Museum of Fine Arts, Boston.

Work of Art (Online)

Last name of artist, First name. *Title of Work.* Date of composition. Institution, City. *Title of Web Site.* Medium. Date accessed.

Cézanne, Paul. *Postman Joseph Roulin.* 1888. Museum of Fine Arts, Boston. *Museum of Fine Arts, Boston.* Web. 23 Feb. 2009.

Government Document

Government [Country]. Department. Agency [if any]. *Title of Document.* Place: Publisher, year. Medium.

United States. Dept. of Justice. Federal Bureau of Investigation. *Crime in the United States, 2005.* Washington, DC: GPO, 2006. Print.

Government Document (Online)

Government [Country]. Department. Agency [if any]. *Title of Document.* Place: Publisher, year. *Title of Web Site* [if different from document]. Sponsor of Web Site, date. Medium. Date accessed.

United States. Dept. of Justice. Bureau of Justice Statistics. *Homicide Trends in the United States*. Washington, DC: GPO, 2006. *Office of Justice Programs*. OJP, 2009. Web. 17 Feb. 2009.

Personal Interview

Last name of person interviewed, First name. Personal interview. Date of interview.

Charlier, Terry. Personal interview. 10 Feb. 2007.

Radio or Television Program

"Title of Segment or Episode." *Title of Program* [*or Series*]. Host, By, Narr., Dir., or Perf. First name Last name. Network. Local station, City, date of broadcast. Medium.

"The Super." *This American Life*. Host Ira Glass. Public Radio International. WBEZ, Chicago, 5 Jan. 2007. Radio.

Radio or Television Program (Online)

"Title of Segment or Episode." *Title of Program* [*or Series*]. Host, By, Narr., Dir., or Perf. First name Last name. Network, date of broadcast. *Title of Web Site*. Medium. Date accessed.

"Elif Shafak: Writing under a Watchful Eye." *Fresh Air*. Host Terry Gross. Natl. Public Radio, 6 Feb. 2007. *NPR.org*. Web. 22 Feb. 2009.

Film or Video

Title. Dir. Director's First name Last name. Perf. First and Last name(s) [of lead actor(s)]. Distributor, year of release. Medium.

Crash. Dir. Paul Haggis. Perf. Sandra Bullock, Don Cheadle, and Matt Dillon. Lion's Gate, 2004. DVD.

Online Video Clip

Last name of creator, First name [if any]. "Title of Video Clip." *Title of Web Site*. Sponsor of Web Site, date. Medium. Date accessed.

Murphy, Beth. "Tips for a Good Profile Piece." *YouTube*. YouTube, 7 Sept. 2008. Web. 19 Mar. 2009.

Podcast

Last name, First name [if any]. "Title of Podcast." Host, By, Narr., Dir., or Perf. First name Last name. *Title of Web Site*. Sponsor of Web Site, date. Medium. Date accessed.

"Calculating the Demand for Charter Schools." Host David Guenthner. *Texas PolicyCast*. Texas Public Policy Foundation, 28 Aug. 2008. Web. 10 Jan. 2009.

Advertisement

Name of product or company. Advertisement. Print or online publication information. [See previous relevant models.]

Symantec. Advertisement. *Newsweek* 12 Feb. 2006: 62. Print.

Sound Recording

Last name, First name of the composer, performer, or conductor. "Title of Recording" [if a short work or song]. *Title of Recording* [if a long work or CD]. Perf. First name Last name of performers or musicians. Orchestra [if relevant]. Cond. First name Last name [if relevant]. Manufacturer, year of release. Medium.

Fleck, Bela. *The Hidden Land*. Perf. Bela Fleck and the Flecktones. Sony, 2006. CD.

E-mail Message

Last name of writer, First name. "Subject Line." Message to the author. Date of message. Medium.

Barnes, Phil. "Finding Information." Message to the author. 25 Feb. 2007. E-mail.

Posting to an E-mail Discussion List (LISTSERV) or Newsgroup Forum

Last name of writer, First name. "Title of Posting." *Listserv, Forum,* or *Group Name.* Sponsor of the Web Site, date. Medium. Date accessed.

Smith, Kevin. "Style." *DorothyL.* Diane K. Kovacs, 3 Jan. 2007. Web. 25 Feb. 2007.

Real-time Communication

Last name of writer, First name. Description of event. *Forum name.* Sponsor of Forum, date of event. Medium. Date accessed.

Martin, Lawrence B. Rank Beginner. *Chronicle Live Discussions.* The Chronicle of Higher Education, 10 Jan. 2007. Web. 25 Feb. 2007.

Map or Chart

Last name, First name [if given]. *Title of Map or Chart.* Medium of presentation [map or chart]. Print or online publication information. [See previous, relevant models.]

National Parks System. Map. Washington, DC: US Dept. of the Interior, 2007. Print.

English 100 Program
Student Writing Award Guidelines

We invite students to submit work for the English 100 Program Student Writing Awards. All projects, whether in print (e.g., essays) or in media (e.g., podcasts, videos), developed for English 100 during the 2014-2015 academic year are eligible. Writing that does not receive an award may still be considered for inclusion in *CCC*.

AWARD CATEGORIES

Print

Narrative   This includes writing that engages an idea or a compelling question from a personal point of view. Examples: personal essay, memoir, fiction with a persuasive purpose, place-based observation, reflective writing, etc.

Informative/Synthesis   This includes essays that explore ideas of others, processes, or events; or explains diverse information in a creative, compelling form. Examples: critical reviews, literature reviews, rhetorical analyses, investigative journalism, histories of a word or idea, etc.

Critical/Analytical   This includes essays that perform in-depth critical analysis of a text, event, or policy; or essays that explore a compelling question from a critical perspective or make a critical argument about an issue or idea. Examples: analytical essays, policy analyses, results of a primary research project, argumentative essay supported by outside sources, substantive proposals, etc.

Media

Smart Media/Print Media   This includes projects that may have been written for any part of your English 100 course and that heavily depend on a form of composition other than the written word, such as images, video, audio, etc. Examples: websites, podcasts and audio essays, infographics, posters, theory comics, videos, documentaries, etc.

Note: If you have a narrative, informative, or critical project that incorporates media heavily, please submit it to the "Media" category, not the other categories.

GUIDELINES FOR SUBMISSION

To submit your project, please visit the link to the online submission form available on the English 100 program website, on your section's Learn@UW page, or in the email you receive from your instructor.

All Projects

To be considered for either an award or publication in the English 100 Course Reader, you must go to the link for the online submission form, then

1. complete the informational form
2. click the "permission to publish" check box
3. upload or provide a link to your file.

Before submitting, we encourage you to revise your graded assignment to take into account instructor comments. This will help ensure that your work appears at its strongest.

Print Essay Submissions

Papers should be typed, free of mechanical errors, and clearly legible for photocopying. No grades or instructor comments should appear on the submitted paper. Include only the essay's title and award category on the first page. Sign the form to verify that your essay is your own work and that any research is properly documented.

Media Project Submissions

Media projects should be in a universally recognizable format (e.g., pdf, jpeg, mp3). You will have an opportunity to either upload your media file, or to provide a link to your project if it is already hosted at another site online.

English 100 Program
Outstanding Teacher Award
Guidelines

We invite students to nominate instructors for the English 100 Program's Outstanding Teacher Award.

To be eligible for the award, the instructor will have taught in the English 100 Program during the 2014-2015 academic year.

To nominate an instructor: Please submit a brief paragraph (200-250 words) describing why you find this instructor outstanding in the teaching of English 100.

You may want to consider some of the following in making your nomination:

- Attention to students
- Quality of feedback and advice
- Impact on your learning and development as a writer
- Quality of writing activities and assignments
- Overall course experience

DEADLINE FOR NOMINATIONS

- **For Fall 2014:**   December 15, 2014
- **For Spring 2015:**   April 15, 2015

Please send nominations to Morris Young, Director of English 100 (msyoung4@wisc.edu).